BLUE MARBLE EVALUATION

Also Available

Developmental Evaluation:
Applying Complexity Concepts to Enhance Innovation and Use
Michael Quinn Patton

Developmental Evaluation Exemplars:
Principles in Practice
Edited by Michael Quinn Patton, Kate McKegg,
and Nan Wehipeihana

Principles-Focused Evaluation: The GUIDE
Michael Quinn Patton

BLUE MARBLE evaluation

Premises and Principles

● ● ● ●

MICHAEL QUINN PATTON

THE GUILFORD PRESS
New York   London

Copyright © 2020 The Guilford Press
A Division of Guilford Publications, Inc.
370 Seventh Avenue, Suite 1200, New York, NY 10001
www.guilford.com

Printed in the United States of America

This book is printed on acid-free paper.

Last digit is print number: 9   8   7   6   5   4   3   2   1

Library of Congress Cataloging-in-Publication Data is available
from the publisher.

ISBN 978-1-4625-4194-2 (paperback)
ISBN 978-1-4625-4195-9 (hardcover)

To our grandchildren—
on Jean's side,
Erik, Alek, Dylan, Eli, Henry, and Oliver,
and my foursome,
Calla, Sylvia, Jasper, and little Coconut

And to all the grandchildren,
with a mix of deep worry and great hope
for the future of Earth and humanity

Preface

On December 7, 1972, the first photograph of the whole Earth from space was taken by the astronauts in *Apollo 17*. That photo became known as the *Blue Marble shot*. Blue Marble evaluation takes its name from that whole-Earth image. The Blue Marble perspective means looking beyond nation-state boundaries and across sector and issue silos to connect the global and the local, connect the human and ecological, and connect evaluative thinking and methods with those trying to bring about global systems transformation. Blue Marble evaluation focuses on transforming evaluation to evaluate the transformations necessary to reverse negative climate change effects and make human life on Earth more sustainable and equitable.

Before there was the Blue Marble shot, there was the *Earthrise* photo from *Apollo 8*, the first crewed mission to the moon. The space capsule entered lunar orbit on Christmas Eve, December 24, 1968. The astronauts—Commander Frank Borman, Command Module Pilot Jim Lovell, and Lunar Module Pilot William Anders—held a live broadcast from lunar orbit in which they showed pictures of the Earth and moon as seen from their spacecraft. One of those photos, showing a partial Earth and some of the moon's surface, was dubbed *Earthrise*. Nature photographer Galen Rowell declared it "the most influential environmental photograph ever taken."

It was the first image of our planet captured by a human from beyond Earth's orbit. "We came all this way to explore the moon, and the most important thing is that we discovered the Earth."

Earthrise evokes perspective. The Blue Marble principles presented in this book highlight the importance of how we see

things and think about them, inviting us to think, engage, design, and evaluate with global consciousness.

At the time, I was in Burkina Faso (then Upper Volta), one of the poorest countries in the world, both then and now. I was doing agricultural extension work with subsistence farmers as a Peace Corps volunteer and my wife, Karen Wilson, was doing nutrition and prenatal education through the maternity clinic of Fada N'Gourma, the town where we lived for 2 years. We listened to the space broadcast on our short-wave radio, but did not see the photos until later.

In 1969, Neil Armstrong on *Apollo 11* became the first human to walk on the moon. My African (Gourma) counterpart, M. Lompo Bernard, was fascinated by the idea of humans going to the moon so I asked friends to send me information for him in French. His mother lived 30 kilometers (18.6 miles) from the town of Fada N'Gourma. On the eve of the moonwalk, I accompanied him to see her. She had never been out of the region in which she was born. Her whole life had been spent in that place and it was all she knew.

As we sat on short, hand-carved stools, drinking millet beer, he pointed to the moon and told his mother, "Tomorrow the Americans are going to the moon."

She turned to me nonchalantly and said in the Gourma language, "Have a good trip?"

I was struck by her openness to the idea of my going to the moon and her complete lack of understanding of what space travel involved. The next day, July 16, 1969, during the actual moon landing, I was on a remote dirt path with my broken-down motor scooter. I had to walk 5 kilometers (3.1 miles) to find help. The technological juxtaposition made an impression.

A week following the moonwalk, I was in the capital city, Ouagadougou, and saw a news magazine with a photo of Earth taken from *Apollo 11*, a precursor of the 1972 photo from *Apollo 17* that was dubbed the *Blue Marble shot*. Seeing the Earth from

that vantage point made a deep impression and stuck with me. I was 24 years old and impressed with how country borders vanished when the Earth was seen from space. This was the time of the Vietnam War and the country of Upper Volta was a French colonial creation only recently independent. The French arbitrarily divided the people of the Gourma tribe between Niger and Upper Volta, severely hampering interactions among villages and people going back centuries.

I traveled throughout West Africa during the late 1960s, deeply cognizant that the countries created by colonial powers were artificial, disruptive, unstable, and often in conflict. The Biafran War (1967–1970) was going on then, a war between the government of Nigeria and the secessionist state of Biafra, home of the Igbo people. The Nigerian government imposed a blockade that led to severe famine. During the 2½ years of the war, military casualties were estimated at more than 100,000, while between 500,000 and 2 million Biafran civilians were estimated to have starved to death. Refugees fleeing the conflict reached Upper Volta with tales of horrible suffering.

Fast forward 45 years later through a career as a professional evaluator, trainer, author, and storyteller. What a long, strange trip it's been, not to the moon, but around the world. The trip continues and now the world itself is in danger. In 2015, when the United Nations declared the International Year of Evaluation, tremendous resources were poured into strengthening national evaluation capacities. I was involved in training evaluators around the world. I came to see a growing disparity between the emphasis on building evaluation capacity at the nation-state level and the evidence that global problems cannot effectively be addressed solely at the nation-state level. We also need evaluators who can think, act, and evaluate globally. I developed a training program to prepare evaluators to evaluate global systems change. The need, it seemed to me, was for evaluators trained, engaged, and supported to be *global, dynamic systems* thinkers—in essence, *world savvy evaluators* who demonstrate *global competence*, and engage knowledgeably in addressing *world systems issues* through evaluation. I've had the privilege of working with a diverse team of international evaluators and development professionals engaged around the implications of taking a Blue Marble perspective. This book reports what has emerged from that inquiry and this ongoing journey into Blue Marble thinking and engagement.

Acknowledgments

The material in this book has been developed and tested over the last 4 years in a variety of workshops, webinars, keynote addresses, and seminars. The many and diverse supporters of and participants in those events have helped shape the Blue Marble perspective you'll find in these pages. I'll review a few of the highlights of support I've experienced to give you a sense of the scope and depth of input that has led to this book.

In 2015, *Utilization-Focused Evaluation*, in partnership with the nonprofit educational organization *World Savvy*, received a grant from Michael Scriven's Faster Forward Fund to develop a course and training materials for Blue Marble evaluation. Charmagne Campbell-Patton, my daughter and Blue Marble evaluation energizer and collaborator from the beginning, and I developed pilot training modules. We taught the first workshops together at the Minnesota Evaluation Studies Institute (MESI) and then at the International Program for Development Evaluation Training (IPDET) in Ottawa in 2016. Jean King for MESI, and Linda Morra Imas and Ray Rist, IPDET codirectors and cofounders, were early supporters of Blue Marble evaluation development and training. Verena Friedrich, Stefanie Andrea Krapp, Wolfgang Meyer, and Reinhard Stockmann, as leaders in the revitalized IPDET taking place at the University of Bern, supported my teaching a new course on Evaluating Transformation in 2019.

In 2017, I was invited by Glenn Page and Ioan Fazey to provide a final keynote to the Transformations 2017: Transformations in Practice conference in Dundee, Scotland, that allowed me to further develop several principles of Blue Marble evaluation and engage with a community that was working on these issues largely outside of traditional evaluation practice. Jess Dart arranged for me to present Blue Marble evaluation as part of the Australasian Evaluation Society (AES; *aes.asn.au*) 2018 conference in Tasmania where the theme was *Transformations*, the focus of Part III of this book. Rob D. van den Berg, President of the International Development Evaluation Association (IDEAS), contributed ideas and resources to conceptualizing Blue Marble evaluation and provided opportunities to do workshops and presentations at the 2019 IDEAS conference in Prague, where the theme was *Evaluation for Transformative Change*, the focus of the concluding chapter in the book.

Dana Mortenson, founder and Director of World Savvy, an early adopter of developmental evaluation, understood immediately the niche and trajectory for Blue Marble evaluation, and her pioneering work on global competencies has informed our work in that area. Stewart Donaldson, as President of the American Evaluation Association (AEA), included Blue Marble evaluation in the opening and closing plenaries of the 2015 AEA annual conference. That was the first introduction of the idea to the larger evaluation community and came in the International Year of Evaluation as designated by the United Nations. With Stewart's support, I subsequently taught a Blue Marble evaluation workshop in the Claremont Evaluation Summer Program.

Charmagne, as Director of Organizational Learning and Evaluation for Utilization-Focused Evaluation, developed our Blue Marble evaluation website, which has provided a way of connecting with people from around the world who are interested in Blue Marble evaluation. Since then, she has been working closely with Glenn Page, who has been developing a new Blue Marble website and, more importantly, a strategy for further co-creation of Blue Marble case studies, webinars, trainings, learning journeys, and a wide range of other virtual and in-person meetings to create a Blue Marble community of practice. The site address is *blumareval.com.*

Blue Marble evaluation moved from idea to implementation in 2017, when the Global Alliance for the Future of Food adopted Blue Marble evaluation as its framework for evaluating its strategy, then created the first Blue Marble evaluator position, filled by Pablo Vidueira, whom you'll meet in the first chapter. Ruth Richardson, Executive Director of the Global Alliance for the Future of Food, has shown great vision and leadership in integrating Blue Marble evaluation into the organization's core functions and way of thinking.

Jane Maland Cady of the McKnight Foundation brought the Blue Marble evaluation idea to the Global Alliance for the Future of Food. The McKnight Foundation, based in Minnesota, was a founding member of the Global Alliance, and Jane began serving as co-chair of the Steering Committee in 2019. She has also incorporated Blue Marble thinking in her McKnight program work, as you'll find featured in Chapter 6. A grant from the McKnight Foundation is making possible the creation of a Blue Marble evaluation infrastructure globally. Jane immediately grasped the significance of taking a Blue Marble perspective and has been a stalwart supporter throughout the development of the approach and writing of this book.

Intellectual fellow travelers over a 50-year career are far too many to mention by name, so I will limit my thanks here to those who have played an especially direct and influential role in my thinking about Blue Marble evaluation and global systems transformation as this book emerged. Jer-

ald Hage was my doctoral adviser in sociology at the University of Wisconsin, Madison, in the early 1970s. He introduced me to complexity theory, systems thinking, social innovation, and organizational dynamics when those arenas of inquiry were just emerging. His latest work, a *magnum opus* synthesizing some 300 years of interdisciplinary social science scholarship on those and related issues, constitutes the foundation for the theory of transformation introduced in Chapter 13. I am deeply grateful that he shared his draft manuscript and helped me formulate what I have called the *Hage hypothesis of social transformation*, published here for the first time, a breakthrough premise about how major systems change happens based on an unprecedented integration of theory and research from across disciplines and around the world. His breadth of scholarship exemplifies the Blue Marble principles of crossing boundaries, breaking down silos, and connecting the local to the global through micro, meso, and macro interactions and interdependencies.

Another long-time sociological colleague and inquiry companion is Frances Westley. Frances epitomizes the scholar–practitioner. She has designed and implemented a variety of social innovation programs. I had the privilege of working with Frances on our book *Getting to Maybe: How the World Is Changed* (Westley, Zimmerman, & Patton, 2007), for which she was the lead author and inspiration. Her integration of theory and practice is nonpareil, and as she has turned her attention to transformation, her work, with Hage's, undergirds this book's theory of transformation.

Three long-time evaluation colleagues and friends have brought their special perspectives to bear as I've developed Blue Marble evaluation: Rodney Hopson's work on decolonizing evaluation and cultural responsiveness, Kate McKegg on honoring and valuing local and indigenous perspectives on and experiences of globalization, and Patricia Rogers on theory formulation and the global contributions she makes to evaluation through her critical work on *Better Evaluation* (*www.betterevaluation.org*), the go-to place worldwide where the tried-and-true meets the leading edge in evaluation theory, practice, and ongoing development.

For the last 2 years, a worldwide Blue Marble evaluation team has been developing the Blue Marble principles, reviewing draft chapters of the book and providing insightful feedback. You'll hear from several of these team members in the book. Charmagne Campbell-Patton from Minnesota, Jeph Mathias from India, Marah Moore from New Mexico, Claire Nicklin from Ecuador, Glenn Page from the Gulf of Maine, KaYing Vang from Minnesota, Pablo Vidueira from Spain, and John Wilson from Zimbabwe. Zenda Ofir in Switzerland via South Africa, Deborah Rugg from New York City via the United Nations Evaluation Group, and Mark Cabaj from Edmonton, Alberta, read drafts and provided helpful feedback, ideas, and resources. Fred Carden, John Colvin, and Antony B. Maikuri offered helpful reactions to early chapters.

Writing a book has its ups and downs, like the Northern winter itself, during which most of this was written. A writer needs critical friends to temper flights of fancy and earnest support to navigate the lows. Charmagne Campbell-Patton and Glenn Page were my constant companions throughout the writing, reading every chapter in multiple drafts and responding in depth with insights that have spared readers a lot of tangents and sidetracks while helping to identify and highlight what is central to Blue Marble thinking. I could not be more grateful. My Northwoods neighbor, Terese Wigand, provided expert proofing.

C. Deborah Laughton, Publisher and Senior Editor at The Guilford Press, went through the early chapters in detail, helping shape the format, flow, and fluidity of my writing, including identifying what she called a writing "tic": that I tend to utilize triplets in describing things, a habit I have, under her careful tutelage, at last broken.

Laura Specht Patchkofsky, Senior Production Editor at The Guilford Press, did a phenomenal job of shepherding the book from manuscript to publication in time for launch at the 2019 annual conference of the American Evaluation Association.

My life partner and Minnesota Northwoods companion, Jean Gornick, supported me through the long winter months of writing, with multiple forms of sustenance and fresh insights into the challenges of our time that helped keep me grounded in the real world when I drifted off into the siren clouds of abstract globalism.

The book is dedicated to our grandchildren—on Jean's side, Erik, Alek, Dylan, Eli, Henry, and Oliver, and my foursome, Calla, Sylvia, Jasper, and little Coconut—and to all the grandchildren, everywhere, who will bear the brunt of the legacy we leave behind. For as Tanya Steele, Chief Executive at the World Wildlife Fund, has pointed out, "We are the first generation to know we are destroying our planet and the last one that can do anything about it." This book is about the role evaluators can play in doing something about it.

Logo Art Credit

Glenn Page coordinated the development, review, and approval of the Blue Marble logo featured throughout this book by engaging the creative genius of Lisa Pupa (*lpupadesign.com*). With feedback from the Blue Marble evaluation team, they created an evocative and fitting visual image that incorporates several core principles of Blue Marble thinking, including *GLOCAL* interactions, Yin–Yang harmonization, cross-scale integration, and global transformation, all embedded in the logo.

Cartoon Credits

Cartoons invite us to see things in a different way, both less and more seriously at the same time. Four cartoonists have contributed to this book.

Mark M. Rogers is an experienced facilitator, trainer, mediator, program designer, and evaluator working on peace building around the world. He has contributed cartoons to my previous books and new ones grace these pages.

Chris Lysy is the evaluation profession's unofficial official cartoonist with a huge repertoire of evaluation cartoons on his website (*www.freshspectrum.com*).

Simon Kneebone was the official cartoonist for the AES annual conference in Tasmania in 2018. AES has graciously given me permission to include 10 of the cartoons he did for the conference, for which AES is the copyright holder, one of which, below, was his impression of my keynote on the relevance of complexity theory for evaluating transformations, the theme of the conference and of Part III of this book.

I then commissioned additional cartoons from Simon for this book, which he crafted exquisitely.

Claudius Ceccon (*Claudionor*), a distinguished Brazilian political cartoonist and father-in-law of Brazilian evaluator Thomaz Chianca, illustrated a Portuguese translation (Patton & Guimarães, 2018) of a *New Directions for Evaluation* volume I edited on the pedagogy of evaluation (Patton, 2017). Three of the cartoons from that volume are included here. See the full set of 18 stunningly evocative full-color illustrations in what I've described as perhaps the most beautifully illustrated evaluation publication ever at *https://issuu.com/telecursofrm/docs/avaliacao-incluir-para-transformar-*.

Being world savvy means understanding the butterfly effect from complexity theory by Simon Kneebone. Used with permission of the copyright holder, the Australian Evaluation Society (*aes.asn.au*).

Contents

List of Exhibits

PART I

The Blue Marble Perspective

Four Overarching Blue Marble Principles

Blue Marble refers to the iconic image of Earth from space without borders or boundaries, a whole-Earth perspective. We humans are using our planet's resources, and polluting and warming it, in ways that are unsustainable. Many people, organizations, and networks are working to ensure that the future is more sustainable and equitable. Blue Marble evaluators enter the fray by helping design such efforts, providing ongoing feedback for adaptation and enhanced impact, and examining the long-term effectiveness of such interventions and initiatives. Incorporating the Blue Marble perspective means looking beyond nation-state boundaries and across sector and issue silos to connect the global and the local, connect the human and ecological, and connect evaluative thinking and methods with those trying to bring about global systems transformation.

Blue Marble evaluation integrates design, implementation, and evaluation. Evaluators bring their knowledge and expertise to bear in the design of resilient, sustainability-oriented interventions and initiatives. When an intervention and, correspondingly, an evaluation fail to incorporate an ecological sustainability perspective, both are engaging from a closed-system mindset, disconnected from larger patterns and realities—like turning a crank that isn't connected to anything. It is essential for planners, implementers, and evaluators at the beginning of their work together to routinely analyze the sustainability and equity issues presented by the formulation of the intervention and analyze the implications for evaluation. Blue Marble evaluation premises and principles provide a framework for that initial review, ongoing development and adaptation, and long-term evaluation of systems transformation contributions and impacts.

Blue Marble evaluation looks backward (what has been) to inform the future (what might be) based on the present trajectory (what is happening now). Evaluators examine what has worked and not worked in the past, not just to capture history, but to inform the future. Forecasts for the future of humanity run the gamut from doom and gloom to utopia. Evaluation as a transdisciplinary, global profession has much to offer in navigating the risks and opportunities that arise as global change initiatives and interventions are designed and undertaken to ensure a more sustainable and equitable future.

CHAPTER 1

Global Thinking Principle

> We cannot solve our problems with the same
> level of thinking that created them.
> —ALBERT EINSTEIN

CONTEXT: The Blue Marble

On December 7, 1972, the first photograph of the whole Earth from space was taken by the astronauts on *Apollo 17*. That photo became known as the **Blue Marble shot.** You can't see Earth as a globe unless you get at least 20,000 miles away from it. Seeing from

a *whole-Earth* perspective is what the designation "Blue Marble" connotes.

Taking a Blue Marble perspective means viewing the world **holistically.** It begins with watching for, making sense of, and interpreting the implications of things that are interconnected in the global system, thus thinking beyond nation-states, sector silos, and narrowly identified issues. Blue Marble thinkers see the interconnections between the global and the local, the macro and the micro, and the relationships between worldwide patterns and area-specific challenges. They become adept at zooming out for a big-picture perspective and zooming in to understand and incorporate contextual variations, problems, and solutions. Applying Blue Marble thinking to initiatives aimed at creating a more sustainable, equitable, and just world, at any level and in any arena of action, has implications for how such initiatives are designed, carried out, and evaluated. Thus, the first Blue Marble principle expresses the importance of thinking globally.

Global Thinking Principle Explicated

> **PREMISE:** Global problems like climate change, worldwide pollution, and global disparities require global interventions and, correspondingly, globally oriented and world savvy evaluators.

Global Thinking Principle

Apply whole-Earth, big-picture thinking to all aspects of systems change.

IMPLICATIONS

- Whatever is done, or evaluated, at all levels and for all types of interventions and initiatives, consider its global context and implications both within and beyond nation-state boundaries.
- Think systemically. Conceptualize systems and evaluate systems changes, not just focusing on projects and programs.
- Connect the local to the global, and the global to the local.
- Think across silos by examining how issues, problems, and specific interventions may be interconnected.
- Unpack and bring fidelity to initiatives, organizations, and projects calling themselves "global." Working on one issue in three countries is not global. What are the various ways in which the designation "global" has meaning?
- Select appropriate methods for the situation and nature of the targeted systems changes.
- Time being of the essence, be attentive to varying time horizons by integrating short-, medium-, and long-term sustainability considerations while acting with a sense of urgency, given climate change and related global trends.

This chapter provides an overview of the basis for the global thinking principle—its implications and applications. Subsequent chapters present and discuss the other Blue Marble principles that, together, constitute the Blue Marble perspective.

Global Interconnectedness

The Blue Marble perspective flows from our global interconnectedness. Consider these news stories as examples of global interdependence:

- Slave labor in the Amazon has been linked to suppliers of Lowe's and Walmart (U.S. retail stores). An investigation has revealed U.S.-based companies bought timber from Brazilian traders where loggers worked under slave labor conditions. (Campos, 2017).
- China's ban on importing contaminated waste leaves Australia awash in rubbish (Smyth, 2018).
- Dramatic warming of the Gulf of Maine due to increased freshwater flow from the Arctic into the Labrador Current is dramatically changing the ecological and socioeconomic future of this once-abundant fishery (Poppick, 2018).
- Though the details vary from continent to continent, the global refugee crisis has roots in climate change, the differential effects of economic globalization, changing global power dynamics, and social media communications (Werz & Hoffman, 2016).
- Central banks in industrialized countries raised interest rates. Workers in Mexico and merchants in Malaysia suffered. Rising interest rates in the United States and Europe drove money out of many developing countries, straining governments and pinching consumers around the globe ("The Fed Acts," 2017).

Now let's zoom out to the future and the whole Earth. An international team of 23 multidisciplinary scientists reviewed more than 3,000 papers on various effects of climate change. They identified 467 ways in

Zoom in, zoom out by Simon Kneebone.

which expected changes in climate affect human physical and mental health, food security, water availability, infrastructure, and other facets of life on Earth. The effects include heat waves, wildfires, sea level rise, hurricanes, flooding, drought, and shortages of clean water. Loss of life, increasingly desperate living conditions, and forced migration are worst for the poorest people around the world. Mammoth economic burdens for climate mitigation will hit wealthier countries, demonstrably diminishing growth and prosperity (Mora et al., 2018).

We're all affected by more severe weather. But let's get even more personal. We all use plastic. Everyone reading this uses plastic at some level in some way. In 2018, the Earth Day Network featured the effects of plastic pollution locally and globally. Their website (*www.earthday.org/plastic-calculator*) offers a personal evaluation tool to measure your level of plastic consumption. Why does this matter? Here's why.

Plastic pollution is permeating oceans and threatening marine wildlife. Microscopic plastic particles are absorbed by fish that humans eat. Land animals are trapped by plastic debris or eat it and become sick. The main source of marine plastic is improperly managed waste, especially from badly managed landfills that overflow directly into waterways and oceans.

> The negative impacts of improper or insufficient waste management are immense, and the growing scale of the problem is pushing this issue towards an environmental and humanitarian crisis. . . . It is estimated that of all the world's waste, 40 percent ends up in uncontrolled dump sites. Many of these dump sites are so poorly regulated that the waste overflows directly into the ocean. This phenomenon is the main source of the problem of plastic pollution in our oceans.
>
> The growing scale of the problem of mismanaged waste means that by 2020 we will see a tenfold increase in the amount of plastic in the oceans and by 2050 marine plastic will outweigh the fish in the sea. Mismanaged waste also contributes to global warming. By 2025, dump sites and landfills will account for a staggering eight to 10 percent of global greenhouse gas emissions. (Earth Day Network, 2018)

Plastic pollution is but one example of global interconnectedness. However manifest, global interdependence has implications for businesses, governments, nonprofits, philanthropic foundations, communities, and people in general. Globalization and the resulting global interconnectedness influence international development initiatives, including evaluation of those initiatives. Designing, carrying out, and evaluating change initiatives from a Blue Marble perspective requires a deepened capacity to understand global patterns and their implications.

The Blue Marble Worldview

The Blue Marble worldview constitutes a paradigm, so let's do a quick review of what paradigms do and why they matter. Paradigms tell us what is important to pay attention to, thereby guiding us in how to think and behave. Therein resides the power of paradigms—they provide a belief system that facilitates action. The shadow side of paradigms is that the very reasons for our choices are hidden in the unquestioned assumptions of the paradigm. Paradigmatic behavior becomes thoughtless and routine. Operating within a paradigm provides the comfort of familiarity. Being conscious of one's paradigmatic premises supports evaluative thinking. Blue Marble evaluation, based on Blue Marble perceptions, thinking, and principles, constitutes a paradigm, a mindset, a way of making sense of things.

Paradigms are distinguished by both what they assert and what they contrast with. Humans' dominion over nature is a paradigm perspective. That humans and nature are fundamentally and deeply interconnected and interdependent is an alternative paradigm. Laissez-faire capitalism is a paradigm that self-interest, profit, and unfettered markets should be the mechanisms for distributing wealth, the basis of neoclassical economic theory that undergirded the development of modern global financial markets. Social democratic economics is an alternative paradigm that elected governments should regulate markets and redistribute wealth from those with much to those with little. Nationalism is a paradigm that makes national sovereignty and nation-state interests primary. Globalism is an alternative paradigm that places priority on the well-being of humanity as a whole. These paradigmatic contrasts draw stark comparisons. There is lots of room in the middle. But what constitutes the middle is defined by the contrasts. The Blue Marble paradigm sometimes constitutes a clear alternative to currently dominant mindsets and at other times harmonizes opposites to seek common ground. Either way, Blue Marble thinking is a mindset. It is a mindset defined by a set of principles. Let me explain the principles-focused nature of the Blue Marble perspective and then we can get into the substance of the worldview and its implications.

Why Principles?

Blue Marble evaluation is principles based because to deal with the complexities of global issues and problems we need principles to guide us, not a rule book to tie us down. Principles-focused thinking is for principles-driven people engaged in principles-based change. An effectiveness principle provides guidance about how to think or behave toward some desired result (either explicit or implicit) based on norms, values, beliefs, experience, and knowledge. A high-quality principle provides guidance about what to do, is useful for informing decisions and actions, provides inspiration as an expression of values, is relevant to diverse contexts and situations, and can be evaluated. Just as examining contrasting paradigms illuminates each, examining contrasting principles illuminates why adhering to one principle versus its alternative matters. I'll present those comparisons. Evaluating a principle involves examining its meaningfulness to those expected to follow it, whether it is being adhered to in practice, and, if adhered to, whether it leads to desired results (Patton, 2018d).

Distinguishing Overarching from Operating Principles

Part I of this book presents and explains four overarching Blue Marble principles. Part II examines and elaborates the implications of the **overarching principles** with 12 operating principles. The distinction between overarching principles and operating principles is like the distinction between goals and objectives. Overarching principles provide big-picture, general guidance. **Operating principles** provide more specific guidance. For example, an overarching principle providing guidance for an initiative could be: *Build collaborations to increase impact.* Two operating principles that provide more detailed guidance would be

1. Ensure that all voices in the collaboration are heard.
2. Share leadership among collaboration members.

Principles provide guidance but do not specify structures or procedures for following that guidance because such details are context dependent.

The first overarching principle, introduced in this chapter, is the Global Thinking principle: *Apply whole-Earth, big-picture thinking to all aspects of systems change.*

Two operating principles that provide more specific guidance are the focus of Chapters 5 and 6, respectively:

1. Transboundary Engagement principle: *Act at a global scale.*
2. GLOCAL (global–local) principle: *Integrate interconnections across levels.*

While this book focuses on Blue Marble evaluation, the Blue Marble principles can guide situation analysis, design of interventions, and work to bring about systems changes as well as evaluation of those efforts. It's important to clarify right away that the Blue Marble perspective is both an approach to evaluation and a way of thinking about all aspects of systems change initiatives and interventions, at all levels at which they occur, from local to global.

Practicalities

Before continuing with the Blue Marble principles, let me address some practicalities that arise whenever I speak about this approach or conduct training. Here are quick answers to four common questions.

1. *For what kinds of programs and interventions is the Blue Marble perspective appropriate?* It's simplest to distinguish two levels of application. One is applying Blue Marble thinking to programs and initiatives that are not focused on global systems

change specifically but appreciate that global trends like climate change, environmental degradation, inequitable distribution of wealth, and unsustainable use of resources affect whatever is being done. Increasingly, there are calls for all nongovernmental organizations (NGOs) and all programs at all levels to incorporate attention to and contribute toward global sustainability and equity. Blue Marble thinking and evaluation offers a doorway into greater global awareness and engagement for any program, community, organization, or initiative. For example, understanding and evaluating the collective response to a rapidly warming Gulf of Maine requires a systemic, cross-sector, cross-scale analytical framework embracing both indigenous and Western perspectives.

The second and more direct application of Blue Marble thinking and evaluation is with the thousands of initiatives that are oriented toward global systems change, like the Global Alliance for the Future of Food (GA), the World Wildlife Fund (WWF), the Global Center for X, the Global Initiative on Y, or the Global whatever—you fill in the blank. We'll look at specific examples as we go along. Global efforts of any and all kinds are prime territory for Blue Marble evaluation.

2. *You talk about a Blue Marble perspective, Blue Marble thinking, Blue Marble principles, and Blue Marble evaluation. Is this primarily an evaluation approach or something else?* Let me begin my response with an observation from researchers who study how we make decisions.

> We have a tendency to treat problems in isolation, rather than as part of a larger whole. Just as investors often mistakenly evaluate stocks individually, rather than as part of the portfolio, coaches and fans often evaluate sports decisions in terms of their immediate impact and give less consideration to how those decisions fit in the larger context of the game. (Walker, Risen, Gilovich, & Thaler, 2018, p. 4)

We tend to silo rather than integrate. We deal with things in parts and fail to see the whole. Indeed, the most common advice for dealing with complicated challenges is to break them down into small, manageable parts. That may get the small bits taken care of, but may miss how the parts interconnect as a whole. Complex systems are best understood by examining the quality of interactions among elements, not the quality of the elements in isolation. Working on isolated elements without understanding their relationship to other elements can interfere with the functioning of the whole. Dealing with problems piecemeal can, inadvertently, make the overall situation worse.

Design, implementation, and evaluation are typically treated as separate functions dealt with sequentially by different people with different roles who don't communicate with one another. At the heart of the Blue Marble perspective you'll find a pattern of breaking down silos, integrating separated functions, connecting people and places, and creating linkages across time. In that spirit, Blue Marble evaluation focuses on integrating design, engagement, implementation, and evaluation of programs and interventions of all kinds, especially initiatives working on making global systems more sustainable.

Blue Marble evaluation builds on what we've been learning from developmental evaluation of social innovations in which the evaluator is engaged on an ongoing basis as part of the innovation team supporting redesign, implementation adjustments, and responsive evaluation occurring together, mutually reinforcing, as the innovation unfolds. Likewise, with principles-focused evaluation, the evaluator is typically involved in helping to craft evaluable principles, support their application and adherence in practice, and provide feedback about the results of adherence, or lack thereof. Blue Marble evaluation has emerged from these innovative approaches to evaluation in which evaluation becomes part of the intervention because it is embedded in and integral to the innovation and change efforts being developed. That degree of evaluation engagement is controversial, to be sure, and asks more of the evaluator, so I'll address those concerns along the way. For now, it's sufficient to understand the evolution of Blue Marble evaluation and its niche in the evaluation and global systems change landscapes.

3. *Who is Blue Marble evaluation for? Is this something just for evaluators?* This isn't a private party for evaluators only. The whole world is invited: development practitioners and specialists, social innovators, policymakers, program designers, leaders and directors in government, philanthropy, NGOs, the private sector, grassroots activists, researchers, think tank experts, sustainability scientists, equity advocates, sustainable development goal (SDG) implementers, commissioners of evaluations, and certainly funders and social impact investors. Have I left anyone out? If so, I apologize. Everyone is invited.

While evaluators are a prime audience for Blue Marble evaluation, evaluators can't effectively and usefully undertake Blue Marble evaluations unless others engage in Blue Marble thinking. Transformation for sustainability and equity connects all of us together. In putting forth Blue Marble evaluation, we are joining others in addressing the 2030 global systems change agenda adopted by the United Nations (UN) in 2015 and expressed in the overarching vision of *No One Left Behind,* operationalized in the 17 SDGs. Blue Marble evaluators join others in working toward that vision and, hopefully, increase its likelihood of being realized by supporting knowledge generation, learning, and adaptive actions along the way. To make such contributions, however, evaluation will have to be transformed to systematically and holistically evaluate transformation, the premise that undergirds Blue Marble evaluation and is the focus of Part III of this book.

4. *Is any organization actually doing Blue Marble evaluation?* Many are, but not necessarily by that name. Thinking globally is not exclusive to Blue Marble evaluation, to be sure, but naming it helps make the perspective explicit. Social innovation is propelled by early adopters. In research, the first documented manifestation of a phenomenon is called an *index case* (Patton, 2015, p. 266). The world's first official Blue Marble evaluator was chosen to fulfill that responsibility by the GA, which adopted Blue Marble evaluation as well aligned with its mission and strategy. The 23 major philanthropic foundations that make up the GA adopted a three-pronged strategy informed by a global perspective:

a. Forge new insights and strengthen evidence for global systems change.

b. Convene key food-system actors, facilitate meaningful dialogue, and strengthen interconnections.

c. Stimulate local and global action and interaction for transformational change in collaboration with other committed stakeholders to realize healthy, equitable, renewable, resilient, and culturally diverse food systems.

In support of this strategy, the GA created the world's first Blue Marble evaluation position and brought on board the world's first Blue Marble evaluator, Pablo Vidueira. The notion of Blue Marble evaluation conducted by Blue Marble evaluators is not some distant pipe dream. It is happening. The future is now. The index case (first ever) has emerged. You can meet Pablo in the sidebar accompanying this discussion.

The engagement of a Blue Marble evaluator with global team support helps embed global systems change thinking in the work of the GA. In every activity, the question of how that activity relates to global transformation is always asked, and the theory of transformation to which the GA is committed (see Chapter 13) stays front and center

Pablo Vidueira Reflects on Being the World's First Official Blue Marble Evaluator

Pablo Vidueira studied agronomy as an undergraduate at the University of Madrid. His master's focus was in international development in which he studied social development processes in rural areas of Spain as part of a European program called Erasmus Mundus involving universities in Copenhagen, Montpelier, Cork, Madrid, Wageningen, and Catania. Pablo's doctorate specialization in evaluation focused on systems methods for impact evaluation in the European Union. His work included working with small farmers in Puebla state in Mexico. In his engagement as Blue Marble evaluator, he is supported by a team of people who have adopted the Blue Marble perspective. Here, Pablo comments on how he has come to view Blue Marble evaluation.

Being the first-ever Blue Marble Evaluator and doing so with the Global Alliance for the Future of Food is an honor. I could tell you a million things about this, but for now I want to share two personal views that I hope may contribute to better understanding and framing Blue Marble evaluation.

In my PhD, I tried to understand how impact evaluation was being done in the European Commission (EC) programs, then considering the extent to which systems concepts and methods might overcome some of the limitations I found. My main concern was that, in order to assess the impacts of programs implemented all across the European Union (EU), a set of indicators was being quantified at each Member State level, and then those were being added up at the EU level. At the same time, discussions around how to evaluate the Sustainable Development Goals were following the same "monitoring-focused path." This narrow approach did not seem to me to take advantage of the wealth of evaluation approaches and resources that have been developed. I felt that the lenses being used to make sense of and evaluate these interventions were not allowing evaluators to contribute all we could. We were, as I wrote in one of my papers on the EC programs, enclosed in evaluation "as a legal requirement instead of as the opportunity to make policy development more transparent, to implement better programs and to use public money to make a difference to people's lives." I quickly came to see Blue Marble evaluation as a way to address these concerns and limitations. This is what appealed to me the most at my entry point to Blue Marble evaluation.

When first introduced to the idea of Blue Marble evaluation, I thought it probably meant developing fancy computer-based simulation models about global systems. It took me a while to understand that the point is not tools—and never was. The point is how we look at and make sense of global interventions, how we understand the role that evaluation should play, how we pose meaningful questions that help to critically assess potential improvements, how we understand the ways in which interventions are interrelated with each other and with broader contexts, how different stakeholders understand the same thing in many different ways, how boundaries matter, and how it all affects our profession and our contribution to improving the world we live in, from the smallest to the largest interventions and evaluations. It is all about the lenses we use, first to understand, then to evaluate. This was the biggest breakthrough of Blue Marble evaluation for me—it has changed how I look at interventions, evaluation, and our world, all together.

Note. Chapter 10 features the Blue Marble evaluation framework that Pablo Vidueira has developed for the Global Alliance for the Future of Food.

in strategy implementation and evaluation of the GA. That's what it means to have a Blue Marble perspective taken seriously and embedded in the ongoing work of an organization or initiative. The GA executive director explains:

> We believe that transformational change requires that we craft new and better solutions at all scales through a systems-level approach and deep collaboration between philanthropy, researchers, grassroots movements, the private sector, farmers and food systems workers, Indigenous Peoples, government, and policymakers. Transformation means realizing healthy, equitable, renewable, resilient, and culturally diverse food systems shared by people, communities, and their institutions. (Richardson, 2019)

Such an organizational commitment expresses a commitment to thinking and acting globally and constitutes fertile ground for Blue Marble evaluation. The call for global systems transformations is grounded in facing the realities of threats to humanity's future in what has come to be called the Epoch of the Anthropocene, the focus of the second overarching Blue Marble principle in the next chapter.

Global Thinking by Simon Kneebone. Used with permission of the copyright holder, the Australian Evaluation Society (*aes.asn.au*).

CHAPTER 2

Anthropocene as Context Principle

The current epoch, the Holocene, is the 12,000 years of stable climate since the last ice age during which all human civilization developed. But the striking acceleration since the mid-20th century of carbon dioxide emissions and sea level rise, the global mass extinction of species, and the transformation of land by deforestation and development mark the end of that slice of geological time, the experts argue. The Earth is so profoundly changed that the Holocene must give way to the Anthropocene.

—DAMIAN CARRINGTON (2016, p. 1)

CONTEXT: Global Challenges in the Anthropocene

More people inhabit Earth today than at any time in human history. Fewer different plant and animal species exist today than at any time since *Homo sapiens* emerged on Earth. These two facts are related. Welcome to the Anthropocene.

The context for Blue Marble evaluation is that we have entered a new geological era, dubbed the Anthropocene, characterized by dramatic and demonstrable human impacts on the planet, impacts of sufficient scale and scope that the future of humanity is in doubt. Three decades of integrated research on the functioning of global systems has led to the conclusion that planet Earth and her human inhabitants have entered an era of measurable and lasting human impact on Earth. A substantial and growing body of evidence concludes that the sustainability and resilience of Earth's systems, both natural and human, are now at risk due to cumulative negative human actions (Brannen, 2018; Nakicenovic, Rockström, Gaffney, & Zimm, 2016).

The term *Anthropocene* was coined in 2000, by Nobel prize–winning scientist Paul Crutzen with Eugene Stoermer:

This name change stresses the enormity of humanity's responsibility as stewards of the Earth and recognizes the *great acceleration* of human impacts on the planet from the mid-20th century. (Crutzen, quoted by Carrington, 2016, p. 1; original emphasis)

In August 2016, the Working Group on the Anthropocene presented its recommendation to the International Geological Congress meeting in Cape Town. Erle Ellis, Professor of Geography and Environmental Systems at the University of Maryland, Baltimore County, and a member of the Anthropocene Working Group of Future Earth, explains:

Overwhelming evidence now confirms that humans are changing Earth in unprecedented ways. Global climate change, acidifying oceans, shifting global cycles of carbon, nitrogen, and other elements, forests and other natural habitats transformed into farms and cities, widespread pollution, radioactive fallout, plastic accumulation, the course of rivers altered, mass extinction of species, human transport and introduction of species around the world. These are just some of the many different human-induced global environmental changes that will most likely leave a lasting record in rock: the basis for marking new intervals of geologic time. (2018, pp. 2–3)

Anthropocene as Context Principle Explicated

We are the first generation to know we are destroying our planet and the last one that can do anything about it.
—TANYA STEELE (2018), chief executive of the World Wildlife Fund

> **PREMISE:** Human actions have created the global problems humanity faces; human actions are necessary to resolve these problems—thus, there are things for evaluators to know about global sustainability in the context of the Anthropocene to undertake evaluations knowledgeably and credibly.

Anthropocene as Context Principle

Know and face the realities of the Anthropocene and act accordingly.

IMPLICATIONS

This principle calls on evaluators and those with whom we work and engage to understand the realities of the Anthropocene and use evaluative thinking and evaluation processes to contribute to more sustainable and equitable human/ecosystem trajectories for the future.

- Apply systematic Anthropocenic analysis in designing and evaluating interventions and initiatives.
- Make a balanced assessment identifying the bad things that are happening and acknowledging the good things that are happening, and use that assessment to identify priorities and opportunities.
- Use methods appropriate to map and track Anthropocenic challenges.
- Be transparent and assertive about what is at stake for all involved, including the evaluators. Evaluators are not outside looking in. Evaluators, their families, and communities are affected by Anthropocenic trends. *Evaluators have skin in the game* (see Chapter 12).

Ten Overlapping Realities of the Anthropocene

Global problems transcend national borders, agency boundaries, and specific sector goals, like reducing poverty, disease, or pollution. Consider these 10 global issues as examples of the challenges humanity faces.

1. *Climate change and global warming.* Many agencies around the world have produced evidence of global changes in sea and land surface temperatures. The five warmest years in recorded history have been the last five (Schwartz & Popovich, 2019). These warming trends are also confirmed by other independent observations, such as the melting of mountain glaciers on every continent, reductions in the extent of snow cover, earlier blooming of plants in spring, a shorter ice season on lakes and rivers, ocean heat content, reduced Arctic sea ice, and rising sea levels (National Oceanic and Atmospheric Administration, 2018). The UN Intergovernmental Report on Climate Change projects that 2030 is roughly the time when global warming will reach an irreversible tipping point.

2. *Rising sea levels.* The Artic is warming at twice the rate of the rest of the planet. Greenland's ice melt is accelerating. Research reported in late 2018 forecasts that "if all of Greenland's vast ice sheet, which is nearly 2 miles thick in places, were to melt, global sea levels would rise by more than 20 feet, inundating coastal communities" around the world ("Greenland's Fast-Melting Ice Sheet," 2019).

3. *Growing concentration of wealth and economic inequality.* The wealth of 62 people is equal to the wealth of the poorest 3.5 billion people, and the richest 1% have more wealth than the other 99%. Humanity as a whole has had much less impact on Earth than the 1% who acquires more than 80% of the world's wealth generated in a year (Oxfam, 2019; Quackenbush, 2019).

> Wealthy nations and wealthy people use vastly more energy and emit far more carbon dioxide than the poor. . . . The consequences have been wealthy, carbon-intensive lifestyles for some, and a carbon-filled atmosphere for all. (Ellis, 2018, p. 133)

4. *Virulent infectious diseases and evolving super-viruses.* Epidemiologists talk not of whether there will be a new global pandemic but when and how extensive it will be. The 1918 flu epidemic killed more people than all the military deaths in World Wars I and II combined (Barry, 2017). The next one will be worse, possibly brought on by superbugs resistant to antibiotics that are already killing thousands every year (Groopman, 2018; McKenna, 2017).

5. *Deadly pollution.* "Approximately 9 million people die from pollution each year. 94% of these deaths are in lower-middle-income countries. Pollution also imposes substantial economic costs, frequently in the range of 4–5 percent of a country's GDP—often exceeding the amounts countries received in terms of overseas development aid" (Independent Evaluation Group, 2018, p. 1).

6. *Global terrorism, international drug cartels, global human trafficking, and global arms merchants.* The infrastructure of global criminal organizations uses the latest communications technology, political corruption, and sophisticated money laundering to operate with near impunity throughout the world. All nations are targeted, all are affected. The Global Terrorism Index shows global effects of increased terrorism (Institute for Economics and Peace, 2018).

7. *Refugees.* In 2019, there were 65 million refugees worldwide, more displaced people in the world than at any time since World War II. A major World Bank report (Rigaud et al., 2018) modeled climate change-induced migration in three regions—sub-Saharan Africa, South Asia, and Latin America—that together represent 55% of the developing world's population. The report projected that climate change will push tens of millions of people to migrate within their countries by 2050 and that without concrete climate and development action, over 143 million people—or around 2.8% of the population of these three regions—could be forced to move within their own countries. They will migrate from less viable areas with lower water availability and crop productivity and from areas affected by rising sea level and storm surges. The poorest and most climate-vulnerable areas will be hardest hit. The report finds that internal climate migration will likely rise through 2050 and then accelerate, unless there are significant cuts in greenhouse gas emissions and robust development action (Ober et al., 2018).

8. *Major cities running out of water.* Cape Town, Mexico City, São Paulo, Atlanta, and Melbourne are among the cities facing potential water shortages related to climate change. The World Resources Institute reports that more than a billion people currently live in "water-scarce" regions and "3.5 billion could experience water scarcity by 2025" (Baker, 2018, p. 35).

9. *Extensive loss of biodiversity.* Loss of biodiversity includes both diverse ecosystems and diversity of food we consume.

> About 75 percent of the world's food comes from just 12 plants and 5 animal species. Almost half of our plant-derived calories come from just three foods: wheat, corn, and rice. From over some 30,000 edible plants, we only eat 150 of them. 30% of livestock breeds are at risk of extinction, and six breeds are being lost each month. (Gould, 2019, p. 1)

In a regional report on Africa, the Intergovernmental Science-Policy Platform on Biodiversity and Ecosystem Services (IPBES) forecast that all flora and fauna are threatened by human-induced and natural causes such that by 2100, climate change alone could reduce by half Africa's bird and mammal species, along with a significant loss of plant species. In the next 30 years, Africa's population is expected to double to 2.5 billion people, accelerating loss of habitat and biodiversity (IPBES, 2018).

The Sixth Extinction describes the current and ongoing loss of species during the present epoch, mainly due to human activity, spanning numerous families of plants and animals, including mammals, birds, amphibians, reptiles, and arthropods. The International Union for Conservation of Nature and Natural Resources estimates the present rate of extinction may be up to 140,000 species per year (Kolbert, 2014).

- *Wildlife apocalypse.* It's not just climate change. "Demand for wildlife body parts for scientifically unproven medicinal remedies and paranormal trinkets is causing a worldwide crisis for many endangered species, including rhinos and elephants" (Ladendorf & Ladendorf, 2018, p. 30). Humans making their own short-term perceived needs and wants primary epitomizes the Anthropocene.

- *Insect apocalypse.* "Insects are responding to the transformation of the world, not just a changing climate but also the widespread conversion, via urbanization, agricultural intensification and so on, of natural spaces into human ones, with fewer and fewer resources left over for nonhuman creatures to live on. What resources remain are often contaminated. The life of many modern insects constitutes trying to survive from one dwindling oasis to the next with poisoned deserts in-between. . . . The insect apocalypse is here" (Jarvis, 2018, pp. 41, 67). The collapse of bee colonies has received widespread attention (e.g., Hanson, 2018), but the problem is greater than the loss of pollinators, as severe as that is.

10. *Ongoing threat to humanity from nuclear weapons* (Ellsberg, 2018). "Major nuclear actors are on the cusp of a new arms race, one that will be very expensive and will increase the likelihood of accidents and misperceptions. Across the globe, nuclear weapons are poised to become more rather than less usable because of nations' investments in their nuclear arsenals" (Bronson, 2018, p. 1). The withdrawal of the United States in early 2019 from the Intermediate-Range Nuclear Forces Treaty with Russia has increased the danger of nuclear engagements, either intentional or accidental.

The preceding are but a sample of global challenges. We could add feeding the world, unsustainable and insecure food systems, cyberterrorism and threats to the World Wide Web, multinational corporate influences, global financial turbulence, more extreme weather patterns, and world population growth. Experts may argue about the severity, scope, and urgency of specific challenges, but when considered together, the essentially global nature of these problems is not in doubt and the overall implications for human well-being are profound. For the first time in human history, we now know the scope and scale of change we have wrought and are bringing to our home planet as a collective species.

The Smithsonian National Museum of Natural History in Washington, DC, has spent over $45 million on an exhibit de-

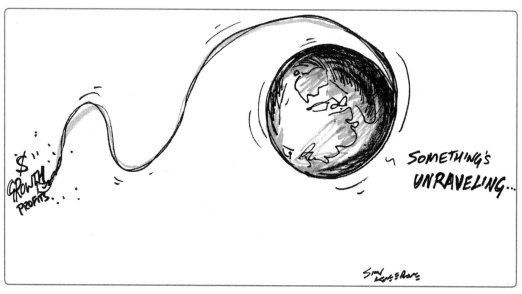

Something's unraveling by Simon Kneebone. Used with permission of the copyright holder, the Australian Evaluation Society (*aes.asn.au*).

scribed as a new story of human history. "This provocative exhibit will focus on the Anthropocene—the slice of Earth's history during which people have become a major geological force. Through mining activities alone, humans move more sediment than all the world's rivers combined. *Homo sapiens* has also warmed the planet, raised sea levels, eroded the ozone layer and acidified the oceans" (Hickman, 2016).

Toward a Balanced Assessment

New technologies and approaches are merging the physical, digital, and biological worlds in ways that will fundamentally transform humankind. The extent to which that transformation is positive will depend on how we navigate the risks and opportunities that arise along the way.
—Klaus Schwab, founder and Executive Chair of the World Economic Forum

It's not all doom and gloom. Examining the state of the world generates urgent calls for transformation, as well as beacons of hope. There are good things happening all over the world in response to ecosystem change,

as well as efforts to measure, evaluate, and accelerate them. Blue Marble design and evaluation supports finding balance and seeing both the challenges ahead and positive developments already underway. The last few years have included major increases in solar energy use, millions of acres of forest restoration, significant initiatives aimed at pollution reduction, extreme poverty decreasing worldwide, public health breakthroughs, phasing out of coal production and use, policy changes aimed at reducing fossil fuel use, and worldwide commitments to reduce inequality and increase sustainability (Hervey, 2017). In *Inheritors of the Earth*, conservation biologist Chris Thomas (2018) argues that animals and plants are adapting to changes in the world humans are creating, transformations that bode well for the future viability of diverse ecosystems globally. At the beginning of 2019, *New York Times* columnist Nicholas Kristof (2018) cited numerous positive indicators, including fewer people living in poverty, high quality of life for millions, and greater educational opportunities for more people, especially girls around the world, explaining "why 2018 was the best year in human history." In the same vein, Harvard psychologist and best-selling author Steven Pinker (2018) makes the case in his latest book, *Enlightenment Now: The Case for Reason, Science, Humanism, and Progress*, that the world is in the best state it has ever known because of significant and demonstrable worldwide reductions in poverty, illiteracy, disease, hunger, and violence, and he is optimistic that the world will awaken to the dangers of climate change and, ultimately, do what needs to be done to mitigate disaster. (Pinker's analysis of climate data has been strongly criticized; e.g., Monbiot, 2018.) Optimists (e.g., Buffett, 2018; Gates, 2018, 2019), mining global trend data, express confidence in the future as vociferously as pessimists sound alarms. The book written by the innovative global statistician Hans Rosling (2018), crammed full of data and insights, is subtitled *Ten Reasons We're Wrong About the World—and Why Things Are Better Than You Think*. Rosling's book became, and remains, a huge best-seller. *Anthropocene* magazine is devoted to innovations and positive solutions in the "human age." A special issue of *Time* magazine in February 2019 featured "The Art of Optimism," with observations from "34 people changing how we see the world" (Duvernay, 2019).

Good things are happening. Bad things are happening. The momentum of the bad things happening may mean that things will get worse globally before they get better, if they do get better, ever. Balancing positive trends against negative ones, desired outcomes against undesired results, and learning from what's working in contrast to what's not—these are quintessential evaluation challenges. That's what we evaluators do—we create a balanced, informative, and useful synthesis from disparate and often conflicting findings. At least that's what we've been doing at a project and program level for 50 years. Now we are called on to seriously up our game to global evaluation syntheses.

Pessimism/optimism by Simon Kneebone.

Global systems change evaluations will have to attend to diverse perspectives, changing boundaries of problems and possibilities, and dynamic interrelationships. This includes looking at pockets of positive and negative developments locally within the larger context of worldwide trends. An example of such analysis comes from a news interview with Stephen Flynn, Director of the Global Resilience Institute, who concluded in contrasting micro versus macro developments: "I worry that we're creating islands of resilience in seas of fragility." Those islands of resilience are bounded projects and programs. The sea of fragility is the whole Earth. That expresses well my own sense of the situation, thus this chapter has leaned more toward listing the negative trends than positive ones, but the balance between positive and negative, always a matter of interpretation and judgment, will be in play for some time to come. Being neither Pollyannaish nor absolute doomsayers, our work goes on somewhere in the muddled middle, acknowledging the challenges and working to identify solutions at both micro and macro levels.

One of the positive forces, hopefully, is new directions in global systems change design and evaluation. The point of examining both negative and positive trends is to see what emerges from taking a global perspective, which is the basis for Blue Marble thinking. It is important to note that there are powerful people benefiting from the negative trends—finding balance among competing views is difficult for the average person. Still, the evidence points overwhelmingly, in my judgment, to a severe and growing crisis.

Facing Reality

The Anthropocene as Context principle calls for knowing and facing the realities of the Anthropocene. The significance of knowing and facing reality is based on two of the most insightful observations about humankind in the history of social science:

"We've got her on a respirator, a detox diet and an IV. She keeps complaining she feels like she's aged fifty millenniums since the industrial revolution. Oh, and she doesn't like being referred to as a marble."

Planetary intensive care unit by Mark M. Rogers.

If [people] define situations as real, they are real in their consequences.

—Thomas theorem (Thomas & Thomas, 1928, p. 572)

If a thing is not recognized as true, then it does not function as true in the community.

—Merton corollary (Mead, 1936, p. 29)

Distinguished sociologist Robert K. Merton (1976, p. 380) explained that "theorem" in this case refers to

an idea that is being proposed or accepted as sound, consequential, and empirically relevant. . . . I had fastened on the term *theorem* rather than such less formidable terms as *dictum, maxim, proposition,* or *aphorism* in order to convey my sense that this was "probably the single most consequential sentence ever put in print by an American sociologist."

The magnitude, direction, and speed of transformations envisioned and undertaken to deal with the realities of the Anthropocene depend on perceptions of those realities. Blue Marble evaluators carry a responsibility with others to make those realities—their implications and potentially dire consequences—known, understood, and acted upon. That responsibility takes us to the third overarching Blue Marble principle: the Transformative Engagement principle.

CHAPTER 3

Transformative Engagement Principle

In the kind of world we have today, transformation of humanity might well be our only real hope for survival.
—STANISLAV GROF, Czechoslovakian psychiatrist

CONTEXT

Climate change changes everything. There are many scenarios being spun that portray varying degrees of catastrophe—some sooner, and some later. Any straight-line projections of current climate trends conclude with disaster. Humanity is consuming Earth's resources unsustainably. The numbers will continue to be updated and new scenarios will be generated, but they all lead to the conclusion that transformational change is needed for human life on Earth to be sustained—and those transformations need to happen sooner rather than later.

Transformation means dramatic, radical change on a global scale. It means transforming energy consumption, agriculture, power structures, distribution of resources and wealth and creating fundamentally different relationships between human beings and the environment to achieve both sustainability and greater equity for the people of the world. It means everyone doing their part wherever we find ourselves. People calling for transformation in the face of climate change speak with a sense of urgency.

In essence, two conclusions inform widespread calls for global systems transformation:

1. Humanity's use of Earth's resources for both production and consumption is unsustainable.

2. Transformation globally is urgently required to avoid catastrophe for humanity.

Chapter 1 focused our thinking at the global level. Chapter 2 presented the evidence for these conclusions given the realities of the Anthropocene. This chapter examines the implications of the evidence that undergirds the third overarching Blue Marble principle, on transformative engagement.

Transformative Engagement Principle Explicated

PREMISE: Global, Anthropogenic problems are so severe, threatening the future sustainability of the planet and humanity, that major and rapid systems transformations are needed. Susanne Moser (2017), at the Stanford Woods Institute for the Environment, has stated the premise for transformation:

> Before we went to transformation conferences, we went to adaptation conferences, mitigation conferences, sustainability conferences, but now we have arrived at a place where we know we need transformation, we need to do much deeper work. Transformation is not just a faddish word or idea. It captures the scale and scope of what must change if it is life we want, for the future of life is in doubt and cannot be taken for granted.

Transformative Engagement Principle

Engage and evaluate consistent with the magnitude, direction, and speed of transformations needed and envisioned.

IMPLICATIONS

Business as usual will not suffice. Major systems changes at a global scale are needed, given the trends of the Anthropocene. Program and project interventions affect narrowly targeted outcomes that are important in their own right but are insufficient to achieve transformation. Likewise, the tools, methods, and thinking that dominate program and project evaluation will be inadequate to evaluate transformation. Individual theories of change will have to be synthesized into a higher-impact, broader-scale theory of transformation. Evaluating transformation is different from evaluating projects and programs. Blue Marble evaluation aspires to be part of taking evaluation to a new level, a global level, to contribute to transformation.

Transformation of global systems includes, and may even begin with, individual transformation. Each of us is called on to change our lifestyle. If we are to become part of the movement for global systems transformation, individual mindsets, knowledge, and behavior are part of the larger global systems transformation process. Small local programs to large global programs are all part of transformation.

Complexity rules. No one is in charge, no one can exercise control, the path forward is uncertain and unpredictable, and will surely be both emergent and nonlinear. Blue Marble evaluation is based on complexity theory and systems thinking.

This chapter lays out the case for transformation. Chapter 13 presents a theory of transformation. Chapter 14 focuses on evaluating transformation. The final chapter, Chapter 15, makes the case that to stay relevant and useful, transforming evaluation will be necessary to evaluate transformation.

Calls for Transformation: Scrapbook Entries for the Future

Let me take you on a quick tour of the global transformation landscape to get a sense of who is advocating for systems transformation and what case they are making. Then, we'll look at the implications for evaluation. I'm highlighting a few voices and perspectives from among hundreds through which we can glimpse the scale and scope of the calls for global systems transformations. These are some of the people and initiatives I've encountered on the journey to understanding and appreciating transformation as a distinct focus for both action and evaluation. Think of what follows as a small selection of distinct calls to action—1 week's worth of excerpts from my *transformation scrapbook*.

Transformations: The Only Option for Future Survival

Here are highlights from three participants at *Transformations 2017,* the third in a series of international interdisciplinary conferences focused on transformations toward sustainability, this one held in August 2017 at the University of Dundee, Scotland. (Terry A'Hearn and Kumi Naidoo gave keynote addresses.)

> In Scotland, we are living as if we have the resources of three planets when we only have one. Australia is consuming five planets of resources. For the world as a whole, we are consuming Earth's resources as if we have 1.7 planets. We only have one.
>
> We are all heading in the wrong direction. There isn't a single country that has reversed its over-use of the planet yet. Incremental change isn't enough. We need transformational change. We need to transform our society and world to one that lives within what one planet can support.
>
> —TERRY A'HEARN, CEO, Scottish Environment Protection Agency (2017)

> I globe trot from one meeting to another. Some of us are caught up in this cycle and there seems to be no way out of it. Anyway, this year (2017), I participated in nine international meetings. I was active in all of them either as part of the organizing group or as a presenter. There is one thread connecting all of them: *transformation.*
>
> At last there is a realization that change, fundamental change in the way we are living, is needed. . . . I think that the majority of us are all caught up in this paradox of deeply understanding the kind of transformation that is needed but being part of perpetuating the same system that we hate so much.
>
> —MILLION BELAY, Coordinator of the Alliance for Food Sovereignty in Africa[*] (2017; emphasis added)

---

[*]The Alliance for Food Sovereignty in Africa (AFSA) is a broad alliance of different civil society actors that are advocating for and working toward food sovereignty and agroecology in Africa.

Transformation Requires Social and Economic Justice

> The most important challenge for leadership of our time, whether the leaders are from the private sector, from government, or from civil society, is how we can tell it like it is, speak truth to power, say that *we are five minutes till midnight on climate change.*
>
> When we look at the question of inequality in the world today, it is crazy. You have 85 people in the world who have amassed more wealth than the bottom 65%.
>
> The problem is that most of the interventions we have are at the level of delivering projects and programs, not enough on policy change, and certainly not enough on governance change, partly because of the funding trap that progressives, as well as others, are caught in.
>
> —KUMI NAIDOO, Launch Executive Director of the African Civil Society Support Initiative (2017; emphasis added)

Transformation Means "No One Left Behind"

> In September 2015, leaders from around the world adopted the ambitious 2030 Agenda for Sustainable Development at a historic United Nations Summit. Agenda 2030 calls for global transformation that focuses on ending poverty, protecting the planet, and ensuring prosperity for all. . . . A call on all countries to mobilize efforts to end all forms of poverty, fight inequalities, and tackle climate change, while ensuring that "no one is left behind." (Segone & Tateossian, 2017, p. 24)

Transformations 2050: Transformations to Achieve the Sustainable Development Goals

The first report prepared by *The World in 2050* (International Institute for Applied Systems Analysis, 2018) initiative identifies six transformations critical for achieving long-term sustainability:

1. The digital revolution.

2. Smarter cities.

3. Sustainable transformation of resource use.

4. Widespread education and human development.

5. Transformation of human production and consumption practices.

6. Decarbonization and energy use transformation.

Sustainable Development Goals Transformation Forum: Statement of Need

Many pressing challenges require transformation, rather than incremental change and trade-offs. The knowledge, tools, and action for achieving transformative change are, however, inadequate and fragmented across disparate disciplines, issues, organizations and people. There is, therefore, an urgent need to develop, nurture and connect ways of working and learning for transformative change.

Transformation involves redefinition of goals (e.g.: from producing energy to producing sustainable energy) which arise from a new understanding about the way things work (e.g.: carbon emissions result in climate change) and produce fundamental change in operating logics (e.g.: from "mining" of nature, to harmony with nature). This usually involves deep shifts in power structures (e.g.: away from carbon extractors).

—SDG TRANSFORMATIONS FORUM (2017, p. 1)

Transformational Leadership

A process through which an individual, organization, or collective guides large, fundamental, radical transitions from one existing state to a more positive, desired state. This kind of leadership takes a systems approach, employing holistic, comprehensive, collaborative, and multi-disciplinary methods to make effective, demonstrable change that then scales to large groups of people. Those who practice Transformational Change Leadership (2019) embody it fully in the way they live their lives, carry out their work, and communicate their philosophies.

—*https://tcleadership.org/introduction*

Transform NGO and Nonprofit Missions

Put Climate in Every Nonprofit Mission

—Headline in the *Nonprofit Quarterly* blog by MARIAN CONWAY, Executive Director, New York Community Bank Foundation (2019)

It follows that putting attention on climate change in every nonprofit organization and

Trans formation by Simon Kneebone. Used with permission of the copyright holder, the Australian Evaluation Society (*aes.asn.au*).

program mission would mean putting attention on climate in every evaluation of nonprofits.

Transformation, Transformation, Transformation

The seven scrapbook selections calling for global systems transformation that I just presented fill up only a week if you read but one per day. I could easily have offered enough to fill a year of daily warnings. Urgent calls for transformation seem to be everywhere. In less than two decades, scientific scholarship has shifted from calling for adaptations to the social, political, and ecological shocks and stressors faced globally to recognizing that adaptation to some of the world's most intractable problems may be insufficient (Adger & Barnett, 2009; Kates, Travis, & Wilbanks, 2012; Moser & Ekstrom, 2010).

Funders are increasingly calling for, and even requiring evidence of, transformations (see Belmont Forum, 2017; International Science Council, 2018; Schwab Foundation for Social Entrepreneurship, 2017). Policymakers have begun to recognize transformation as a goal (e.g., UN, 2015; Welsh Assembly Government, 2009). Geographers, political scientists, ecologists, indigenous governance scholars, organizational theorists, business schools, and more are studying and engaging in transformations for sustainability while building empirically based evidence about the potential of certain initiatives to provide transformative solutions (e.g., Charli-Joseph, Siqueiros-Garcia, Eakin, Manuel-Navarrete, & Shelton, 2018; Corntassel, 2012; Heras & Tàbara, 2014; Scoones et al., 2018). If one considers the number of "incubators," "hubs," "labs," networks, and more (Schäpke et al., 2018), it could also be argued that social innovators, social entrepreneurs, and "change makers" have begun to create an entire industry around the idea of transformation. (Moore, Westley, & Olsson, 2019).

An Uncertain Future

Urgent calls for transformation make it difficult to find balance and see both the challenges ahead and positive developments already underway. The last few years have included major increases in solar energy use, millions of acres of forest restoration, significant initiatives aimed at pollution reduction, extreme poverty decreasing worldwide, public health breakthroughs, phasing out of coal production and use, policy changes aimed at reducing fossil fuel use, and worldwide commitments to reduce inequality and increase sustainability (Hervey, 2017).

To gain some perspective, Chris Kutarna, coauthor of *Age of Discovery* (Goldin & Kutarna, 2016), advises:

The thing to step back and challenge ourselves with, is to recognize that in a disruptive moment, linear expectations of the future are not going to cut it, are not going to help us to navigate and set good expectations for what's to come, that the better mindset is to recognize that this is a deeply contested moment, that this is both the best time and one of the most fragile times to be alive and to decide and to act forward from that perspective. It's challenging ourselves to recognize that there are a lot of positive forces operating in the world right now.

One of those positive forces, hopefully, is new directions in Blue Marble evaluation addressing transformation. Here are the major themes arising from the Transformative Engagement principle that we explore in future chapters and add details to through the operating principles.

- Base transformational interventions on a research-informed theory of transformation knitting together relevant theories of change.
- Ensure that what is called transformation *is* transformational.
- Catalyze, connect, track, map, and evalu-

ate networks and initiatives worldwide to generate critical mass tipping points toward global transformation.

- Apply systems thinking and complexity theory to transformational engagements.
- Transform evaluation to evaluate transformation.

Transformation as Value Neutral

The Anthropocene, whether called that ultimately or not, is a scientific fact. Humans are having a dramatic, measurable, decisive, and lasting impact on Earth. Thus, *transformation* is a descriptive term for major systems change. That change can be toward greater sustainability and equity, or it can also be toward greater concentrations of power and wealth, resurgence of nationalism and white supremacy, and long-term environmental degradation. Rendering judgment about the direction of transformation, and whether it is good or bad, requires a value judgment and application of

human and environmental ethics (Attfield, 2018).

What's at Stake

Humanity has reached a critical juncture—the most important in the relatively short existence of our species. Unless we are willing to let global problems fester to the point where violence and intolerance appear to be the only realistic ways of confronting our unevenly integrating world, we must link the future of globalization to a profoundly reformist agenda. . . . However, these transformative social processes must have a moral compass and an ethical polestar guiding our collective efforts: the building of a truly democratic and equalitarian global order that protects universal human rights without destroying the cultural diversity that is the lifeblood of human evolution.

—MANFRED STEGER, globalization scholar (2013, pp. 136–137)

Ethical guidance for transformation includes connecting humans and the natural

Barrier Reef transformation by Simon Kneebone. Used with permission of the copyright holder, the Australian Evaluation Society (*aes.asn.au*).

A Michael Quinn Patton/Mark M. Rogers collaboration

"Can we get back in balance?"

Teeter totter by Mark M. Rogers.

world in mutually sustainable ways. A call for democratic processes is not advocacy for a particular form of government but, rather, for participatory processes that involve people in decisions that affect their future and that consider both local interests and a sustainable trajectory for humanity and the planet. Blue Marble evaluation aspires to contribute to realizing that vision, making evaluation part of the solution rather than part of the problem. To do so will mean integrating the Blue Marble principles, not treating them as a pick-and-choose list. That leads us to the fourth and final overarching Blue Marble principle, the Integration principle.

CHAPTER 4

Integration Principle

The most notable distinction between living and inanimate things is that the former maintain themselves by renewal.
—JOHN DEWEY, *Democracy and Education* (1944, p. 360)

CONTEXT

Blue Marble evaluation is guided by four overarching principles, each based on a premise about the state of the world. Chapters 1–3 presented the first three overarching Blue Marble principles. This chapter introduces the fourth, the principle of integration. Given that the Blue Marble perspective emphasizes holism, interconnectedness, interdependence, and thinking across borders, boundaries, and silos, it will perhaps not be surprising that to reinforce the Blue Marble perspective, the final principle is integration.

Integration Principle Explicated

PREMISE: Transformation requires multiple interventions and actions on many fronts undertaken by diverse but interconnected actors.

Integration Principle

Integrate the Blue Marble principles in the design, engagement with, and evaluation of systems change and transformation initiatives.

IMPLICATIONS

This fourth principle integrates the previous three, making it clear that this is not a pick-and-choose menu of options but rather an integrated and comprehensive approach in which all the principles are important and, together, constitute a complete package. As we proceed in subsequent chapters to introduce and explain the 12 operating principles, the Integration principle will apply to those as well. The Integration principle provides coherence to Blue Marble evaluation. Exhibit 4.1 presents the premises and overarching principles together.

EXHIBIT 4.1. Four Overarching Blue Marble Premises and Principles	
Premises	**Overarching principles**
1. Global problems like climate change, worldwide pollution, and global disparities require global interventions and, correspondingly, globally oriented and world savvy evaluators.	***Global Thinking principle:*** *Apply whole-Earth, big-picture thinking to all aspects of systems change.*
2. Human actions have created the global problems humanity faces; human actions are necessary to resolve these problems; thus, there are things for evaluators to know about global sustainability in the context of the Anthropocene to undertake evaluations knowledgeably and credibly.	***Anthropocene as Context principle:*** *Know and face the realities of the Anthropocene and act accordingly.*
3. Global anthropogenic problems are so severe, threatening the future of the planet and humanity, that major and rapid systems transformations are needed.	***Transformative Engagement principle:*** *Engage and evaluate consistent with the magnitude, direction, and speed of transformations needed and envisioned.*
4. Transformation requires multiple interventions and actions on many fronts undertaken by diverse but interconnected actors.	***Integration principle:*** *Integrate the Blue Marble principles in the design, engagement with, and evaluation of systems change and transformation initiatives.*

The principles provide guidance for Blue Marble evaluation thinking, knowing, and doing. Exhibit 4.2 depicts these four overarching principles in dynamic interaction. Exhibit 15.2, in the final chapter, presents the full set of overarching and operating principles.

Blue Marble Evaluation Perspective

Blue Marble evaluation looks backward (what has been) to inform the future (what might be) based on the present trajectory (what is happening now). Evaluators examine what has worked and not worked in the past, not just to capture history, but to inform the future. As discussed in previous chapters, forecasts for the future of humanity run the gamut from doom and gloom to utopia. Evaluation as a transdisciplinary, global profession has much to offer in navigating the risks and opportunities that arise as global change initiatives and interventions are designed and undertaken to ensure a more sustainable and equitable future.

While conducting evaluations worldwide, evaluators have learned a great deal about what is needed to *design* effective interventions and then what it takes to implement them. This knowledge informs the Blue Marble approach as design, implementation, and evaluation are integrated on the basis of knowledge about these relationships. That said, emphasizing that the Blue Marble principles encompass design, implementation, and evaluation makes writing about the principles wordier and somewhat cumbersome. For the sake of brevity, I refer most often to Blue Marble evaluation with the understanding that design thinking and attention to implementation, execution, engagement, and adaptation are included and embedded.

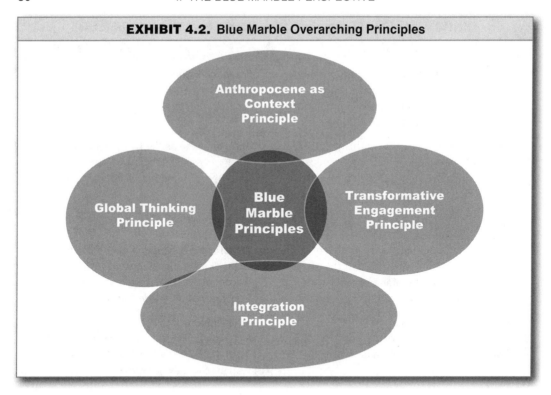

EXHIBIT 4.2. Blue Marble Overarching Principles

Transforming Evaluation

Integrating design, engagement, and evaluation is but one way Blue Marble evaluation transforms evaluation. Traditional project and program evaluation will not suffice to address systems change on a global scale. Traditional—and still dominant—performance measurement and monitoring techniques are likewise inadequate. Static and rigid randomized control designs—emphasis on control—are irrelevant to the uncontrollable dynamics of complex systems. Indeed, these traditional approaches to evaluation can create barriers to systems change by forcing transformational visions into narrow project boxes amenable to methods evaluators are comfortable with (e.g., logic models and specific, measurable, achievable, relevant, time-bound [SMART] goals). Innovations in evaluation include eclectic approaches created by tapping into a vast array of many-splendored, diverse, and innovative knowledge-generating and learning-oriented processes. You'll find those throughout the book, then brought together in the synthesis chapter (Chapter 15), at the end, subtitled "Transforming Evaluation to Evaluate Transformation."

In short, evaluation is no longer just a back-end activity assessing whether goals have been attained. By integrating design, engagement, and evaluation, a Blue Marble evaluation team can support accomplishing a range of tasks in developing both local and global systems change initiatives. The next section provides a checklist of Blue Marble contributions that can be used as both a reminder of possibilities for evaluators and a menu of options for those designing and implementing systems change initiatives.

Blue Marble Design, Engagement, and 12-Point Evaluation Checklist

1. *Situation analysis and statement of the problem.* What is the empirical evidence that delineates the scope, status, and pa-

rameters of the problems to be addressed? To what extent and in what ways do these global issues reflect Anthropocenic, regional, and local trends? A Blue Marble perspective brings global data, expertise, relevant research, indigenous knowledge, and local insights to bear on problem delineation at whatever level an initiative is operating—local, regional, statewide, national, or multinational.

2. *Asking the right questions.* What evaluation questions are useful to answer? There are more possible questions about any initiative than can possibly be answered. Utilization-focused evaluation navigates through the maze of possibilities to keep the spotlight on what's truly useful to know from a Blue Marble perspective for improvement and decision making. The Blue Marble perspective enlarges the context for decision making by adding overarching attention to global systems transformation. This means understanding the important questions to local and global stakeholders, capital city policymakers, indigenous people on their own lands, and the variety of stakeholders who have an interest in the evaluation and a right to have their questions addressed.

3. *System(s) to be changed.* What are the boundaries, interrelationships, dynamics, and perspectives that delineate the systems that an intervention or initiative aspires to transform? Global subsystems like climate, the global economy, worldwide population dynamics, land systems, ocean systems, flora and fauna subsystems, and human systems (economic, political, cultural) make up the whole Earth system.

4. *Theory of transformation.* What research and evaluation findings support, explain, and justify the proposed approach to systems transformation? A theory of transformation is not just a brainstorming idea, creative fabrication, or vision of hope. A theory of transformation should be knowledge based, research supported, and evaluable. A Blue Marble theory of transformation includes specification of how

Indigenous evaluators by Simon Kneebone. Used with permission of the copyright holder, the Australian Evaluation Society (*aes.asn.au*).

global trends, factors, and influences will be handled in the initiative. And when the target is transformation, multiple theories of change may be knitted together into a *theory of transformation,* the focus of Chapter 13.

5. *Budget development.* What are the likely costs of a proposed intervention or initiative? Evaluators can help find cost comparisons and budget projections based on similar efforts. Initial cost-effectiveness calculations help guide decisions about feasibility and viability. Blue Marble budgets must identify and include the real costs of operating globally.

6. *Contextual analysis.* What larger contextual factors—social, cultural, environmental, political, and economic—should be taken into account and factored in through strategic thinking, then monitored as the initiative unfolds? The context for Blue Marble design and evaluation includes the effects of having entered the *Anthropocene epoch.* The Anthropocene is an essential context for global systems change initiatives, as elaborated in the next chapter. And the point here is not just to do situation and contextual analyses as freestanding, check-off-the-box-as-done activities. The point is to use those analyses to inform the evaluation, focus evaluation questions, and interpret findings—and that situation and context analyses need to be regularly revisited and updated.

7. *Implementation strategy.* What has to happen to move from proposed idea to in-the-real-world action? Evaluative thinking helps connect the dots to portray the pathway toward intended change and success. The global dimensions of thinking and acting from a Blue Marble perspective takes into account that implementation of systems transformation initiatives will be more complex and uncertain than more narrowly conceived traditional projects and programs.

8. *Adaptive learning and ongoing course corrections.* How can engagement and implementation be monitored to allow for ongoing development and timely learning, allowing course corrections in the face of complex systems dynamics, emergent developments, and unanticipated consequences? Especially important is how to reflect on global developments and experiences that give a global edge to lessons learned.

9. *Reality testing.* How can those working at change know whether what they hoped would happen is really happening, and what they aspired to accomplish is being accomplished? All of us, as humans, are subject to selective perception, seeing only what we want to see. Evaluation is the antidote to self-congratulatory reality distortion. It is easy to slide back into a narrow project and program mentality away from global systems change thinking and engagement. The Blue Marble perspective stays focused on global realities and the interconnections between local and global realities.

10. *Extracting insights and lessons to inform trajectory adjustments.* What revisions in actions, strategy, theory of change, and theory of transformation are needed to reflect what is being learned and guide adaptation in the face of unfolding realities? A theory of transformation is not a wall decoration. Evaluative findings, interpreted through the lens of the theory of transformation, support deepening understanding of what is happening and why, and the implications going forward. Blue Marble evaluation generates lessons that can be applied to adapting what is already being done, taking advantage of new opportunities, and facing emergent challenges. Blue Marble evaluation findings and lessons can also support connecting transformative initiatives to one another as a collective response to global trends.

11. *Timing and focusing reporting.* When will evaluation findings be synthesized and

reported to which intended users and stakeholders for what intended purposes, to optimize evaluation use? Boilerplate time lines (e.g., quarterly and annual reports) may not align with the need for timely evaluation feedback that can make the greatest difference. Blue Marble evaluators also monitor global and local situational developments that may affect time lines.

12. *Principles-focused evaluation.* To what extent and in what ways have the Blue Marble principles been meaningful, adhered to, and integrated? To what extent and in what ways have the Blue Marble principles provided useful guidance, been inspiring, and supported developmental adaptation? Principles-focused Blue Marble evaluation invites evaluation of the utility and effectiveness of the principles.

Integrating Overarching and Operating Principles

Blue Marble evaluation consists of four overarching principles, which are implemented through specific operating principles. As explained in the opening chapter, the distinction between overarching principles and operating principles is like the distinction between goals and objectives. Overarching principles provide big-picture, general guidance. Operating principles provide more specific guidance. Each overarching principle and each operational issue is a chapter in this book. The first four chapters have presented the four overarching Blue Marble principles. This concludes Part I of the book. Part II turns to the operating principles. The Integration principle applies to the integration of overarching

The Four Horsepersons of the Blue Marble, each working alone, felt they were fighting a losing battle and so set off to find a Blue Marble evaluator to help them become more effective working together.

Four horsepersons by Mark M. Rogers.

and operating principles. It also applies to the integration of values and strategies as the cartoon depicting the *Four Horsepersons of the Blue Marble* shows. This is cartoonist Mark Rogers's takeoff on and hopeful counter to the *Four Horsemen of the Apocalypse: Pestilence, Famine, War, and Death*. When not drawing imaginative cartoons, Mark is an international development professional working on peace-building initiatives. He knows of what he draws.

We turn now to Part II with this admonition from William Easterly (2013), longtime critic of top-down development projects and author of *The Tyranny of Experts: Economists, Dictators, and the Forgotten Rights of the Poor*:

It is critical to get the principles of action right before acting. (p. 1)

Blue Marble Operating Principles

Part I challenged evaluators to think globally in the face of the realities of the Anthropocene and support, through evaluation, the global systems transformations necessary to create a more sustainable and equitable future for humanity. The overarching Blue Marble principles are interrelated and mutually reinforcing and, in accordance with the Integration principle, need to be integrated with the more specific operating principles. That's what Part II of this book aspires to do.

Overarching Blue Marble Principles
1. *Global Thinking principle*
2. *Anthropocene as Context principle*
3. *Transformative Engagement principle*
4. *Integration principle*

Blue Marble Operating Principles

- CHAPTER 5. Transboundary Engagement Principle
- CHAPTER 6. GLOCAL Principle
- CHAPTER 7. Cross-Silos Principle
- CHAPTER 8. Time Being of the Essence Principle
- CHAPTER 9. Yin–Yang Principle
- CHAPTER 10. Bricolage Methods Principle
- CHAPTER 11. World Savvy Principle
- CHAPTER 12. Skin in the Game Principle

Systems Thinking and Complexity Theory

Systems thinking is central to Blue Marble evaluation. Bob Williams, a leader in applying systems thinking to evaluation, monitors systems approaches from his global sensing station in New Zealand. He coedited the first expert anthology on *Systems Concepts in Evaluation* (Williams & Iman, 2007). He estimates that as many as a thousand separate frameworks and methods "fall under the systems banner." Why? "Because there is no single agreed-upon definition of a 'system.'" Nor is there ever likely to be. Indeed, Bob argues, at the core of systems thinking is attention to the inevitable arbitrariness of boundaries, a variety of perspectives, and dynamic, entangled interrelationships, all of which apply as much to the complex world of systems theories, frameworks, and approaches as to other phenomena. (For comprehensive reviews of different approaches to systems thinking, see Midgley, 2003; Systems in Evaluation, 2018; Williams & Hummlebrunner, 2011; Williams & Iman, 2007).

The overarching principles of systems thinking focus on system boundaries, interrelationships of system elements, diverse perspectives, and system dynamics (Systems in Evaluation, 2018). The ways in which Blue Marble evaluation draws on systems thinking is explained below.

1. ***Boundaries.*** Blue Marble evaluation extends boundaries beyond traditional projects and programs to global initiatives, transboundary systems, natural and human ecosystems, and global networks. The evaluand (focus of evaluation) for Blue Marble evaluation can be the whole Earth and global–local interconnections and interactions among subsystems of the whole Earth (food systems, ecological systems, ocean systems, land systems, governance systems, economic systems, and so forth).

2. ***Interrelationships.*** Blue Marble evaluation examines the nature and consequences of interactions across sectors (public sector, private sector, NGOs, philanthropic foundations, and both formal and informal networks) and across and between arenas of action and interaction (e.g., education, health, poverty, environment, SDGs).

3. ***Perspectives.*** Blue Marble evaluation constitutes a perspective. Other perspectives come into play when designing and evaluating global interventions. Competing, conflicting, and mutually reinforcing perspectives about globalization, sustainability, resilience, innovation, scaling, and transformation, to name but a few examples, come into play in an integrated Blue Marble perspective.

Systems thinking and complexity theory by Chris Lysy.

4. *Complex dynamics.* Complex dynamics focus on the patterns of change that emerge within the global system to understand their influence and significance for global transformation. Global systems are characterized by turbulence, uncertainty, unpredictability, nonlinearities, adaptations, and multiple levels of change. Blue Marble evaluation maps and assesses those dynamics and their implications for long-term sustainability.

Systems Thinking and Complexity Theory Resources

Resources include Bamberger, Vaessen, and Raimondo (2016); Capra and Luisi (2014); Eoyang and Holladay (2013); Meadows (2008); Parsons, Dhillon, and Keene (2020); Patton (2011); Westley, Zimmerman, and Patton (2007); Williams (2005, 2008, 2019); Williams and Hummelbrunner (2011); and Williams and Iman (2007). Also visit the Human Systems Dynamics Institute website at *https://www.hsdinstitute.org.*

CHAPTER 5

Transboundary Engagement Principle

> Every nation must now develop an overriding loyalty
> to mankind as a whole in order to preserve what is
> best in their individual societies.
> —MARTIN LUTHER KING, JR.

CONTEXT

The first *overarching* principle is global thinking. This first *operating* principle aims to ensure that engagement and action follow thinking at a global scale. Chapter 2, on the realities of the Anthropocene, documented the kinds of global problems that transcend national and agency boundaries. Consider, as a beginning point, these 10 challenges to humanity's future.

1. Climate change
2. Global economic turbulence
3. Refugees at record levels
4. Virulent infectious diseases
5. Loss of marine life, dying coral reefs, and loss of biodiversity
6. Global cyberterrorism
7. International drug cartels
8. Human trafficking
9. Weapons trafficking
10. Hunger and poverty worldwide

The definitions of these problems are disputed. Possible solutions are vehemently debated. The "facts" are argued as a matter of "perspective." Politics and special interests dominate intervention proposals and strategy development. Nation-state interests, multinational corporate priorities, international agency agendas, and competition for scarce resources delay concerted action. The stakes are nothing less than the future well-being—indeed survival—of humanity. Blue Marble evaluation provides a framework of principles, practices, knowledge, and methods for evaluators to contribute to sustainable and just transformation for both the planet and its people.

These global challenges epitomize Einstein's observation, cited in Chapter 1, that "We cannot solve our problems with the same level of thinking that created them." The mantra that expresses the essence of this chapter—*Think globally, act globally*—has two parts. Thinking globally is the first overarching principle, explicated in Chapter 1. The current chapter emphasizes acting globally.

The terms *international* and *multinational* refer to working in several countries. In contrast, **global** involves working throughout the world to change the nature and dynamics of global systems, both human (social, economic, political) and ecological (land, water, air, flora, fauna). For Blue Marble evaluation, this means assessing the extent and ways in which an intervention or initiative calling itself "global" is truly global in design, implementation, and impact. A great many initiatives that call themselves "global" turn out to be working in three countries on one issue. Fully global initiatives work across geographic systems and sector silos. On the other hand, a global initiative that doesn't necessarily work in many countries may bring a decidedly global perspective to those places where it does work. Engaging globally can include looking at nation-state interactions but also beyond to transboundary systems. The next chapter looks at how a global perspective can inform local change efforts and how local knowledge and experience can inform global transformations. Keep the global–local interconnection in mind as we look at what it means to act globally in this chapter.

Transboundary Engagement Principle Explicated

PREMISE: Globalization has increased the scope and depth of global problems. Global problems require global responses. The interests of nation-states do not necessarily correspond with what is good for planetary sustainability and the well-being of humanity. Nation-states are not about to disappear and will play a role in dealing with global issues, but to some degree and in some ways global problems require globally oriented initiatives and

interventions. This means thinking globally and acting globally.

Transboundary Engagement Principle
Act at a global scale.

IMPLICATIONS

- Blue Marble evaluation is especially aligned with and appropriate for truly global initiatives, interventions, and systems transformation efforts.

- Global actions will occur within inherently complex dynamic systems, which means that Blue Marble evaluators must be able to engage beyond conventional project and program evaluation approaches by employing systems thinking, complexity theory, and network understandings.

- Global thinking and acting must remain connected to local, national, and regional thinking and acting without losing the global perspective.

- Thinking globally, acting globally, and evaluating globally need to be integrated to address the global realities of the Anthropocene.

- The Blue Marble perspective means understanding and tracking global interconnections that both inform and contextualize Blue Marble evaluation.

- Exhibit 5.1 highlights the design and evaluation implications of the Blue Marble Transboundary Engagement principle.

Beyond the Nation-State as the Focus of Change

Nation-state borders have been established through war, imperialism, enslavement, greed, religious persecution, and indigenous cultural suppression. Political, economic, and cultural dominion intersect with geography to create arbitrary and artificial national borders. For example, an analysis of the histories of almost 200

Blue Marble Transboundary Engagement principle	Design guidance	Evaluation criteria and questions
EXHIBIT 5.1. Design and Evaluation Implications of the Blue Marble Transboundary Engagement Principle		
Act at a global scale.	To address global problems, look beyond nation-state borders and boundaries to affect transnational, regional, and global patterns, interactions, and dynamics.	*Global-scale fidelity:* To what extent and in what ways is an initiative or intervention acting at a truly global scale? *Global systems focus:* What global system(s) are the focus for intervention and transformation?

countries in the world found only 22 that had never experienced an invasion by the British (Laycock, 2014). Exhibits 5.2 and 5.3 contrast images of the map of nation-state boundaries and divisions with one Earth undivided, the Blue Marble. Linger for a moment on those contrary images.

Nation-state boundaries have changed significantly over time and continue to change. To witness the drama of changing national borders, see the *History of Europe–6013 Years in 3 Minutes* on YouTube (MOAP, 2013).

These visuals, set to music, portray through changing maps the stunning arbitrariness of nation-state borders. For a more irreverent depiction, see *History of the Entire World, I Guess* (Wurtz, 2017). See also El-Gendi, 2016, for more detail about how nations and empires emerge, disappear, and change borders.

In contrast with nationalist identities and hegemony, the *Universal Declaration of Human Rights* and the *Declaration of the Rights of the Child,* although adopted by nation-states through the UN, constitute a global set of values, practices, and commitments. Operating from a Blue Marble perspective includes being knowledgeable about what these documents contain and how they offer criteria for global action and evaluation.

The Dominance of Nation-States as the Unit of Analysis for Development Evaluation

It is instructive to look at the dominance of nation-states as the unit of analysis for both development strategy and evaluation. Let's begin by examining the focus of the SDGs and, correspondingly, evaluation of the SDGs. The millennium development goals (MDGs) 2000–2015 were targeted at developing countries in what is often called the Global South. In contrast, the SDGs are worldwide in scope in that they are meant to apply to all countries in the world. The deliberations that led to adoption of the SDGs included extensive discussion about the utility of articulating and agreeing to goals that would require commitments by countries. But are the SDGs global? The targets are country-level targets.

The earlier MDGs were also based on *national goals* and *national reports of goal attainment* (United Nations, 2014; United Nations Development Programme, 2015; World Bank, 2015). EvalPartners, the most active collaboration of development-focused evaluators working on SDG evaluations, has as its mission, developing **national** evaluation capacity. All of its goals focus on national monitoring and evaluation (M&E) systems.

EXHIBIT 5.2. Nation-State Map Perspective

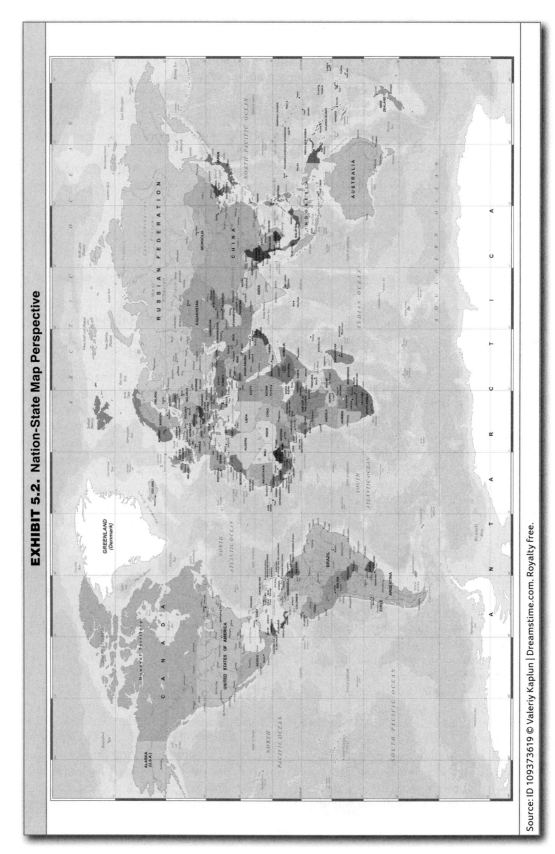

EXHIBIT 5.3. Blue Marble Perspective

Similarly, EVALSDGs is a network of policymakers, institutions, and practitioners who advocate for effective evaluation for the SDGs at the nation-state level. They advocate for voluntary national reviews (VNRs) as an important tool for demonstrating how far countries are progressing toward realizing the SDGs. VNRs focus on building (or refining) national M&E systems to track progress in achieving the 17 SDGs and their 169 targets. This assumes that evaluation results feed into national development plans and enable assessment of how far policies and programs are addressing the SDGs and their targets, given specific country priorities and needs across sectors. "Under this approach, national responsibility for evaluating sustainable development is primarily tied to national follow-up and review processes" (Schwandt, D'Errico, Ofir, Lucks, & El-Saddick, 2018, p. 2).

Truly Global Data

Simply aggregating nation-state data doesn't generate a global picture. Global patterns and transboundary interactions transcend national averages. The amount of carbon added to the atmosphere annually is different from the sum of the average carbon emissions of each country because of the inaccuracies of national data and the multiplier effects of national and subnational carbon releases into the atmosphere that magnify the global impact. The costs of a cyberwar computer virus attack are greater than and different from the sum of nation-state costs when you consider the costs to international agencies, multinational corporations, and NGOs. The same analysis can be made with health, migration, crime, pollution, poverty, and other statistical indicators. Different units of analysis have their own data dynamics. Data at a nation-state level and transboundary/global data are interconnected, but the relationship is complex, dynamic, and nonlinear, so that big-picture, cross-boundary patterns must be studied directly and not just deduced by aggregating nation-state data. The analytical process, as noted throughout this book, is zooming out, zooming in, zooming out, zooming in.

How Much Do Nations Matter?

Wlliam Easterly (2013) has thoughtfully addressed the question, How much do nations matter in development? His answer offers one example of an alternative way of thinking, what I might call taking a Blue Marble

Birds without countries by Simon Kneebone.

perspective, for designing and evaluating global systems change interventions.

Nations do matter for growth and development outcomes, but not as much as usually believed. When they do matter, it is sometimes for the wrong reasons. By overemphasizing the national unit as the place where development happens, the experts wound up interfering with the rights of people from different nations to do mutually advantageous deals with each other.

Development's search for the answer to "what is the right national action to raise growth?" was misplaced. The answer is not the right *national* action; the answer is a system of political and economic rights in which many political and economic actors will find the right actions—both within and across borders—to promote their own development. (p. 216)

The extreme emphasis on national growth performance is misguided, for it shows little evidence of paying off—or even of any way to know whether the national strategy really is paying off or not, according to questionably measured growth rates. (p. 236)

In summary, international development evaluation has been dominated by a nation-state focus. That will continue to be the case. The effectiveness, dominance, and future of the nation-state is much debated (Lechner & Boli, 2015). For our purpose here, it is sufficient to note that a massive international data collection and reporting behemoth has been created to monitor progress on the SDGs at the nation-state level. That serves an important function for nation-state accountability, learning, and trend analysis. Blue Marble evaluation doesn't presume to undermine, criticize, or replace that nation-state emphasis. Rather, Blue Marble evaluation poses different questions based on transnational and global perspectives leading to different global systems change designs and correspondingly appropriate Blue Marble evaluation criteria and questions.

Global Systems Change Designs and Corresponding Blue Marble Evaluations

In general environmental boundaries do not follow jurisdictional boundaries. One ecosystem may spread over several countries, and one country may have several ecosystems. . . . Interventions or actions move from one actor to multiple, from one location to many, from a "local" to a "national" or even "global" level. . . .
— ROB VAN DEN BERG, a founder and President of the International Development Evaluation Association (2017)

A Typology and Continuum of Global Engagement

It is useful to distinguish different dimensions of being global: global in participants, perspective (attitudes, opinions), knowledge, behavior, operations, and/or impacts. For example, the high school enrichment program *World Savvy,* originated by visionary educators Dana Mortenson and Madiha Murshed, offers opportunities for middle school and high school students to learn about the rest of the world. The program operates primarily in three American cities: San Francisco, where it originated; Minneapolis/Saint Paul; and New York City. The operations, then, are quite narrow. The perspective, however, is genuinely global. The program emphasizes global competence, world citizenship, and worldwide knowledge. It is Blue Marble in orientation, though not in operations. Of such distinctions are judgments made about the extent to which an initiative is transboundary or global. Let me elaborate.

A program, organization, agency, or initiative with the term *global* in its name should be expected to be global in perspective, knowledge, behavior, operations, and/ or aspiration.

Evaluating the extent to which a program or initiative that calls itself global is actually global in operation involves assessing fidelity. Fidelity evaluation examines the extent to which the reality of what is done corresponds to how it is labeled and branded. The same issue arises with regard to the designation "world." Baseball's "World Series" is a prominent example. It is a competition among American baseball teams and is a "world" competition only in its marketing. On the other hand, the World Cup of football (soccer in America) is a truly global competition.

The worldwide effort to eradicate polio is a truly global intervention. The World Health Organization (WHO), the Bill and Melinda Gates Foundation, and other partners throughout the world have created protocols for intervening quickly and comprehensively when an outbreak of polio occurs anywhere in the world. As this is being written, the possibility of eradicating polio worldwide appears imminent. While the focus of the eradication campaign is down to a handful of countries, the impact is global. Ironically, this narrowing has resulted in a massive decrease of operations at WHO's world headquarters in Geneva, Switzerland, and increased investment in a few national offices. These types of initiatives invite Blue Marble evaluation.

The World Wildlife Fund's (WWF's) "truly global" strategy emerged in 2013 when the heads of WWF's 75 country programs met in Switzerland to debate what it would take to become "a truly global network," which would mean building capacity in emerging economies. The truly global strategy was a reaction to global trends manifest in WWF's work, including deforestation, endangered and lost species, and climate change. Carter Roberts, chief executive officer of WWF in the United States at the time, explained: "We realized that if we are going to make a difference at a global scale against those issues, if we're going to bend the curve, we need to change the ways in which we work" (Rogers, 2014, p. 1). The new strategy aimed to generate more innovative ideas for global impact and more initiatives at a global scale. Both of these expectations invite Blue Marble evaluation.

Global Greengrants Fund is another "truly global" but also "truly local" organization. It administers over 900 small (around $5,000) grants a year in 90 countries. It is largely operated by volunteers who are deeply connected in their communities' issues and are in the optimal position to find and leverage movement-building opportunities. Often the local movements coalesce around a transnational oil or mining company that can contribute to global systems change.

Later, we examine other variations in what it means to engage globally. The implication is that having "global" in the name of an entity doesn't make it global. The evaluation fidelity challenge is to differentiate and distinguish the extent to which something calling itself global is, in

---

EXHIBIT 5.4. Blue Marble Scale Questions for Initiatives

Stage of initiative development	Blue Marble scale questions
Global design question	To what extent and in what ways is an initiative's design, conceptualization, and theory of transformation truly global in aspiration and action?
Global implementation question	To what extent are an initiative's engagement and implementation processes global in nature and influence?
Global impact evaluation question	To what extent and in what ways is global systems change occurring and, if so, to what extent and in what ways has the intervention contributed to documented global change?

EXHIBIT 5.5. Sample Dimensions for Global-Scale Assessment

Degree to which an initiative or intervention is . . .

1. Global in perspective	7. Global geographically
2. Global in operations	8. Global in staffing
3. Global in participation	9. Global in financing
4. Global in knowledge and content	10. Global evaluation indicators
5. Global in collaborative connections and relationships	11. Global in aspiration
6. Global in networking	12. Global virtually

Note. This list is meant to be suggestive, not exhaustive or definitive. Evaluation of any given intervention will need to define the relevant dimensions for being truly global in scale.

practice, *truly global*. The Transboundary Engagement principle involves asking the three basic Blue Marble evaluation questions presented in Exhibit 5.4. Exhibit 5.5 offers a menu of global dimensions for evaluating global scale.

Globalization

The basic premise that undergirds the Transboundary Engagement principle is that globalization has increased the scope and depth of global problems, and therefore the importance of addressing such problems globally—and evaluating the results globally. Let me close this chapter, then, by making the connection between this Blue Marble principle and globalization more explicit.

> Globalization refers to the expansion and intensification of social relations and consciousness across world-time and world-space. (Steger, 2013, p. 15)

Here are two examples. As climate is making water scarcity a critical security issue globally, wealthier countries have begun to look outside their borders to meet their water needs. Saudi Arabia's largest dairy company, Almarai, has purchased farmland in Arizona, here in the United States, to grow alfalfa—a water-intensive crop—to feed its dairy cows back home. The farm uses water from the Colorado River to irrigate its crops, thereby competing with Americans for water in a region of the country that is already struggling with increasing scarcity of water. Almarai also runs farms in other countries. Saudi Arabia, with vast oil reserves, has one of the world's smallest water reserves, and even that has been dwindling. So, they are looking globally for water (Nesbit, 2018).

Another globalization example concerns China's food imports. China buys more than half the world's soybeans, despite tariff wars ("China Purchases U.S. Soybeans and Sorghum," 2019), another water-intensive crop, from farmers in North and South America (Nesbit, 2018). There is globalization of energy sources, water, and food, plus globalization of pollution, disease, and media. There are four core dimensions of globalization:

1. *Creation* of new social networks and *multiplication* of existing connections that cut across traditional political, economic, cultural, and geographic boundaries;

2. *Expansion* and the *stretching* of social relations, activities, and connections;

3. *Intensification* and *acceleration* of social exchanges and activities; and

4. *New human consciousness.* Without erasing local and national attachments, the compression of the world into a single place has increasingly made global the frame of reference for human thought and action. Hence, globalization involves both the macro-structures of a "global community" and the micro-structures of "global personhood" (Steger, 2013, pp. 14–15).

Thinking Globally, Acting Globally, Evaluating Globally

Globalization challenges us to think globally and act globally. It means designing interventions and initiatives based on an understanding of globalization and evaluating them from a Blue Marble perspective. Globalization scholar Manfred Steger (2013) sums up succinctly and insightfully the importance of the Transboundary Engagement principle:

The central feature of potentially disastrous environmental problems is that they are "global," thus making them serious problems for all sentient beings inhabiting our magnificent blue planet. Indeed, transboundary pollution, global warming, climate change, and species extinction are challenges that cannot be contained within national or even regional borders. They do not have isolated causes and effects for they are caused by aggregate collective human action and thus require coordinated global response. (p. 95)

Blue Marble Evaluators without Borders

Blue Marble evaluators, in implementing the Transboundary Engagement principle, become *evaluators without borders*. There are Doctors Without Borders, Teachers Without Borders, MBAs Without Borders, Librarians Without Borders, and even Clowns Without Borders.

Let there be *Blue Marble Evaluators Without Borders.*

Where are you from? by Simone Kneebone.

CHAPTER 6

GLOCAL Principle

Properly speaking, global thinking is not possible. . . . Look at one of those photographs of half the earth taken from outer space, and see if you recognize your neighborhood. The right local questions and answers will be the right global ones. The Amish question, what will this do to our community? tends toward the right answer for the world.

But

We have lived our lives by the assumption that what was good for us would be good for the world. We have been wrong. We must change our lives so that it will be possible to live by the contrary assumption, that what is good for the world will be good for us. And that requires that we make the effort to know the world and learn what is good for it.

So

To cherish what remains of the Earth and to foster its renewal is our only legitimate hope of survival.
—WENDELL BERRY, American farmer, novelist, poet, and environmentalist (2017a)

CONTEXT

Global systems change must be contextually sensitive and grounded in the interactions between local and global processes and scales of change. The term that has emerged to capture this way of thinking is **GLOCAL**, or glocalization (Steger, 2013, p. 2). The implication for Blue Marble design and evaluation is the importance of assessing global–local interactions and interconnections by observing and documenting contextual variations locally within a coherent global pattern. This involves zooming out for the big picture globally, and zooming in to understand local implications and actions. This chapter takes on the challenge of Blue Marble engagement through the GLOCAL lens.

Here's an example, viewing the challenge of recycling plastic through the GLOCAL lens.

For more than 25 years, many developed countries, including the U.S., have been sending massive amounts of plastic waste to China instead of recycling it on their own. Some 106 million metric tons—about 45 percent—of the world's plastics set for recycling have been exported to China since reporting to the United Nations Comtrade Database began in 1992. But in 2018, China banned plastic waste from being imported to protect the environment and human health. The leftover waste is ending up in local landfills, being incinerated, or sent to other countries "that lack the infrastructure to properly manage it." (Watson, 2018, p. 1)

A major insight from complexity-informed systems change initiatives is that "the global and the local are connected in unexpected ways in distant places and over time" (e.g., Moore et al., 2019, p. 38). Here are three examples of how Blue Marble thinking can inform action.

● A faculty department is designing a new curriculum. Traditionally, the curriculum focuses on the subject matter of the discipline in that department. Blue Marble thinking introduces additional questions to consider: What are the global developments in our discipline that students should know about, engage with, and understand to operate effectively in a global environment? How does our discipline inform and provide insight into global trends and patterns? How do we design a curriculum that prepares our students to be global scholars and practitioners? What other disciplines could be involved?

● A philanthropic foundation is funding a major new initiative aimed at addressing inequality in the United States. Blue Marble thinking asks, How is U.S. inequality connected to global patterns and trends in inequality? What global developments will have an impact on U.S. inequality in the future? Who is engaged in addressing inequality internationally that we can partner with to understand the connections between the United States and global inequality? What would a map look like that illustrated the local-to-global scales, their interdependence, and how would such a map help with strategy?

● A nonprofit agency serving recent immigrants in a local community is undergoing an evaluation of its effectiveness. Blue Marble thinking invites evaluation to include the following kinds of questions: How are global human migration and refugee trends and patterns affecting local immigration? What are the interconnections between what has emerged locally in working with recent immigrants and international issues facing immigrants around the world? Who are the key actors working at different scales on immigration issues and where are they located?

These are the kinds of design and evaluation questions that the Blue Marble perspective invites by infusing global considerations and understandings into local programs and projects; synchronistically, information and action flowing upward means infusing local knowledge into global initiatives. As one of our Blue Marble team members put it:

> There are a lot of talking heads at the national and global level, but they are so far from any real action that they have no idea what is going on at the grassroots level. I think the Einstein quote about problems not being able to be solved at the same level that created them applies to global problems needing to go local to be resolved. Getting the local action right and authentic is surprisingly hard and rare, and should be a Blue Marble skill embedded in thinking globally.

Contextual sensitivity is thus essential for Blue Marble evaluators. That's why there are no "best practices" globally, because the term *best* connotes that context doesn't matter. Context always matters. Global context informs local actions. Local contexts make global understandings meaningful and actionable.

GLOCAL Principle Explicated

> **PREMISE:** Sustainable systems change and transformation are more likely to take hold if there are strong reinforcing interconnections up and down levels of engagement from local to global and from global to local.

GLOCAL Principle
Integrate complex interconnections across levels.

IMPLICATIONS

- Complexity rules. Interactions and interconnections across levels (micro, meso, macro) and scales (local, national, transboundary, global) are inherently complex, dynamic, unpredictable, uncontrollable, and turbulent. Evaluation designs under conditions of complexity must be emergent, adaptable, developmental, responsive, flexible, and nimble (Patton, 2011).

- Blue Marble evaluation is likely to involve teams engaged at different levels with systematic coordination across levels.

- One kind of change—whether local, national, transboundary, or global—is not inherently more important than another. These levels do not constitute a hierarchy; they are an integrated, interdependent, dynamic, multilayered complex system.

- The origin of innovation and change can be at any level and move in any direction (up or down levels). Those interactions may be both linear and nonlinear.

- Movement across levels is likely to lead to adaptions rather than static and rigid transference and adoption from one level to another.

- Exhibit 6.1 highlights the integration of design and evaluation, and implications of the Blue Marble GLOCAL principle for each.

GLOCAL Science

Science progresses through GLOCAL inquiries. Scientists observe local patterns in nature and then synthesize observations from many diverse localities to determine global trends. Charles Darwin's observa-

EXHIBIT 6.1. Design and Evaluation: Implications of the Blue Marble GLOCAL Principle		
Blue Marble GLOCAL principle	**Design guidance**	**Evaluation criterion and questions**
Integrate complex interconnections across levels.	1. When designing an intervention or initiative, look at the interactions, interdependencies, and interconnections across levels (micro, meso, macro). 2. Take into account how people, information, and resources flow from local to global, and global to local.	*GLOCAL fidelity:* 1. In what ways is an initiative or intervention truly or fully **GLOCAL?** In both processes and results? 2. What are the interactions, interdependencies, and interconnections across levels? How do they intersect for mutually reinforcing systems change? Look for both anticipated and unanticipated interactions, both positive (mutually reinforcing) and negative (disjointed and nonaligned).

tions of species differentiation in the Galápagos Islands influenced his formulation of the theory of evolution. Now, as climate change warms the world's oceans, what is happening in the Galápagos Islands generates hypotheses about and is a harbinger of cumulative global effects from thousands of islands and seashores around the world. The Galápagos sit at the intersection of three ocean currents and are thus at the center of one of the world's most destructive weather patterns, El Niño, which causes rapid, extreme ocean heating across the Eastern Pacific tropics. Research published in 2014 by more than a dozen climate scientists warned that rising ocean temperatures were making El Niño both more frequent and more intense (Casey & Haner, 2018). The United Nations Educational, Scientific and Cultural Organization (UNESCO) has warned that the Galápagos, designated among *World Heritage Coral Reefs,* are one of the localities most susceptible to the impacts of climate change (Heron, van Hooidonk, Maynard, Anderson, & Day, 2018). The effects on marine life and land animals are already dramatic with several species threatened with extinction (Casey & Haner, 2018). In the northern hemisphere, the Gulf of Maine is one of the most rapidly warming bodies of water on the planet, which is directly linked to the global effects of climate change and regional warming of the Arctic and increased freshwater flows that are disrupting the ocean circulation patterns.

Looking at similar patterns across many places in the world has led to the hypothesis that Earth has entered the *Sixth Extinction,* a period of accelerating species extinction around the world. The Sixth Extinction describes the current and ongoing loss of species during the present epoch, mainly due to human activity, spanning numerous families of plants and animals, including mammals, birds, amphibians, reptiles, and arthropods. Observing local changes and synthesizing them into global patterns leads to general hypotheses about what is

happening that can be further tested in more localities. Thus does science progress.

The Blue Marble GLOCAL operating principle guides attention to the interconnections among large-scale processes at the macro level (global and transnational), intermediate processes at the meso level (national and regional), and those at the micro level (local), including those of indigenous peoples. The effects of global systems change are manifest across levels from the local to the regional to the national to the cross-national, and ultimately, the global. Blue Marble evaluators must be able to map and track these dynamic interconnections across levels. Here are two dramatic examples of GLOCAL interconnections that are relevant to all of us.

Cobalt as a GLOCAL Phenomenon

Cobalt, according to some financial experts, could supplant gold, diamonds, platinum, and even oil as the world's most precious commodity because it is the essential element in lithium-ion batteries. Digital devices of all kinds run on those batteries. Accelerated production and marketing of electric vehicles, drones, and communication devices are expected to triple demand for cobalt by 2025 and double demand again by 2030 (Walt & Mayer, 2018, p. 106). But two-thirds of the world's cobalt is mined in the Democratic Republic of the Congo (DRC), much of it by child labor, in a country plagued by poverty, corruption, violence, inadequate infrastructure, human rights violations, and oppression. Dozens of multinational companies are involved in the mining operations and global trade that produces the batteries we all use daily. Human rights organizations like Amnesty International are on the ground reporting on abuses of children and multiple forms of human degradation. Journalistic access is extremely regulated and limited. Major research efforts are underway to develop batteries without cobalt as well as to locate new sources of cobalt. Consumer reactions to the mining conditions are a major factor driving those innovative efforts and incentivizing consumer products manufacturers to improve mining conditions and quality of life.

The GLOCAL web around lithium-ion batteries connects micro-level Congolese miners, villagers, and children in the heart of Africa with local consumers of electronic devices worldwide (including everyone reading this book). At the global (macro) level, multiple actors mediate the cobalt trade: international regulatory agencies, trading networks, commodity markets, shipping conglomerates, financial investors, global journalists, consumer education activists, and evaluators of efforts at local reform and community development. At the meso level, often connecting the macro and micro, are national corporations, DRC ministries and agencies, and regional NGOs. (For details and evidence, see Schmidt et al., 2018; Walt & Meyer, 2018.)

Cumulative Effects from Local to Global on Energy Self-Sufficiency

In a mountainous, remote region of Nepal, the Digo Bikas Institute supported a community-owned and community-controlled solar grid in the village of Dhapsung, which was devastated by a 2015 earthquake. In addition to providing much-needed access to energy after the disaster, this climate solution provided it without fossil fuels or harmful greenhouse emissions.

> The grid fuels not just electricity, but self-reliance. By replacing kerosene and fire, the people of Dhapsung now have more time on their hands. Especially at night, they can engage in productive activities such as school work and livelihoods support. There are also more places in the village that are considered safe. (Zavala, 2019)

Reducing carbon emissions to meet Paris Agreement goals will require cumulative action at the local, regional, national, and global levels. Global Greengrants Fund illustrates such GLOCAL synergy for cumulative impact. It administers over 900 small grants a year in 90 countries working largely through volunteers who are deeply connected in their communities so they are well positioned to organize and leverage local action in support of global sustainability issues.

The Collaborative Crop Research Program

The Collaborative Crop Research Program (CCRP) of the McKnight Foundation, based in Minnesota, works in multiple countries across regions in South America and Africa. The CCRP is committed to the flow of local and global knowledge through agriculture research for development. Exhibit 6.2 shows how the CCRP conceptualizes the program interface at the nexus of global and local.

So, how has the CCRP as a philanthropic entity used the Blue Marble evaluation perspective to shape strategy? First, it has funded projects to better understand the impacts of the quinoa boom on growers and the environment. This included a more traditional type of evaluation of how the certification and strengthening of farmer associations influenced social, environmental, and economic impacts. The CCRP also funded a quinoa monitoring network of 300 geographical representative households, where the selected farmers are called every month to provide basic data on yield and management practices to see what problems they are facing and how they are dealing with these issues. The eventual objective of this network is to turn into a crowdsourcing-type mechanism that will provide more global insights on general agronomic principles, as well as local advice.

The global narrative on the quinoa boom has often been that it had a net negative social and economic toll on Bolivian farmers. Taking a GLOCAL stance has led the CCRP to conclude that there has been a

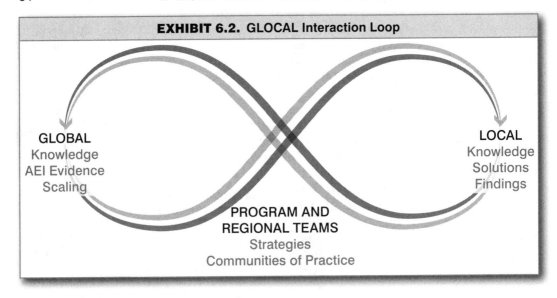

EXHIBIT 6.2. GLOCAL Interaction Loop

GLOBAL
Knowledge
AEI Evidence
Scaling

LOCAL
Knowledge
Solutions
Findings

**PROGRAM AND
REGIONAL TEAMS**
Strategies
Communities of Practice

great deal of diversity in the impacts of the quinoa boom. These diverse impacts need to be understood and embraced. Different options for distinct contexts—at the farm, community, and regional levels—need to be developed and shared. Ultimately, the CCRP supports local action in quinoa and other agroecosystems, but with a global understanding and perspective.

GLOCAL Power Dynamics

It is easier to macrobullshit than to microbullshit.
—NASSIM NICHOLAS TALEB, global financial
analyst and journalist (2018, p. 12)

In his best-selling book entitled *Skin in the Game,* from which this quote is taken, Taleb argues that those who have more at stake should have more power when decisions are made. Local people who live at the micro level, at ground level, have a different stake than global analysts who track macro trends. The GLOCAL principle—*Integrate complex interconnections across levels*–applies to conceptualizing interventions, designing interrelationships across levels, economic flows, cultural interactions, and power dynamics. Governance is a central issue in the

global commons. Blue Marble evaluators have to engage with stakeholders at multiple levels and, in so doing, deal with the inevitable unequal distribution of power. Governance of environmental gene editing provides an informative example of the issues involved as well as a look at the kind of situation that would benefit from Blue Marble evaluation.

The end of malaria. Restored island habitats. Resiliency for species threatened by climate change. Many envisioned environmental applications of newly developed gene-editing techniques such as CRISPR might provide profound benefits for ecosystems and society. But depending on the type and scale of the edit, gene-edited organisms intentionally released into the environment could also deliver off-target mutations, evolutionary resistance, ecological disturbance, and extinctions. Hence, there are ongoing conversations about the responsible application of CRISPR, especially relative to the limitations of current global governance structures to safeguard its use. . . . Largely missing from these conversations is attention to local communities in decision-making. Most policy discussions are instead occurring at the national or international level . . . , even though local communities will be the first to feel the context-dependent impacts of any release. To be fully representative, therefore, local inputs and perspectives must also be considered. (Kofler et al., 2018, p. 527)

Blue Marble evaluation of governance systems includes tracking whose voices are heard, whose are unheard, and the dynamics of how decisions are made, including local–global interactions. Blue Marble evaluation would also track and assess what actions and impacts follow from governance decisions. An example of a framework that has been in development for the past 20+ years that has shifted the paradigm of how to manage natural resources, engage different perspectives, and address global issues such as climate change, is the ecosystem management framework. Ecosystem management is a more holistic and integrated approach to policy, implementation, and M&E that centers on identifying and taking into account interdependencies between natural (marine and terrestrial) ecosystems and human societies, and between economies and institutional systems, as well as among various species, both flora and fauna, within an ecosystem. Ecosystem-based management examines how "ecosystem services" (interventions) flow from human–environment interactions ("coupled socioecological systems") in an integrated fashion rather than looking at actors and actions in a piecemeal manner (McLeod & Leslie, 2009).

One particularly relevant Blue Marble–type framework developed a decade ago by two pioneers in the ecosystem approach, Stephen Olsen and Glenn Page, is a process for measuring governance response to ecosystem change. Their work began with a focus on coastal and marine ecosystems and has been applied in a far wider context because of the simplifying framework they developed to deal with highly contextual issues from the local to the global. For example, loss of biodiversity in marine ecosystems flows from the cumulative effects of multiple actors and actions across different sectors that, taken together, have a compounding effect: overfishing, coastal development, filling and dredging, mining, recreation, pollution, climate change, real estate markets, and other human activities all contribute to the loss of biodiversity and degradation of the ecosystem. While local and global environmental benefits are closely interrelated, support for improved environmental management must provide benefits to local people and be linked to global mandates and support mechanisms (Olsen, Page, & Ochoa, 2009; Uitto, 2019). Determining how people at different levels with varying positions in power structures perceive costs and benefits of interventions is a core evaluation function. Developing a baseline and measuring progress can enhance the functioning of multilayered ecological management and governance.

A GLOCAL Perspective on Scaling

The most common approach to having global impact is "going to scale." This means disseminating models demonstrated to be effective in one or more local contexts and taking them to scale (multiplying them) to have greater and greater impact—ideally, global impact. Because the idea of scaling for impact dominates the thinking of major philanthropic foundations, international aid agencies, and global think tanks devoted to innovation, Blue Marble evaluators need to know the issues involved.

Scaling a model faces the problem that what works in one context doesn't work in another. Scaling means that more people get helped in more places, but the systems that created the need in the first place often remain in place, creating more need and demand for more programs to meet that ever-growing need. **Need**, it turns out, is highly sustainable. Systems that function to eliminate need, not so much. Scaling is typically oriented toward meeting narrowly defined needs, not changing systems in which those needs are embedded.

In 2015, a study was conducted by Riddell and Moore with the J. W. McConnell Family Foundation on an applied dissemination initiative. The purpose was to build grantee capacity to accelerate large-scale systemic change. Leaders of more than a dozen national-level initiatives in Canada convened regularly over a period of several years to learn from one another's efforts on scaling. They documented six different strategies that may be adopted to scale innovation on the pathway to large-scale or transformative change defined as systemic impact, which cut across three different types of "scaling": scaling out, scaling up, and scaling deep (Riddell & Moore, 2015). Scaling out is reaching large numbers. Scaling up is influencing law and policy. Scaling deep is impacting cultural roots based on the recognition that culture plays a powerful role in shifting problem domains, and transformative change must be deeply rooted in people, relationships, communities, and cultures.

Because scaling is such an important issue on the global stage, I conclude with wisdom from the best study I've encountered about scaling, one I featured in *Developmental Evaluation* (Patton, 2011, chap. 6). It is highly relevant to Blue Marble design and evaluation. The heart of the matter is distinguishing adaptation from replication.

Adaptation versus Replication

Lisbeth Schorr (1997), as director of Harvard's Project on Effective Interventions, has made what may be the most comprehensive analysis of the idea of "Spreading What Works Beyond the Hothouse." She found that innovative demonstration projects, even those aimed at major systems change, often innovate only at the margins and thus may serve as no more than a safety valve releasing pressure for change without threatening the status quo. In some cases, an effective demonstration of a new way of doing something has the unintended consequence of alerting the status quo to a poten-

tial innovation, allowing resisters to figure out how to undermine any effort to expand the innovation. The emergence of such organized resistance constitutes a change in context. Of particular importance to evaluation, Schorr found that

> the techniques that work to beat the system when the model program is small and marginal can no longer help when it is time to expand and break through the Ceiling on Scale. . . . Efforts to reach greater numbers bring greater visibility, and greater visibility creates new demands to comply with old rules. That is why innovative programs cannot grow and thrive in an unchanged system. (p. 27)

Schorr (1997) identified several critical mistakes commonly made in efforts to take innovations to scale. The problem begins, she found, with the mental models people have about replication:

> Franchising, mass production, and biomedical science turn out to be misleading analogs; we underestimated the importance of local variation, local ownership, and the subtleties of effective interventions; and we ignored the critical role of the external environment. (pp. 27–28)

> 1. We didn't realize that people-centered interventions can't be turned out like widgets. Most front-line staff in successful programs can testify that while they operate on a body of shared knowledge and skills, a significant portion of what they do cannot be standardized. The good ones are forever responding to contingencies. . . . The most promising interventions rely on at least some components that change from one site to the next, and that evolve with considerable variations over time.

> 2. We didn't realize that local people may have to reinvent parts of the wheel. Even when local people set out to replicate someone else's intervention, they find they have to adapt it to local conditions to make it work. Veterans of successful community-

based programs agree that people implementing programs in new settings must be able in fundamental ways to make them their own.

3. We underestimated the subtleties of effective interventions. Even the best practitioners often can't give usable descriptions of what they do. . . .

4. We failed to see that you can't grow roses in concrete. Human service reformers and educators alike thought the challenge was to develop new ideas, not to change institutions. They assumed an innovation or a "good product" would become part of a mainstream system because of its merit, unconstrained by the system's funding, rule making, standard setting, and accountability requirements—all of which are likely to be inconsistent with the innovation. (pp. 28–29)

Schorr (1997) suggests that the failure to appreciate the importance of context, which is the unifying theme in these failures to achieve scale, derives from oversimplistic ideas about how replication works based upon dissemination of new agricultural products to farmers and naïve efforts to follow private-sector franchising models

> where context is simpler. In the private sector, the context is the market, and profit is the measure of success. Rules and regulations may intrude, but they stop short of prescribing the very essence of what the enterprise does and how it does it. By contrast, human services, education, and community building are shaped by highly complex systems that specify what you may or may not do. (pp. 29–30)

Schorr's astute analysis highlights how complexity emerges as a difference maker. I find that the mental model common among those who use the language of replication and generalization is that of empirically generalizing from a sample to a population. The debate about the conditions under which research findings can be generalized

is relevant and instructive because it is the larger context for considering the extent to which evaluation findings about effective program models can be generalized. The credibility of Blue Marble evaluation processes and findings depends in part on understanding these issues as well as reframing what scaling means from adaptation to replication.

Contextualized Scaling

Contrary to the lessons about scaling that Schorr has shared, agricultural development remains dominated by institutions and funders that seek simple, standardized, one-size-fits-all solutions for problems and opportunities that are extremely diverse. In contrast, the McKnight Foundation's CCRP works with small farmers in Africa and South America using an *options by context* approach to find customized approaches for farmers in distinct agroecological systems. This principles-based approach to agroecological intensification supports a transition from degenerative agriculture to regenerative and sustainable agriculture. Knowledge about options appropriate for dealing with diverse conditions and varying farm household situations is disseminated as contextualized scaling (Sinclair & Coe, 2019). The CCRP agroecologists aim to transform small farming systems research and are engaged in doing so.

> Radical change is needed to facilitate the agroecological intensification of smallholder farming. We propose that large-scale participatory approaches, combined with innovations in information and communications technology (ICT), could enable the effective matching of diverse options to the wide spectrum of socio-ecological contexts that characterize smallholder agriculture. . . . Novel information management capabilities will be required to introduce options and principles, enable characterization of contexts, manage data related to option-by-context interactions and enable farmers to visualize their findings in useful and intel-

Einstein's theory of leveltivity by Simon Kneebone.

ligible ways . . . , [which] could lead to vastly greater capacity for technical innovation, which could in turn enable greater productivity and resilience, and enhance the quality of rural life. (Nelson, Coe, & Haussmann, 2016, p. 1)

Thinking, Acting, and Evaluating GLOCALLY

The McKnight CCRP program has made thinking GLOCALLY a centerpiece of its strategy for agricultural transformation engagement. Likewise, the Global Alliance for the Future of Food (GA) has adopted GLOCAL thinking officially. The 23-member philanthropic foundations and their grantees engage in local contexts around the world while through the GA's international initiatives, convenings, networking, and collaborations, they engage globally. Their strategy explicitly connects the local and global. Both of these major development collaborations *think GLOCALLY, act GLOCALLY,* and *evaluate GLOCALLY.* Their evaluations are based on Blue Marble evaluation principles.

Blue Marble GLOCAL thinking can be applied at any level at which social, eco-

nomic, political, and environmental changes are being initiated. The questions that flow from thinking GLOCALLY vary somewhat at different levels, but at the core, Blue Marble evaluation involves inquiring into the relationship and interconnections from local to global, and across localities, nation-states, and regions. This integrates both theory and practice: theory about interconnections and actually engaging in practice at the grassroots level, as exemplified in the work and reflections of *glocal* thinker and practitioner John Wilson (2018). It also involves interconnections across sector and issue silos, the focus of the next Blue Marble principle and the next chapter. (See Cristiano & Proietti, 2018, for a comprehensive review of the scholarly, applied social science and evaluation research literatures on the critical contribution of multilevel interventions for systems transformations.)

GLOCAL thinking is based on an imagined Einsteinian-type *theory of leveltivity,* that cross-level interactions manifest properties that are more than the linear sum of their parts. From theory to practice, this means that interactions across levels from local to global, and global to local, are crucial for understanding Blue Marble dynamics.

CHAPTER 7

Cross-Silos Principle

> The greatest danger in times of turbulence is not the turbulence—
> it is to act with yesterday's logic.
> —PETER DRUCKER, management consultant

CONTEXT

A silo is a tower on a farm used to store a single kind of grain. The "silo mentality" constitutes an approach and mindset where all the focus is on what is happening within a single sector, intervention, issue, or problem area without regard to interrelationships and interconnections across those focused domains of action. Use of the silo as a metaphor for narrow, closed-system thinking probably far outnumbers the use of actual silos as containers of grain. This chapter adds to the metaphor side of the ledger.

The silo mentality refers to departments in organizations that hoard power, resources, and information. They look after their own interests first and, therefore, do not contribute as much as they could and should to the organization's overall vision and mission (*www.businessdictionary. com/definition/silo-mentality.html*). The silo mentality is pervasive in business, governments, universities, and organizations of all kinds. This mentality in international development and, correspondingly, in M&E,

is manifest in narrowly targeted SMART (specific, measurable, achievable, relevant, time-bound) goals, tightly focused project logic models, and single-issue funding streams. The dominant paradigm is categorical, problem-focused funding, needs assessment, planning, design, and evaluation. Thinking and working *across silos* challenges this dominant paradigm.

The *GLOCAL principle*, presented in Chapter 6, calls for integrating multilevel global–local interactions. The *Cross-Silos principle*, presented in this chapter, advocates understanding interactions across problem areas. Silos take many forms. Siloed problem areas can include sectors (education, health, housing), issues (crime, immigration, poverty), performance indicators (income, nutrition, school graduation rates), goals (equity, sustainability, economic growth), and traditional program areas (agriculture, schools, clinics). For Blue Marble evaluators, engaging across silos means assessing the extent to which global systems change efforts address interrelated factors

59

across problem areas and evaluate interconnected outcomes.

Blue Marble interventions work across sector divisions and program specializations. This means designing and evaluating initiatives to integrate and coordinate interventions across sectors, SDGs, and traditional program areas. It follows, then, that Blue Marble evaluations assess the extent to which initiatives address multiple interrelated factors (across arenas of action) and diverse interconnected outcomes that characterize integrated global systems change. Consider this example:

> Child marriage affects millions of young women worldwide, leading to early pregnancies, reduced education, and significant health risks. Nor is this problem limited to less developed countries. An estimated 248,000 children were married in the United States between 2000 and 2010, mostly to adult men (Reiss, 2017). The minimum age of marriage in most U.S. states is 18, but exceptions in every state allow those younger than 18 to marry. Laws in 25 states do not set a minimum age below which a child cannot marry. Globally, ending child marriage will require changes in economic incentives for families marrying off young girls, significantly increased girls education opportunities, changed cultural and religious practices, new policies and regulations, changed gender dynamics, improved reproductive health services, ending female genital mutilation, intolerance and punishment for rape, financial status changes for both young single women and child brides, and innovations in agricultural systems where women produce much of the food consumed by households. And these are just the obvious factors that must be addressed, in combination, to end child marriage.

Example of Working across Silos

A major philanthropic foundation has programs in population control, agriculture, and girls' education—three distinct issues. Specialized program staff engage in grant making and capacity building in those three arenas of interest. The population program aims to delay childbearing among young girls in developing countries and offers contraception and sex education. The agriculture program focuses on food production, which in many parts of the world is a primary responsibility of women farmers. The girls' education program aims to keep girls in school to complete at least a primary school education, and ideally on through high school.

Now, consider the relationships among these programs. Research shows that the best way to delay pregnancies among young girls is to keep them in school. Many leave school because they are needed to help grow food. Imagine girls' schooling that included serious attention to food production, thereby making the curriculum and activities relevant to the food needs of the girls' families. Such a program would also be an antipoverty program, a gender equity initiative, and, if agroecological approaches to agriculture were the basis of the curriculum, would address issues of water quality, soil conservation, climate change, and farm system sustainability. Enhancing nutrition would also be part of such an initiative.

Cross-Silos Principle Explicated

> **PREMISE:** Problems are embedded in systems. To target the problem without changing the system of which it is a part is to provide only a partial solution and one unlikely to endure. Moreover, problems are often intertwined. Interconnected problems within and across systems require systems change strategies to have lasting impact. Solving problems piecemeal leads to piecemeal solutions.

Cross-Silos Principle

Engage across sectors and issues for systems change.

IMPLICATIONS

- Changing systems is different from implementing projects. Evaluating systems change is different from evaluating projects and programs. Programs and projects are based on a linear logic of causality. Evaluation of programs and projects follows that linear thinking. Systems consist of interdependent elements interconnected in such a way that a change in one element changes connections with other elements and, reverberating through the set of system interconnections, may change the system. Tracking those changes for evaluation purposes requires mapping methods and ways of capturing changes in system interconnections and their dynamics.

- Systems thinking applies to situation analysis, intervention design, engagement, implementation, adaptations, and developmental evaluation.

- Cross-silos design and evaluation tackles multiple issues at once and likely requires a Blue Marble team with diverse knowledge specializations and interdisciplinary capabilities.

- Exhibit 7.1 highlights cross-silos design guidance and sample evaluation criteria and questions.

Vertical versus Horizontal Strategies

Siloed thinking and action constitute a vertical approach to change, focusing intensely on narrow, well-defined outcome targets. The vertical nature of silos is epitomized by an underground chamber in which a guided missile is kept ready for firing on its target. Vertical approaches create closed systems where context and external influences are controlled to maximize focus on predetermined targets. The advantage is focus: focused resources, actions, targets, and results. The disadvantage is that the results tend to be narrow, isolated, and unsustainable. An example is attacking a disease like polio, or a problem like neighborhood burglaries, or reducing high school dropouts. These are worthy endeavors, but results, if attained, have limited effects on larger, underlying system conditions because they only focus on attacking the symptoms of the problem, not root systems causes.

In contrast, a horizontal approach that analyzes and engages with issues as complex constellations of interrelated elements is more effective at changing systems to achieve improved health care, safer communities, and effective schooling for all. The strength of the horizontal approach is attacking fundamental causes aimed at major, sustainable systems change. Weaknesses are the difficulties of changing systems, the lack of institutional capacity to engage in sustained systems change, and the substantial, long-term commitment and resources required to do so effectively.

Integrating the Vertical and the Horizontal: The Case of Polio and Health Systems

> Big donors have long preferred fighting individual diseases, known as a "vertical" strategy. . . . By contrast, the broader, "horizontal" strategy has less well-defined goals and might not move the needle of global health statistics for years. . . . Is humanity better served by waging wars on individual diseases, like polio? Or is it better to pursue a broader set of health goals simultaneously—improving hygiene, expanding immunizations, providing clean drinking water—that don't eliminate any one disease, but might improve the overall health of people in developing countries? (Guth, 2010, p. 1)

In health, vertical approaches target measurable results for specific goals, like eliminating a disease: human immunodeficiency virus (HIV), tuberculosis, malaria, and polio. Horizontal approaches aim more broadly to improve overall health systems (Seager, 2018).

The global effort to eradicate polio provides insights into the contrasts between

EXHIBIT 7.1. Design and Evaluation Based on the Cross-Silos Principle

Blue Marble Cross-Silos principle	Design guidance	Evaluation criterion and questions
Engage across sectors and issues for systems change.	1. Design an intervention to address interconnections across sectors, issues, problems, and SDGs. 2. Consider diverse perspectives about targeted systems. Be intentional and thoughtful about system boundaries. 3. Understand the multidimensional, systemic nature of issues and design for systems change, especially attentive to environmental and human interactions in complex dynamic ecosystems.	*Cross-Silos fidelity:* 1. To what extent and in what ways is an initiative working across silos in both processes and results aimed at systems change? 2. What are the interactions across sectors, issues, indicators, and problems, and how do they intersect for mutually reinforcing systems change? 3. What system boundaries, interrelationships, and perspectives are targets of change—and what changes occur? Look for both anticipated and unanticipated interactions.

vertical versus horizontal approaches, and what it means to integrate these strategies. By 2010, the global effort to eradicate polio had cost $8.2 billion with no end in sight. Polio was proving much harder to eradicate than smallpox had been, the first disease to be eradicated worldwide in 1979 (Guth, 2010). In high-level strategic deliberations among world health leaders, global health organizations, and philanthropic foundations, debate about the relative effectiveness of vertical versus horizontal approaches came to the forefront.

Evidence was mounting that a single, massive campaign like that against polio could weaken health systems more generally by concentrating resources and people on one effort while leaving other needs inadequately attended. Moreover, evaluations found that "once polio had been ended in some countries, weak health-care systems let it return" (Guth, 2010, p. 1). After much deliberation and review of the evidence, global leaders, including the World Health Orga-

nization and the Gates Foundation, agreed to a new holistic strategy that integrated vertical and horizontal approaches. The new strategy was based on the cross-silos premise that "disease-specific wars can succeed only if they also strengthen the overall health system in poor countries" (p. 1).

Yes . . . And . . .

The Cross-Silos principle is not an absolute attack on silos. It is an attempt to highlight the need for and nature of a *systems change strategy* when changing systems is what will lead to more sustainable and equitable results. For better or worse, siloed programming and funding will remain the dominant way of attempting to solve problems because, for better or worse, that's what funders, designers, implementers, and evaluators mostly know how to do. Cross-silos systems change is an alternative, but the Blue Marble position is "yes . . . , and . . ."—integrating vertical and horizontal efforts where both are being done, and understanding the contribution of each.

Cross-Silos Principle Applied to Interconnections among the SDGs

Let's look at the implications of the Cross-Silos principle for the 2030 Sustainable Development framework that dominates the international development landscape. To reiterate, the 17 SDGs have yielded 169 targets and 230 indicators, 90 of which are mandated to be reported on periodically. Technical specialists measure and report on CO_2 emissions, rates of school attendance and graduation, poverty levels, numbers of refugees, agricultural productivity statistics, changing demographics, energy consumption, and nutrition indicators. A massive infrastructure has been created within each SDG to collect data and report progress toward targets on indicators. The monitoring of indicators is important, but targeting performance indicator by indicator and nation by nation scarcely begins to tap into and make use of the potential of evaluation to inform and assess global system changes, both processes and results, in support of strategic leadership decisions and collective action. Doing so requires analyzing the interconnections among goals and indicators across SDG silos.

From a Blue Marble perspective, holistic analysis and synthesis involves examining deep and complex interactions across the SDG domains. Focusing on siloed SDGs, both in designing interventions and evaluating them, risks missing synergies, interconnections, spillover and side effects, and reinforcing alignments, as well as undermining misalignments. "A holistic perspective helps to prevent lock-ins and mobilizes opportunities to accelerate and leverage the transformation towards sustainable development" (International Institute for Applied Systems Analysis, 2018, p. 5).

Sometimes the interconnections are relatively simple, as when examining the rela-

tionship between two arenas of change: climate change and human health. Consider this headline:

> **Climate change will make hundreds of millions more people nutrient deficient: Crops grown in a high CO_2 atmosphere are less nutritious, containing less protein, zinc and iron.** (Davis, 2018)

Integrating Social, Economic, and Environmental Dimensions of the SDGs

Experienced development evaluator Juha Uitto (2019) emphasizes three closely interlinked dimensions—social, economic, and environmental—arguing that all three dimensions are central for sustainable development. "Environmental issues are intricately intertwined with economic growth, people's livelihoods, and health: the entire social and economic development process, with its political, power, and intergenerational dimensions. Sustainable development occurs in the nexus for human (social and economic) and natural (environmental) systems" (pp. 54–55). Applying this thinking to the SDGs, Uiotto emphasizes the importance of assuming "an integrated perspective," one in which attention is paid to "the interlinkages at different levels: across sectors (e.g., finance, agriculture, energy, and transport); across societal actors (local authorities, government agencies, private sector, and civil society); and between and among low-, medium-, and high-income countries." Exhibit 7.2 shows the 17 SDGs grouped together in three layers: four biosphere goals (life on land, life below water, clean water and sanitation, and climate action), eight societal goals (no poverty; zero hunger; good health and well-being; quality education; gender equality; affordable and clean energy; sustainable cities and communities; peace, justice, and strong institutions), and four economic goals (decent work and economic growth; industry, innovation, and infrastructure; responsible

EXHIBIT 7.2. SDG Cake

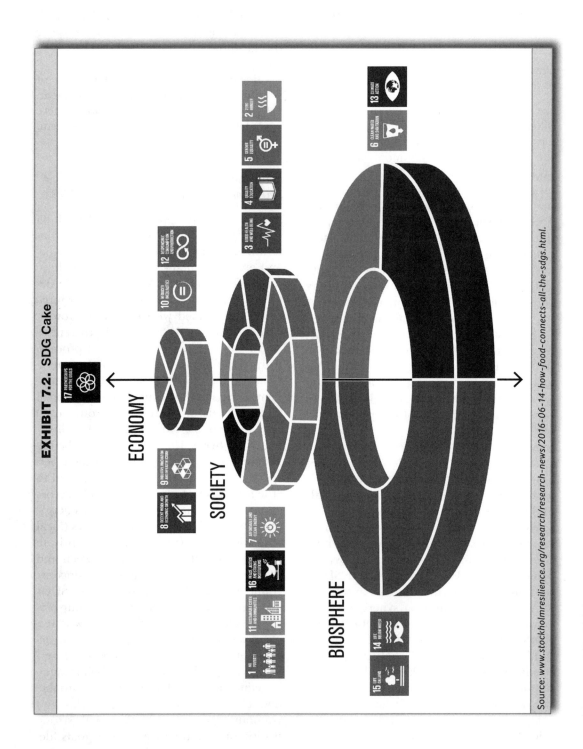

Source: www.stockholmresilience.org/research/research-news/2016-06-14-how-food-connects-all-the-sdgs.html.

production and consumption; and reduced inequalities). Partnerships to achieve these goals sit atop the framework.

Why Are Interactions Important?

You think that because you understand "one" that you must also understand "two" because one and one makes two. But you must also understand "and."
—SUFI TEACHING (quoted by Meadows, 2008, p. 12)

A particularly informative and useful guide to SDG interactions was published by the International Science Council (Nilsson, Griggs, Visbeck, Ringler, & McCollum, 2018). The framework developers take seriously the conceptualization of the 2030 Agenda for Sustainable Development as a holistic agenda—an "indivisible whole" integrating the three "pillars" of economic development, social development, and environmental protection as intertwined and cutting across the entire agenda. They find that most of the 17 SDGs embed all three dimensions within their targets. They then ask, What does this mean in practice?

> For example, SDG2 "End hunger, achieve food security and improved nutrition and promote sustainable agriculture" contains targets with social (e.g. malnutrition and vulnerability), economic (e.g. agricultural productivity and agricultural trade) and environmental dimensions (e.g. genetic diversity and climate resilience). Second, there are significant interactions between SDGs. Continuing with the example of SDG2, a commonly discussed set of interactions lies in the nexus between food, water and energy as reflected in the linkages between SDG2, SDG6 and SDG7. For instance, water is required in the energy sector for cooling in thermal power plants and for generating hydro-electricity; energy is required for residential and industrial water usage, and for pumping water for irrigation; and water is needed for all food and bioenergy production. Third, because of the strength of these linkages, achieving targets under these goals can lead to trade-offs between competing interests: for example, food production may compete with bioenergy production for the same land or water. Finally, the SDG targets interact with a much broader set of targets and goals, such as those preventing childhood death (target 3.2), reducing food waste (target 12.3), encouraging sustainable business practices (target 12.6), conserving marine areas (target 14.5) and ensuring rights to control over land and natural resources (target 1.4). Articulating and understanding the many interlinkages helps to explain why the 2030 Agenda must indeed be treated as an "indivisible whole." . . . Yet, there can be conflicts and trade-offs between goals. (Nilsson et al., 2018)

Evaluating the interactions among SDG targets and indicators, both actual and aspirational, positive and negative, and short term and long term, offers significant opportunities for Blue Marble thinkers, designers, and evaluators to contribute to the 2030 Agenda.

The International Science Council report highlights such tensions as those between preserving forests to reduce atmospheric carbon versus converting rain forests to agriculture to increase food production. The tensions are also transnational, as discussed in Chapter 6. There could be increased lumber harvesting and resulting deforestation in some countries as a result of enforced logging bans in neighboring countries. Support for biofuels in one region can drive up prices of food crops elsewhere, increasing food shortages and hunger for the poorest. Analyses that involve thinking deeply about SDG interactions, including different types of interactions, provide a conceptual framework for evaluation of those interactions. The nature and dynamics of the interactions, if better understood and documented through evaluation, could inform policy formulations, including the setting of context-specific (such as regional, national, or local) targets and indicators.

The Urgency of Integration across Problem Domains

Paula Caballero, as senior director of the World Bank Environment and Natural Resources Global Practice, called for "connecting the dots for sustainable development"—her eloquent vision of an integrated approach to an interconnected world.

> This is a year in which the health of the planet is finally understood to be of central concern to the future of people. A year in which the management of natural resources—from fish stocks and fresh water, to fertile soil, forest habitats and the carbon in the atmosphere—is understood to have significant national, international and inter-generational consequences.
>
> Climate change, water shortages and other environmental crises are bringing home the message loud and clear: we need to connect the dots between human actions across the landscape and seascape, or the earth will cease to care for us. It will cease to grow food, to store water, to host fish and pollinators, to provide energy, medicine and timber. Changing temperatures will stress systems already overwhelmed by unsustainable patterns of production and consumption, while a growing middle class will further strain planetary boundaries.
>
> Many of the solutions however will require breaking down the walls of specific sectors—forestry, agriculture, energy, transport, health—and working with a variety of stakeholders across landscapes, seascapes and cities to achieve multiple goals at once. There simply isn't enough time or money to pursue isolated and contradictory solutions.
>
> The world is getting smaller—more constrained and interconnected. We have an opportunity to apply system-wide thinking and leverage data to solve the challenges of our time. (2015)

The Web of Climate Change and Poverty

The Blue Marble perspective looks for and makes sense of systems and their interconnections. An example of such systemic analysis is a World Bank report that examined the relationship between climate change and poverty in South Asia and concluded that by 2050, if global greenhouse gas emissions continue on their current trajectory, 800 million will be thrust ever more deeply into poverty (Mani, Bandyopadhyay, Chonabayashi, Markan, & Mosier, 2018). The people affected will not just be coastal people vulnerable to rising sea levels but also people living in the vast rural areas of India, Pakistan, and Bangladesh, who would see their living standards measurably decline. The study looked at all six countries of South Asia, where average annual temperatures are rising steadily and rainfall patterns are already changing. It concentrated on changes in day-to-day weather, rather than sudden-onset natural disasters, and identified "hot spots" where the deterioration is expected to be most severe. The study found that these hot spots tend to be the poorer areas characterized by low household consumption, poor road connectivity, poor schools, inadequate health services, limited access to markets, and other development challenges. Higher temperatures as a result of climate change are forecast to lower labor productivity and worsen public health. In the central belt of India, hotter days and changes in rainfall patterns are expected to dramatically affect the already limited productivity of small farmers.

Somini Sengupta, a *New York Times* climate reporter, has written extensively about her firsthand observations of the effects of climate change in Asia. She has concluded that

> unchecked climate change . . . would amplify the hardships of poverty. And most jarring for someone like me who has reported from those countries: The people who will feel the most severe impacts are some of the world's poorest and hungriest people—those whose carbon footprints are tiny. (Sengupta & Popovich, 2018)

Reflections on Evaluating across Silos

Margaret (Meg) Hargreaves is a Senior Fellow in the Economics, Justice, and Society Department of NORC at the University of Chicago. Her work focuses on evaluating complex social change initiatives.

One of my favorite Google Map functions is the ability to switch from a two-dimensional road view to a three-dimensional satellite view. When I want to look at a location from a higher vantage point, I can zoom out to the point where I can see the location in context and understand its connection to other elements of the landscape. Even though this feature has limits, I can imagine zooming out until I can see the entire world as one big blue marble.

This reminds me that the boundaries, divisions, or silos that we see and experience when we are close to a situation are not permanent; they are human constructs that can be changed as we shift perspective. It allows me to use a systems lens, paying attention to differences between groups and interdependencies between parts, considering the whole from new angles not previously seen.

Traditionally, programs have been the focus, privileging individual-level change over changes occurring at other levels. But, as the complexities of mass incarceration, childhood adversity, racial inequities, climate change, and other issues are embraced, funders, policymakers, and practitioners are linking individual, community, and regional strategies. Instead of focusing only on increasing individual or organizational capacity, new initiatives are building the collective capacity of groups to work together across sectors and levels. Understanding the limited and potentially unsustainable impact of a single message, program, or policy, new initiatives are intervening at multiple points for greater leverage.

Portraits of Possibility

Once again, the GA constitutes an exemplar. The six principles adopted by the GA are interrelated as an integrated whole. The statement of principles (see Exhibit 7.3) is adamant that the six principles are not a pick-and-choose list, not a menu, but a comprehensive and holistic vision for the future of food. Evaluating adherence to the principles is a focus of the GA Blue Marble principles-focused evaluation (see Chapter 14 in this book; see also Patton, 2018d, Chap. 28, for a global scale example).

The McKnight Foundation CCRP, in projects in Africa and South America, works to integrate soil health, seed systems, water management, ecosystem sustainability, integrated pest management, agroecological practices, nutrition, food security, marketing, and gender inclusion and equity, among other subsystem elements, through participatory small-farm agroecological research organized, in part, through farmer research networks.

Both the GA and McKnight's CCRP exemplify engagement through Blue Marble principles: thinking, acting, and evaluating globally and locally (GLOCALLY) and across silos for systems change at a global scale.

Cross-Silos Themes

So where are we? I've looked at a number of examples of cross-silos thinking and action, only a few of which I have had space to re-

EXHIBIT 7.3. Global Alliance for the Future of Food: Integrated Set of Principles

Renewability

Address the integrity of natural and social resources that are the foundation of a healthy planet and future generations in the face of changing global and local demands.

Diversity

Value our rich and diverse agricultural, ecological, and cultural heritage.

Healthfulness

Advance the health and well-being of people, animals, the environment, and the societies that depend on all three.

Resilience

Support regenerative, durable, and economically adaptive systems in the face of a changing planet.

Equity

Promote sustainable livelihoods and access to nutritious and just food systems.

Interconnectedness

Understand the implications of the interdependence of food, people, and the planet in a transition to more sustainable food and agriculture systems.

Source: *https://futureoffood.org/about-us/how-we-work.*

port to you here. That said, *keep the baseline in mind!* Most development funding, design, and evaluation remains silo based. I have found some beacons of cross-silos possibility against a landscape dominated by issue, sector, and problem silos. What do those beacons of possibility have in common?

1. All integrated frameworks see sustainability as *multidimensional.* Though they identify key dimensions in different ways, resulting in varying numbers of dimensions, they all conceptualize problems as *multifaceted.*

2. All think in systems emphasizing the *interconnections* among the multiple dimensions identified, while being intentional about relevant systems boundaries and perspectives.

3. Each framework conceives of the problem to be addressed, analyzes the situa-

tion, and offers potential interventions through a *complex dynamic systems* lens.

4. Each framework emerged from a baseline analysis that siloed analysis is dominant and problematic, thus the attention to *cross-silos integration.*

5. All the frameworks identify integrating environmental and human dimensions as essential for transformation toward planetary sustainability.

Visualizing Cross-Silos Interconnections

Visual depictions and mapping of interventions, systems, and data are increasingly important for communicating with diverse stakeholders (Azzam & Evergreen, 2013a, 2013b; Evergreen, 2017, 2019). I conclude this chapter with three examples of cross-silos visualizations in Exhibits 7.4, 7.5, and 7.6 on pages 70–72.

An Integrated Perspective on Climate Change and Food Systems

Food and agriculture are significant contributors to and heavily impacted by climate change, but they also offer opportunities to mitigate greenhouse gas emissions. The GA commissioned a report to review key literature about how food and agriculture affect climate change and how climate change is affecting food systems. The findings illuminate how "a food systems approach to climate change adaptation and mitigation can drive positive changes and inform decision making to avoid unintended effects from narrowly targeted interventions" (Niles, Esquivel, Ahuja, & Mango, 2017, p. 5). The report documents specific interventions throughout the food system that support adaptation and mitigation in the short term that can support longer-term food systems transformation.

> Approaching adaptation and mitigation through a food systems approach broadens the range of opportunities and facilitates consideration of systems-level effects and interactions. Food systems include growing, harvesting, processing, packaging, transporting, marketing, consumption, and disposal of food and food-related items. These include preproduction activities like developing and delivering inputs like fertilizer, seeds, feed, farm implements, irrigation systems, information and research and development; production of crops, fish, and livestock; post-production activities like storage, packaging, transportation, manufacturing and retail; consumption activities either in homes or dining establishments; and waste and disposal that occurs throughout the system. Food systems operate within and are influenced by social, economic, political and environmental contexts, and people are involved throughout as producers, information providers, policymakers and regulators,

workers in health, forestry, trade, finance and in companies, and as consumers. (Niles et al., 2017, p. 5)

The centerpiece of the report is a depiction of the complex, multifaceted nature of food systems components, activities, and processes. Exhibit 7.4 shows a visual cross-silos depiction of the complex food system.

Healthy Planet, Healthy People

For too long we've put health and the environment in different boxes. The work of our generation is to bridge the two, to understand that in fact, they belong in the same box—that planetary health defines human health—and that as we improve one, we will improve the other as well.

—COURTNEY HOWARD, vice president, Canadian Association of Physicians for the Environment (2018)

This chapter has looked at examples of integrated thinking. *One Health* is an initiative based on the understanding that the health of people is connected to the health of animals and the environment. It aims to integrate work across these three systems (Lamielle, 2010; Raufman & Machalaba, 2018). Exhibit 7.5 visually depicts the One Health integrated framework. A Blue Marble evaluation would inquire into the extent to which such integration actually occurs, how it occurs, if it does, and with what results.

A Holistic Integrated Depiction of Security Domains

Food systems involve food security, which is connected to health security, political security, economic security, environmental security, educational security, community security, and, ultimately, personal security. A network mapping exercise in India depicts the interconnections among diverse organizations working in these various security domains (see Exhibit 7.6 on page 72).

EXHIBIT 7.4. Food System Components, Processes, and Activities

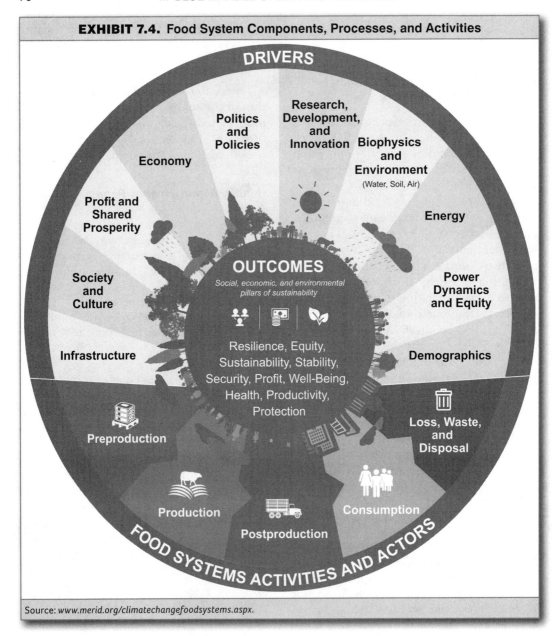

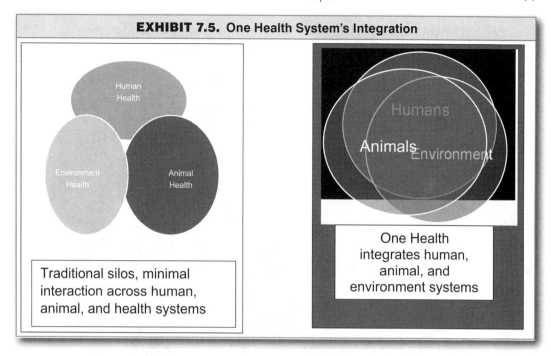

EXHIBIT 7.5. One Health System's Integration

Traditional silos, minimal interaction across human, animal, and health systems

One Health integrates human, animal, and environment systems

Crossing Academic Silos: Evaluation as a Transdiscipline

The silos of academia are disciplines. Disciplines, given birth by the mother of all disciplines, philosophy, can be distinguished by their core burning questions. For sociology, the burning question is the Hobbesian question of order: What holds society or social groups together? What keeps societal groups from falling apart? Psychology asks why individuals think, feel, and act as they do. Political science asks, What is the nature of power, how is it distributed, and with what consequences? Economics studies how resources are produced and distributed. Disciplines and subdisciplines reveal layers of questions. Biologists inquire into the nature and variety of life. Botanists ask how plants grow, while agriculturists investigate the production of food, and agronomists narrow their focus still further to field crops.

To be sure, reducing any complex and multifaceted discipline to a single burning question oversimplifies the focus of that dis-

cipline. But what is gained is clarity about what distinguishes one lineage of inquiry from another. Combining disciplines for inquiry makes the approach interdisciplinary. Sustainability science draws on several natural and social sciences.

A *transdiscipline* is a discipline that both stands on its own as a body of knowledge and—this is key—is essential to other disciplines. Pioneering evaluator and philosopher of science Michael Scriven (2008) eloquently and forcefully positions evaluation as a transdiscipline: evaluation sits atop the disciplinary, scholarly, and academic hierarchy with philosophy, logic, and statistics as bodies of knowledge, theory, and methods that are essential for the scholarship and knowledge creation of all other disciplines. Evaluation is a transdiscipline because "its domain includes the methodology of the task of validation of any discipline's claim to legitimacy as a discipline: it is the master of credentials" (2013, p. 175).

Evaluation is another candidate for the transdisciplinary crown since it is, first, an

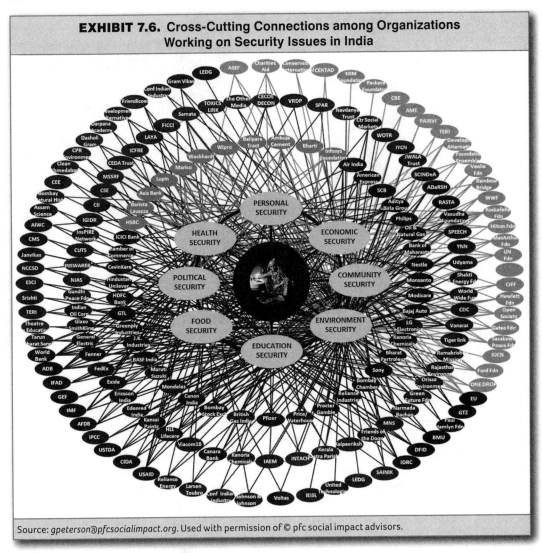

EXHIBIT 7.6. Cross-Cutting Connections among Organizations Working on Security Issues in India

Source: gpeterson@pfcsocialimpact.org. Used with permission of © pfc social impact advisors.

essential element in all other academic disciplines, as the tool that distinguishes them from pseudo-disciplines, that distinction being based on the ability to distinguish high-quality data and hypotheses from shoddy ones in order to distinguish, for example, science from pseudo-science. (2008, p. 66)

Evaluation, the ugly frog, turns into a prince when the spell on us is broken. Evaluation is all that distinguishes astronomy from astrology, good explanations from bad ones, good experimental designs—or bridge designs—from inferior ones, good scientists

and engineers and technologists from run-of-the-mill ones. It is a discipline that is part of every discipline because it distinguishes the discipline from pretentious jargon, just as one distinguishes good food from garbage. (1993, pp. 47–48)

Academics will argue among themselves about whether, and the extent to which, evaluation is a transdiscipline. Arguing about definitions and boundaries is what academics do, and I've had my share of fun so indulging. That said, the assertion that evaluation is essential to every other dis-

Let the silo go by Simon Kneebone. Used with permission of the copyright holder, the Australian Evaluation Society (*aes.asn.au*).

cipline is irrefutable. Thus, to the outside world, when I talk about evaluation, I proclaim without reservation evaluation's transdisciplinary status as a theory-based body of knowledge. Our peer-reviewed journals capture, adjudicate, and report that body of knowledge, and being a reservoir of that knowledge should be part of our public persona and identity to the larger world. Blue Marble evaluation is a transdisciplinary specialization within evaluation that cuts across sector and issue silos, nation-state boundaries, local–global scales, and, as we shall see in the next chapter, cuts across time, encompassing the short-, medium-, and long-term perspectives.

CHAPTER 8

Time Being of the Essence Principle

The future depends on what you do today.
—MAHATMA GANDHI, Indian philosopher
and activist

CONTEXT

A sense of urgency emerges when faced with how we respond to issues of sustainability, resilience, adaptability, and, indeed, human survival in the Anthropocene. It is worth emphasizing that the Intergovernmental Panel on Climate Change (IPCC; 2018) scientific consensus is that humanity has no more than a decade (until 2030) to significantly reverse greenhouse gas emissions before reaching the point of no return on global warming. That is the point where the acceleration of the effects of climate change will be beyond reversal. That is the point where planetary sustainability becomes problematic for much of humanity over the next century. If you are uncertain about just how urgent a sense of urgency is, have a look at Amitav Ghosh's (2016) *The Great Derangement: Climate Change and the Unthinkable,* David Wallace-Wells's (2019) *The Uninhabitable Earth: Life after Warming,* Nathaniel Rich's (2019) *Losing Earth,* Bill McKibben's (2019) *Falter: Has the Human Game Begun to Play Itself Out?,* and *The Madhouse Effect* by climate scientist Michael Mann, subtitled *How Climate Change Denial Is Threatening Our Planet, Destroying Our Politics, and Driving Us Crazy* (Mann & Toles, 2018).

Time Being of the Essence

Nothing evokes time like the threat—or reality—of extinction. For the men and women around the world engaged in trying to conserve species, the sense of despair and loss when the last member of a species dies is real and very personal.

> "On one occasion, I was taken out of school by my father to see the last pure-bred Norfolk Horn ram before he died," one conservationist remembers. The next morning the breed was extinct. The sense of loss was very tangible. (Westley et al., 2007, p. 100)

That memory is from Ulysses Seal who, in 1997, became chair of the Conservation

Breeding Specialist Group (CBSG), a sub-committee of the huge, voluntary, science-driven International Union for Conservation of Nature, a Switzerland-based organization. He recruited scientists, zoo directors, wildlife managers, and environmental activists to work together to save endangered species worldwide. Even as they worked tirelessly, and often successfully, they knew with certainty that they would fail, ultimately, to save all the species they loved. But faced with the imminent demise of an animal, they did what they could to preserve the species for the immediate future. Their mantra became "Not on my watch."

> One CBSG member explained it like this: I do not believe for a moment that we are going to win. I do not openly say this . . . but it is not going to happen. I continue to work because, even if the desired result is not forthcoming, I have still done my duty . . . I have done whatever I could to bring it about, regardless of anything. This is important to me spiritually." He copes by setting boundaries around his own efforts, asserting that a certain animal will not disappear "on my watch." That watch will last his lifetime, but by thinking about his mission in this way, he makes it human-scaled—manageable enough to carry without succumbing to despair. (Westley et al., 2007, pp. 167–168)

The Fourth Dimension

Time is the fourth dimension in the Blue Marble evaluation space–time continuum. The three Blue Marble operating principles presented thus far correspond, analogously, to three dimensions of space: Engaging globally makes the whole Earth the *all-encompassing space* for Blue Marble evaluation; engaging GLOCALLY *connects local and global spaces*; engaging across silos *expands the space for evaluation* across sectors and issues. The *Time Being of the Essence principle* adds learning from the past to engage with a realistic sense of urgency in the present to inform a thoughtful view of the future.

Time Being of the Essence Principle Explicated

PREMISE: Understanding the past provides a perspective on present realities and future possibilities. Future scenarios include both doomsday and utopian possibilities. Evaluative thinking (Patton, 2018c) applied to the present can be joined with futuristic thinking (Patton, in press) to illuminate forward-looking patterns and trajectories. Monitoring how interventions and initiatives unfold can inform adaptations along the way.

Time Being of the Essence Principle

Act with a sense of urgency in the present, support adaptive sustainability long term, grounding both in understanding the past.

IMPLICATIONS

This principle stands in sharp contrast to the dominant practice in evaluation that looks at short-term goal achievement instead of long-term consequences, and stresses continuity of results instead of adaptive capacity for the future. The Blue Marble evaluation approach to time reframes traditional evaluation thinking from conceptualizing initiatives and evaluations within time frames defined by when activities begin and end to intentionally and systematically thinking backward and forward across longer time frames. This means, for example, understanding antecedents and trajectories from the past, thereby learning from the past, and forecasting results and consequences into the future, thereby being ever mindful of the challenges of the future, even while engaged in work in the present. Other ways in which this principle reframes traditional evaluation thinking and practice include moving from:

• Taking pre–post snapshots to capturing dynamics all along the way.

• Ending evaluations with stand-alone recommendations to tracking what is revealed as the future unfolds, being especially mindful of the urgency of transformation, thus being ever watchful for sustainable trajectories.

- Engaging beyond narrow project and program time boundaries to incorporating a global ecological sustainability time frame applied within the local context (GLOCAL principle).

- Moving from a static approach to sustainability (continuity) to a dynamic one (adaptive capacity).

- Shifting from short-term to long-term thinking, recognizing that everything done today has ripples going out in time.

- Past-time (Holocene) complacency to real-time (Anthropocene) urgency.

Exhibit 8.1 offers additional implications of this principle for design and evaluation. The rest of this chapter looks more deeply at these implications.

Time as an Essential Construct in Evaluation

The nature and logic of evaluation make attention to time essential. The most fundamental evaluation framing has always involved determining the status of some

EXHIBIT 8.1. Design and Evaluation: Implications of the Blue Marble Time Being of the Essence Principle		
Blue Marble Time Being of the Essence principle	**Design guidance**	**Evaluation criterion and questions**
Act with a sense of urgency in the present, support adaptive sustainability long term, grounding both in understanding the past.	1. Develop a thoughtful and multidimensional time line from past to present to understand context and stimulate thinking about patterns that may influence the design of interventions. 2. Design interventions to accomplish shorter-term results while enhancing capacity for long-term adaptive sustainability and resilience. 3. Design initiatives with attention to how larger systems dynamics, both human and environmental systems, will affect the development and adaptation of the intervention over time. 4. Design interventions to contribute to global planetary sustainability. 5. Include in the intervention design expected and evaluable trajectories of sustainability progress.	*Time Being of the Essence fidelity*: 1. How does the design address past patterns, both those that need to be changed and those on which to build? 2. To what extent and in what ways does an initiative systemically address the relationship between shorter-term results and longer-term adaptive sustainability? 3. How are larger systems dynamics, both human and environmental, tracked to support adaptability? 4. To what extent, in what ways, and within what time frame does an initiative contribute to global planetary sustainability? 5. How and when are evaluation activities and reporting timed to ensure timeliness of feedback on trajectories toward sustainability?

phenomenon at a beginning point compared to its status at some ending point—for example, participants' knowledge, attitudes, and behaviors at the beginning and end of a program. Getting good baseline data can be challenging, but without a baseline it is impossible to know what has changed over time. With baseline and end-of-program data, an evaluative judgment can be made about whether any observable differences between pretest and outcome measurements were desirable, attributable, significant, and replicable. Blue Marble evaluation adds to this traditional framing the value of a retrospective time line that portrays how the present has emerged from the past and a prospective time line about trajectories for the future.

When to measure outcomes for a program is a matter of how much time is supposedly needed and available to achieve desired results. The length of a program is determined by its theory of change, resources available, funding time line, and nature of the outcomes being targeted. Changing knowledge and attitudes typically takes less time than changing behaviors. Changing individuals takes less time than changing institutions and systems. Changing paradigms takes an even longer time. A hypothesis that includes assumptions about the time required for change ought to be specified in a program's theory of change. Learning a new workplace skill may be attainable in a week. Improving agricultural practices will take a growing season at a minimum, often several growing seasons. Supporting a student's graduation from secondary school will take years. Changing the behavior of an entire fishing community to follow an integrated ecosystem approach to fisheries management can take generations. But always, *always*, some sense of time is an essential part of a program design and, correspondingly, an evaluation design. That much is straightforward. From there it quickly becomes complicated.

Evaluators are typically commissioned to evaluate as if there is an endpoint—a project cycle, the end of the study. But Blue Marble evaluators must think beyond such endpoints. Looking from a baseline to an endpoint provides two snapshots. Capturing data about developments throughout an initiative provides a trajectory. Following the implications of that trajectory for the future becomes part of Blue Marble evaluative thinking. The different evaluation perspectives are like that between snapshots versus panoramic movies.

Sustainability over Time: Alternative Perspectives

There isn't a single country that has reversed its over-use of the planet yet.
—TERRY A'HEARN, chief executive officer, Scottish Environment Protection Agency (2017)

The Conference of the Parties to the Paris Agreement on Climate Change included 14,000 delegates from 195 countries convened to negotiate how countries can meet the Paris Agreement targets. At the opening session, UN Secretary-General António Guterres warned: "We are in trouble. It is hard to comprehend why we are collectively still moving too slowly—and even in the wrong direction." COP24 produced a "rule book" for putting into practice the Paris Agreement of 2015. "But after all is said and done, the 2°C goal, let alone the 1.5°C aspiration, remain distant prospects. The world is on course for more or less 3°C of warming with Kiribati and the Marshall Islands being the first countries at risk of submersion" ("COP24," 2018).

I regularly speak at conferences where, following my presentation on the urgency of dealing with climate change, those in attendance acknowledge the crisis but tell me that no funders of evaluation are interested in addressing climate change in the projects they fund. But funders do demand that evaluations address sustainability—not Blue Marble (whole Earth) sustainability but project sustainability. The difference is huge. Let me explain why.

Traditional and Still Dominant Evaluation Criteria for Sustainability

The criteria formulated in 1991 by the Development Assistance Committee (DAC) Network on Development Evaluation of the Organisation for Economic Co-operation and Development (OECD) may well be the most widely used set of evaluation criteria in the world. International agencies worldwide apply these criteria, which call for evaluations to examine a program's (1) relevance, (2) effectiveness, (3) efficiency, (4) impact, and (5) sustainability.

> Sustainability is concerned with measuring whether the benefits of an activity are likely to continue after donor funding has been withdrawn. . . . [so] it is useful to consider the following questions:
>
> • To what extent did the benefits of a programme or project continue after donor funding ceased?
> • What were the major factors which influenced the achievement or non-achievement of sustainability of the programme or project? (DAC, 1991, p. 1)

The DAC definition above conceptualizes sustainability as continuity of the funded program and its achieved results. This has been and remains the dominant perspective on sustainability by funders, those who receive funds, and, therefore, of evaluators. This criterion is quite understandable from a funder perspective. Funders want to see change and want those changes to be maintained. Evaluators are commissioned to determine both whether the intended changes occurred, and if so, whether they can be sustained. This is fundamentally an accountability perspective imposed from

the perspective of funders who must demonstrate that they have made good use of the assets entrusted to them. But *sustainability as continuation* is linear, mechanistic, and static. It is a logic of moving from one condition (a problem) to a new condition (a solution) in a way that the problem does not recur and the solution lasts. This is how evaluators have come to think and practice, but this way of conceptualizing and evaluating sustainable change is a fundamental barrier to the future sustainability of Earth.

The Blue Marble view of sustainability begins by acknowledging that change is constant, which means that interventions aimed at systems change must be flexible and adaptable, which makes adaptability and resilience critical evaluation criteria. What has not been sufficiently acknowledged, in my view, is how dramatically such a dynamic and complex perspective of sustainability departs from the dominant paradigm under which most evaluations operate. Let's look at the alternative to DAC's criterion of sustainability as continuity over time.

Resilient and Adaptive Sustainability

> Long-term ecological sustainability is dynamic and adaptive. Ecosystem *resilience* is defined as "the magnitude of disturbance that can be absorbed before the system changes its structure by changing the variables and processes that control behavior." (Gunderson & Holling, 2002, p. 28)

> Resilience is the capacity to experience massive change and yet still maintain the integrity of the original. Resilience isn't about balancing change and stability. It isn't about reaching an equilibrium state. Rather it is about how massive change and stability paradoxically work together. (Westley et al., 2007, p. 65)

How we think about and understand resilience is connected to how we think about major systems change in complex adaptive systems, which has implications for how we *evaluate* the sustainability of systems change over time. Framing sustainability as a function of resilience and adaptability over time makes it dynamic rather than static, and directs us to look at the systems dynamics that surround an intervention and how they change rather than just examining the continuity of the intervention by itself, even with thoughtful contextual considerations.

The Resilience Alliance (RA) focuses on ecological sustainability. Established in 1999, the RA describes itself as an international, multidisciplinary research organization that explores the dynamics of socioecological systems. RA members collaborate across disciplines to advance the understanding and practical application of resilience, adaptive capacity, and transformation of societies and ecosystems in order to cope with change and support human well-being. The RA distinguishes itself in its capacity for comparative research and synthesis at a global scale, rooted in local and regional context-specific studies. The RA (2019) defines resilience as follows:

> Resilience is . . . the ability to absorb disturbances, to be changed and then to re-organise and still have the same identity (retain the same basic structure and ways of functioning). It includes the ability to learn from the disturbance. A resilient system is forgiving of external shocks. As resilience declines the magnitude of a shock from which it cannot recover gets smaller and smaller. Resilience shifts attention from purely growth and efficiency to needed recovery and flexibility. Growth and efficiency alone can often lead ecological systems, businesses and societies into fragile rigidities, exposing them to turbulent transformation. Learning, recovery and flexibility open eyes to novelty and new worlds of opportunity.

Gunderson and Holling (2002) distinguish two fundamentally different ways of thinking about resilience: *engineering resilience* versus *ecosystem resilience*. Engineer-

ing resilience has traditionally focused on "stability near an equilibrium steady state, where resistance to disturbance and speed of return to the equilibrium are used to measure the property." In contrast, ecosystem resilience "emphasizes conditions far from any equilibrium steady state, where instabilities can flip a system into another regime of behavior—i.e., to another stability domain. In this case resilience is measured by the magnitude of disturbance that can be absorbed before the system changes its structure by changing the variables and processes that control behavior" (pp. 27–28). Exhibit 8.2 summarizes the contrasts between engineering resilience versus ecosystem resilience.

Gunderson and Holling (2002) argue that sustainable relationships between humans and nature require an emphasis on ecosystem resilience. This not only shifts the management and policy emphasis from micro, command-and-control approaches to adaptive management ones, but it correspondingly *shifts the evaluation emphasis from fidelity and persistence of a program to adaptability and responsiveness of systems change interventions, the essence of ongoing developmental evaluation* (Patton, 2011). The stakes for which approach dominates the worlds of policy, programming, and evaluation are high, indeed, and at the heart of discussions and debates about sustainable development.

> Exclusive emphasis on the first definition of resilience, engineering resilience, reinforces the dangerous myth that the variability of natural systems can be effectively controlled, that the consequences are predictable, and that sustained maximum production is an attainable and sustainable goal . . . [and] that leads to the pathology of resource management. . . . As ecosystem resilience is lost, the system becomes more vulnerable to external shocks that previously could be absorbed. . . . (Gunderson & Holling, 2002, p. 28)

EXHIBIT 8.2. Contrasting Views of Resilience over Time

Engineering resilience	Ecosystem resilience
• Focuses on efficiency, control, constancy, and predictability in conditions of low uncertainty. • Aims at optimal performance of systems by minimizing threats to performance and maintaining steady-state equilibrium. • Concentrates on stability near an equilibrium steady state, where resistance to disturbance and speed of return to the equilibrium are used to measure sustainability. • Management and policy emphasize micro, command-and-control approaches. • Evaluation focuses on stable and consistent elements of the system.	• Focuses on persistence, adaptiveness, variability, and unpredictability under conditions of high uncertainty. • Aims to adapt by absorbing and adjusting to disturbances by evolving absorptive and adaptive structures and processes. • Concentrates on the magnitude of disturbance that can be absorbed before the system changes its structure and processes, and the reality of more than one equilibrium. • Management and policy emphasize the adaptive interplay between stabilizing and destabilizing forces for resilience. • Evaluation focuses on adaptability of the system.

Source: Adapted from Gunderson and Holling (2002).

As these examples illustrate, criteria for resilient sustainability (ecosystem resilience) focus on adaptability and responsiveness:

- Awareness of current and emergent needs.
- Ability to address emergent needs within the realm of the organization's mission and priorities.
- Capacity to adjust to changing contexts.
- Flexibility to adjust to unanticipated negative impacts and side effects (e.g., environmental degradation).
- Continuous adaptation of intervention to optimize benefits and minimize harm.
- Concern of potential harms of an intervention to future generations (intergenerational equity, inclusion of children and youth specifically; Schröter, 2009).

Resilience and Adaptability

Resilience is the capacity to absorb shocks and return to the same essential system constellation and functioning. Adaptability is the capacity to evolve into a new system constellation and functioning if needed because the context has fundamentally changed. These capacities are distinguishable but interrelated. The combined capacities are dynamic in contrast to the static criterion of continuity.

Let me reiterate by way of summary because these distinctions are critical. Sustainability is narrowly focused if it only concerns the continuation of an initiative or intervention. That is sufficient for traditional project-oriented evaluation. But from a Blue Marble evaluation perspective, the resilient adaptability of a change endeavor should be the focus of evaluation *as well as its contribution to planetary sustainability.*

Short-Term versus Long-Term Thinking

In 1980, Dominica was hit by two hurricanes. Hurricane Allen, with gale force winds, devastated trees and tore the roofs off more than half the island's housing. Hurricane David, 6 weeks later, brought torrential rains leading to large-scale erosion and mudslides. Dominica's agriculture was dominated by citrus and banana trees, virtually all of which were uprooted. With international funding, a major initiative was undertaken to replant the island's trees. A retired British military officer led the initiative using a disciplined, carefully planned, and rigorously implemented *management by objectives* approach in which very specific targets for the number of trees planted each day were set. The targets were met and the project was lauded as an example of the value of setting targets and enforcing them. It soon became apparent, however, that to meet the targets, many of the trees were planted in lower, more accessible areas on land most suitable for growing food crops instead of on the steep hillsides of this volcanic island. The short-term goals were met at the expense of longer-term ecosystem appropriateness. The trees planted in the lower areas had to be uprooted and transplanted up the hillsides, a process that incurred twice the expense and took three times longer than if the initiative had been done correctly the first time. The short-term target accountability focus (deliver results) undermined long-term sustainability.

The Dominica cautionary tale carries a larger message. What passes for long-term thinking among philanthropic foundations and international agencies is that what they support should persist (continuity-focused, engineering resilience). This converts into evaluation criteria of sustainability defined in static terms as persistence, which is essentially an operationalization of the engineering resilience mindset. Sustainability from an engineering resilience mindset is inherent in these widespread criteria for evaluating sustainability:

- Persistence of the institution.
- Persistence of program activities, services, and interventions (this includes transferability to other contexts or replication of programming).
- Persistence of resulting changes for individuals (humans), society (e.g., culture, institutions), the economy, and the environment (Schröter, 2009).

The irony is that this seemingly long-term focus on persistence derives from short-term thinking in actual funding practices. Philanthropic foundations and international development agencies typically eschew long-term funding of programs. They like to support pilot innovations and have them demonstrate effectiveness and stability, then turn them loose, like baby birds pushed out of the nest to fend for themselves. In the past, foundations hoped that some government agency would be impressed by what they had funded and pick up the demonstrations to make them ongoing and therefore sustainable. But given the ongoing fiscal crisis at all levels of government, legislators and bureaucrats are looking to shed programs, not add them. Nor do foundations like to pick up the leavings of other foundations. They each want to do their own thing. So nonprofit programs have developed expertise in reframing what they do just enough to repackage and propose it as innovation worthy of new funding, an adaptation to the realities of how philanthropy works. Large nonprofits and international agencies around the world have full-time development staff who manage these gyrations and conceptual gymnastics; they have become adept at making the case that their proposals are both innovative and sustainable—that is, they will persist when the current foundation's funding ends, usually after 3–5 years, in some cases longer, and in others, shorter. What they don't say is that the way they will persist is to repackage what they're doing as new and sell it to a new funder as innovative, fostering an insidious cycle of innovative illusion. Becoming skilled at creating illusions of innovation and sustainability/persistence is all part of the philanthropic and international development assistance funding game:

Those receiving grants pretend that they have a viable strategy for sustaining funding. Those making the grants pretend to believe them.

The actual nonprofit strategy is to promise whatever it takes to get the money and worry about getting more funding later. The actual foundation strategy is to accept promises of sustainability as addressing the sustainability criterion while avoiding any follow-up evaluation that would actually assess whether sustainability has occurred. All of this feeds the shared delusion that a program meriting funding at some point in time should go on indefinitely—be "sustained"—as evidence of wise initial funding.

Short-term thinking dominates Western society. American and multinational corporations report quarterly results that immediately affect stock prices. Two of the world's most successful investors, Warren Buffett and Jamie Dimon, who run large multinational corporations, penned an editorial in the *Wall Street Journal* advocating that corporations stop providing quarterly earnings guidance. They observed that companies often hesitate to spend on technology, hiring, and research and development but rather divert investments to meet quarterly earnings forecasts, even though short-term (quarterly) results can be affected by seasonal factors beyond their control.

> Quarterly earnings guidance often leads to an unhealthy focus on short-term profits at the expense of long-term strategy, growth and sustainability. (Buffett & Dimon, 2018, p. 1)

Likewise, monthly government reports on inflation, unemployment rates, econom-

ic growth, and related economic indicators get a great deal of attention in the press and media and affect corporate decision making, and, again, the movement of stock prices. The instantaneous gratification of sports competitions feeds the short-term mania.

In contrast, Brian Dumaine, a *Fortune* business magazine editor, has cowritten a book titled *Go Long: Why Long-Term Thinking Is Your Best Short-Term Strategy* (Carey, Dumaine, Useem, & Zemmel, 2018). This is but one example of the vast literature that deals with and offers advice about short-term versus long-term thinking. We are counseled to develop long-term strategies while adapting in real time to emergent, short-term trends. The tension we experience between long-term and short-term thinking is embedded in how our brains process information, according to Nobel Prize–winning decision scientist Daniel Kahneman. In his best-selling book *Thinking, Fast and Slow* (2011), he documents how intuitive, short-term thinking dominates longer-term more deliberative thinking. Blue Marble evaluation must deal with both the shorter term and the longer term. Short-term results tell us whether we are on the strategic path to desired long-term results. Short-term climate change trends foreshadow long-term planetary disaster. Resilient sustainability involves examining how dynamic adaptations to short-term challenges and turbulence create long-term patterns of effectiveness or ineffectiveness.

Examining these global trends, the Club of Rome, an organization of individuals who share a common concern for the future of humanity, concludes that we need a "new enlightenment" that leaves behind working in silos to generate a balance between humans and nature, as well as a balance between markets and the state, and the short versus long term (von Weizsäcker & Wijkman, 2018). That's a good description of the Blue Marble evaluation perspective.

Thinking long term, Parts 1 and 2; System–make our own pathways by Simon Kneebone.

Blue Marble Evaluators as Both Historians and Futurists

Sustainability intrinsically requires thinking long term. For something to be sustained, it must endure, even if in some adapted form. The challenge for evaluation, then, is to incorporate a futures perspective into evaluation, which, by its very nature, provides a historical perspective. The fields of futures studies and evaluation include a broad range of people who use a wide variety of techniques to make inquiries into how the world is changed. Futurists conjure the future in order to alter perceptions and actions in the present that affect the future. Evaluators study the past (what programs have already done) in order to alter perceptions and actions in the present that affect the future. In this sense, then, both futurists and evaluators are interested in altering perceptions and actions in the present, the impact of which will be a changed future. Evaluators do so by looking at what has already occurred; futurists do so by forecasting what may occur, often imagining alternative scenarios. Assessing the likelihood of various future scenarios requires evaluative thinking and judgments. Given the common interests that futurists and evaluators share in affecting the future and that both fields employ evaluative thinking in making interpretations and rendering judgments, Blue Marble evaluation integrates futures thinking into evaluative designs and findings reports.

How do we use what is learned from evaluations to inform future actions? Evaluations identify past and present patterns of effectiveness (and ineffectiveness). Futurists generate alternative trajectories about what may lie ahead. But using the past to inform the future is no straightforward process. Imagining future scenarios requires what philosopher Thomas Nagel (2018) calls "as if" thinking. This involves evaluating backward from an imagined future, *as if* we were in that future time and evaluating what had already unfolded. This requires creating idealized trajectories for the future *as if* we had expertise born of hindsight, but lacking that prescience, is manifest as foresight. Scholars of decision making and expertise have found that what distinguishes people with great foresight is not that they have more expertise (answers) than others, but they are more adept at situational recognition and more intentional about their forecasting processes (Patton, 2014, 2019). We can, in fact, come to recognize our analytic tendencies and learn to identify the thinking processes that determine our imaginings and idealizations. In so doing, we can learn to be alert to the biases to which our thought processes make us liable (Kahneman, 2011; Tversky & Kahneman, 1974, pp. 1124–1125).

We can do this through ongoing and in-depth reflective practice. Perhaps, then, if we as evaluators can reflect on and become more aware of how we assess situations and arrive at evaluative judgments, we can use those insights when we are called on to play the role of futurists. For called on as such we shall surely be. How is this so? How do we get from evaluating to futuring?

Distinguished psychometrician and evaluation pioneer Lee J. Cronbach (1980) observed that "results of a program evaluation are so dependent on the setting that replication is only a figure of speech; the evaluator is essentially an historian" (p. 7). A completed evaluation study describes what has occurred. But in addition to portraying what has been, evaluators are routinely asked to make recommendations. In so doing, evaluators move from being historians to become futurists.

Recommendations constitute a forecast of what will happen if certain actions are taken. These forecasts are based on evaluators' foundational analysis and interpretation of what has occurred in the past. The accuracy of such forecasts, as with any predictions about the future, is subject to error due to changed conditions and the validity of assumptions that are necessarily made. Futurists have developed approaches for dealing with the uncertainties of their forecasts. Some of these approaches, I have found, hold promise for evaluation. For example, futurists have developed techniques for constructing alternative scenarios that permit decision makers to consider the consequences of different assumptions and trends. These are variations on "if . . . then . . ." constructions. There are often three to four different scenarios constructed: a pessimistic scenario, an optimistic scenario, and one or two middle-of-the-road or most likely case scenarios. The very presentation of scenarios communicates that the future is uncertain and that the way one best prepares for the future is by preparing for a variety of possible trajectories ahead (Patton, 2008, 2012).

General Robert E. Lee is reputed to have said, "I am often surprised, but I am never taken by surprise." That is the essence of a futures perspective—being prepared and able to adapt to whatever emerges by having reflected on different possibilities, even those that are unlikely. That is also the foundation for resilient sustainability—being prepared to adapt to whatever emerges.

These premises can inform evaluation practices as follows: *Continuously monitor, evaluate, and revise forecasts and plans in light of new data and conditions in order to improve real-time frameworks for making long-term decisions and strategies.* That counsel insightfully integrates evaluative thinking and futuring. What follows suggests some ways this can be done.

Foresight

Three Horizons is a "foresight tool" for working with change. The first horizon describes the current way of doing things, and the way we can expect the world to unfold if we all keep behaving in our current unsustainable patterns. The third horizon envisions a transformed future based on new, sustainable patterns, practices, and policies. The second horizon "is the transition and transformation zone of emerging innovations that are responding to the shortcomings of the first horizon and interested in the possibilities of the third horizon" (Sharpe, 2013, p. 13).

> This is the core idea of Three Horizons—to shift from our simple, one-dimensional view of time stretching into the future and instead adopt a three-dimensional point of view in which we become aware of each horizon as a distinct quality relationship between the future and the present. We call the move into this multi-dimensional view, and the skill to work with it, the step into *future consciousness.* (p. 15; original emphasis)

The Seventh Generation Principle

The Great Law of Peace was codified by the Iroquois Confederacy in the 12th century to bring peace to the warring tribes of five nations in what is now the northeastern United States: the Mohawk, Seneca, Oneida, Onondaga, and Cayuga. The Constitution of the Iroquois Confederacy states that chiefs consider the impact of their decisions on the seventh generation to come. Western society generally considers a generation to be 25 years. The Seventh Generation principle considers one generation to be 100 years. Widely embraced by Native Americans generally, and many other indigenous people around the world, the Seventh Generation principle advises that in every decision—be it personal, family, or tribal—thoughtful consideration should be given to how it will affect descendants seven generations into the future (Larkin, 2013).

What Gets Measured Gets Done

Evaluating for resilient and adaptive sustainability increases the likelihood that intervention designs will address resilient and adaptive sustainability. Under the performance measurement mantra that "What gets measured gets done," if static continuity is the evaluation criterion that is measured, that's how interventions will be designed and implemented, as fixed models to be carried forward. If resilient and adaptive sustainability is the success criterion, that's how interventions will be designed, implemented, and evaluated.

Bottom line: Think about how time is of the essence in everything that is done, and act accordingly.

Urgency

At a 2015 member gathering of the GA, 10 experts in agroecology, agricultural development, and food systems were asked to identify priorities for action toward a more sustainable global food system. Having heard and reacted to one another's presentations, each was asked for a closing statement articulating the most important thing they had to say to those assembled and, indeed, to the world. While the priorities they had offered differed, suddenly there was consensus. Each articulated a *profound sense of urgency*: the urgent need to get beyond complacency, to take seriously the likelihood that there is a point of no return for humanity's depletion of Earth's resources and contributions to climate change, a point of no return that, if not already passed, looms closer and closer.

How close? At the global conference on transformations at the University of Dundee in Scotland in 2017, Kumi Naidoo, launch executive director of the African

Doomsday clock by Simon Kneebone.

Civil Society Support Initiative, offered in his keynote address a concrete estimate through a clock metaphor:

> The most important challenge for leadership of our time, whether the leaders are from the private sector, from government, or from civil society, is how can we tell it like it is, speak truth to power, say that *we are five minutes till midnight on climate change.* (emphasis added)

But thermonuclear destruction may trump climate change as a threat to the future of humanity. Members of the Bulletin of the Atomic Scientists updated the "Doomsday Clock" on January 25, 2018, in Washington, DC. For the first time in the 70-year history of the Doomsday Clock, a metaphorical estimate of the danger of a nuclear Armageddon, they moved the clock forward 30 seconds to *2 minutes before midnight,* their estimate of the likelihood that humanity will self-destruct.

The Ghost of the Present

This chapter opened with the story of conservationists working to preserve endangered species. "Not on my watch" was their commitment to at least delay extinction. This chapter closes with a sense of urgency, for time is running out for humanity. The *Time Being of the Essence principle* evokes Charles Dickens's (1843) Ghost of Christmas Present, who says the following to Scrooge:

> There is never enough time to do or say all the things that we would wish. The thing is to try to do as much as you can in the time that you have.

CHAPTER 9

Yin–Yang Principle

THE YIN–YANG OF LIFE

At birth, a person is flexible and flowing.
At death, a person becomes rigid and blocked.
Whatever is flexible and flowing will tend to grow.
Whatever is rigid and blocked will atrophy and die.
—LAO TZU (in Heider, 1985, p. 151)

CONTEXT

The Blue Marble is an image of wholeness. The Blue Marble perspective embraces that whole by recognizing and harmonizing opposites. For example, *life* is given meaning by *death,* and vice versa. *Up* cannot exist unless there is a correspondingly opposite *down.* Though they are opposites, they define each other. Indeed, they give meaning to each other; they are interconnected.

Yin–Yang Philosophy

Emergent from ancient Chinese philosophy, the image of Yin and Yang capture how seemingly opposite or contrary forces may actually be complementary, interconnected, and interdependent. They illuminate each other in relationship together. Yin–Yang thought emerged in the third century B.C.E. from contemplating nature. The moon was associated with Yin (陰陽) and the sun was associated with Yang (阴阳) (Wang, 2012) The *taijitu* symbol, above, comprises two large teardrop shapes, with the black representing Yin and the white representing Yang. Within the white Yang is a small black circle, and within the black Yin is a small white circle, symbolizing that within Yin there is Yang, and within Yang there is Yin.

Blue Marble Logo

The Blue Marble evaluation logo features a green Yin–Yang symbol that both divides and connects the two halves of the blue Earth. The Yin–Yang wave represents the greening of the Blue Marble. That greening process expresses Yin–Yang elements that are central to Blue Marble evaluation thinking and action. This chapter explores the significance of the Yin–Yang principle for Blue Marble engagement. Yin–Yang understandings provide guidance for conceptualizing, designing, implementing, and evaluating global systems transformations.

Notice that the Yin–Yang principle of harmonization applies to opposite concepts like global and local, a "dialectics of harmonization" (Huang, 2016, p. 847).

Opposite political opinions and beliefs—for example, climate change deniers versus climate change science—are another matter and may not permit harmonizing. We can engage controversies knowledgeably, respectfully, and diplomatically, but as a practical matter, political polarities are distinguishable from conceptual opposites. This chapter focuses on harmonizing conceptual opposites.

Yin–Yang Principle Explicated

PREMISE: We live in a divided world. What is striking about the iconic Blue Marble photo from space is its wholeness. No nation-state divisions. No sector silos. No global–local boundaries. The image is neither long term nor short term, but now. Blue Marble evaluation aims for that wholeness of perspective as a guide to wholeness of understanding to inform holistic action. To achieve that sense of wholeness necessitates seeing and engaging with different perspectives, harmonizing opposites, integrating divisions, transcending boundaries, and overcoming polarities.

Yin–Yang Principle
Harmonize conceptual opposites.

IMPLICATIONS

- How you harmonize depends on circumstance, the nature of polarities you encounter, the depth and degree of opposition, and myriad other factors.

- The Yin–Yang operating principle provides specific guidance for adhering to and applying the overarching Blue Marble Integration principle: *Integrate the Blue Marble principles in the design, engagement with, and evaluation of systems change and transformation initiatives.*

- The Yin–Yang principle is a philosophical mindset, not a procedural technique; it provides conceptual guidance for harmonizing opposites as appropriate and useful, but it is not a rule that all opposites must be harmonized.

- Design and evaluation are not intrinsic opposites, but are typically treated as separate and sequential. Integrating design and evaluation has been a theme throughout this book. The Blue Marble perspective of wholeness and integration applies to design and evaluation.

The Yin–Yang operating principle connects in harmony with the other Blue Marble operating principles.

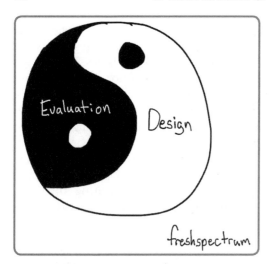

Yin–Yang and design/evaluation by Chris Lysy.

Harmonizing as Manifest in Blue Marble Principles

Let's begin with Yin–Yang implications for the four Blue Marble operating principles covered in Chapters 5–8.

1. *Transboundary Engagement principle.* This principle makes thinking about the entire Earth the focus for intervention and evaluation, not nation-states. But nation-states remain the focus for indicators of progress toward SDGs. The point of the Transboundary Engagement principle is not to ignore or dismiss the influence of nation-states. Rather, this is a classic "yes . . . , and . . ." Yin–Yang interaction. *Yes,* examine nation-state indicators *and* examine transnational and global patterns. *Yes,* look at national patterns, *and* disaggregate the data for a close look at regional variations within countries.

2. *GLOCAL principle.* Integrating the local and global into a GLOCAL perspective epitomizes Yin–Yang harmonization. In any given context at any given time, global and local forces are unlikely to be balanced or even congruent. But whatever the nature of the interrelationship, Blue Marble evaluation examines the nature and implications of global–local interactions.

Global–local interactions often involve a tension of perspective, looking down from outside versus looking up from inside, sometimes characterized as top-down versus bottom-up perspectives and processes. Blue Marble evaluators adopt a skeptical perspective about the extent to which far-away experts are able to understand local context and complexities while at the same time being skeptical that local knowledge is all-encompassing and sufficient. Advocates pushing for adoption of externally developed interventions purport to disseminate the best of modern knowledge, but in asserting claims of having discovered best practices, they can easily overgeneralize and overreach, paying too little attention and sensitivity to indigenous knowledge and local context. On the other hand, I have long since shed any romantic notions that the locals know all that one needs to know about what is going on and that all one has to do is liberate and tap into local knowledge to solve local problems. I respect and want to hear local knowledge, but hear it as what it is, a perspective—one that contains a fair mix of wisdom and bias, insight and untested assumptions, practice-based and time-tested effective practices with old, ineffective patterns deeply ingrained in local belief systems. My value added as an independent and external evaluator is not to advocate wholesale adoption of external models or bow uncritically to local views, but to engage with them in reality testing in which together we see, examine, and test both externally conceived possibilities and locally generated solutions, understanding and evaluating each in context.

3. *Cross-Silos principle.* The Yin is a silo. The Yang is the larger environment around the silo, including other silos. The Yin–Yang principle does not direct us to ignore individual silos. Each silo has goals and indicators and it is important to understand what is happening within a silo, like ocean health. So, *yes,* examine data within silos,

and examine the context within which the silo has taken hold as well as the interdependencies across silos.

Environmental engineer Jenna Jambeck published a study in the journal *Science,* reporting that 8 million metric tons of plastic enters the oceans each year, the equivalent of "five grocery-sized bags filled with plastic for every foot of coastline in the world" (quoted in Kormann, 2019, p. 44). Ocean pollution affects marine life, but the plastic doesn't originate in the ocean. It originates on land. Most of it doesn't come from dumping along the coast, but flowing from inland rivers that empty into the oceans. Agricultural practices, food packaging, industrial production, the effectiveness of recycling programs, and economic policies, to name but a few factors, affect the flow of plastics into the oceans. In this context, harmonizing means looking at multiple sources of data across relevant arenas of action across silos.

4. ***Time Being of the Essence principle.*** Classic opposites: fast versus slow, urgent versus lackadaisical, long term versus short term, and learning from the past versus the future is unwritten. The crisis of the Anthropocene rightfully evokes a sense of urgency, and urgent action is certainly needed, but such action must also be appropriate, relevant, and thoughtful. Being thoughtful involves thinking and, it turns out, there is fast thinking and slow thinking.

Fast Thinking and Slow Thinking

Brain research reveals these different thinking modalities.

- [*Fast thinking*] operates automatically and quickly, with little or no effort and no sense of voluntary control.
- [*Slow thinking*] allocates attention to the effortful mental activities to demand it, including complex computations. (Kahneman, 2011, pp. 20–21)

When we think of ourselves, we identify with [slow thinking], the conscious, reasoning self that has beliefs, makes choices, and decides what to think about and what to do. . . . [Slow thinking] believes itself to be where the action is. . . . , the automatic operations of [fast thinking] generate surprisingly complex patterns of ideas. (p. 21)

We cannot live and work without both fast and slow thinking. We live and work more deliberately when we harmonize these opposing systems. Harmonizing can involve paradoxes. My favorite evaluation facilitation paradox is "go slow to go fast" (Patton, 2018b, pp. 241–242). Facilitators find that slow thinking together in a group builds mutual understanding and shared trust that makes it possible to move quickly in bringing closure to the group process and achieving desired results. *Go slow to go fast* means that, at the group level, the learning that comes from slow thinking and fast thinking together builds a foundation for efficient decision making in the end.

John Wilson is an experienced facilitator who spent his career working on food security issues in Africa. He is a Zimbabwean currently working as a free-range facilitator in East and South Africa with community-based organizations, national NGOs, small farmers, and regional or continental networks. Wilson has also been an active member of our Blue Marble evaluation team. He said:

In reflecting on the admonition to *go slow to go fast,* what I've realized over many years of being connected to community development work is that often "urgency" can undermine sustainability. Social sustainability depends very much on the building of various relationships. This usually can't be done well with only a sense of urgency. (personal communication, 2019)

Blue Marble evaluators aim to harmonize the shorter term with the longer term, and vice versa. Short-term climate change trends foreshadow long-term planetary disaster. Resilient and adaptive sustainability involves examining how dynamic adaptations to short-term challenges and turbulence create long-term patterns of effectiveness or ineffectiveness. Or as the ancient Chinese proverb advises: "If you are in a hurry, you will never get there."

The Yin–Yang of Human and Natural Systems

The coupled human and natural systems (CHANS) framework is defined as "systems in which human and natural components interact" (Liu, Dietz, Carpenter, Folke, & Alberti, 2007b, p. 639). In CHANS, "people and nature interact reciprocally and form complex feedback loops" (Liu et al., 2007a, p. 1513).

What emerges from those interactions cannot be derived from examining the human and natural systems separately. "Social scientists have often focused on human interactions . . . whereas ecologists have traditionally focused on pristine environments in which humans are external and rarely dominant agents" (Liu et al., 2007b, p. 639). But intertwined "emergent phenomena" are not understandable from examining human and natural systems separately. Socioecological interactions require interdisciplinary expertise positioning sustainable development as occurring "in the nexus where human (social and economic) and natural (environmental) systems meet" (Uitto, 2019).

Two-Eyed Seeing

Two-eyed seeing refers to learning to see from one eye with the strengths of indigenous knowledge and ways of knowing, and from the other eye with the strengths of Western knowledge and ways of knowing, and learning to use both these eyes together, for the benefit of all (Marshall, 2017). A distinguishing theme of many in-digenous ways of knowing is the integration of humans and nature, understanding the human–nature relationship as one of stewardship with responsibility to respect and sustain other species and natural things, and seeing humans as part of the natural world rather than having dominion over it.

Demarus Tevuk Sandlin (2019) examined the relationship between indigenous knowledge and Western science as part of her internship at the Environmental Protection Agency's National Center for Environmental Assessment. Her findings emphasize the ethical core of indigenous knowledge about an approach to sustainability. *Sustainability* is a noun in Western culture and a verb, a form of action, in indigenous cultures.

> Traditional sustainable values are relationship, respect, responsibility, reciprocity, appreciation, and low consumption. . . . Indigenous sustainability is more than sustaining resource use for human benefit, it is about creating abundance in nature for the health of ourselves and our animal and plant relatives. (pp. 17–19)

Freirean Principles and Ecopedagogy

Paulo Freire left us the legacy of ethical–political roots to support our practices—wings, that is, a theory to go beyond his work; and many dreams—the utopia of a society of equals; or, as he affirms at the end of *Pedagogia do Oprimido* (*Pedagogy of the Oppressed*): "the creation of a world in which it will be easier to love."
—MOACIR GADOTTI, director, Instituto Paulo Freire, São Paulo, Brazil

Paulo Freire was born in Brazil in 1921 at a time of world economic crisis in which he experienced hunger and poverty at a young age. He became an activist working for a more democratic and universal approach to education in Brazil. In 1964, he was imprisoned in Brazil for 70 days as a traitor and subsequently exiled. In 1968, he wrote his famous *Pedagogy of the Oppressed,* published in Spanish and English in 1970, but not in Brazil until 1974.

Freirean principles, as I've extracted them from his writings (Patton, 2018e), exemplify Yin–Yang harmonization, though he did not articulate his philosophy in that way. Freire framed his perspective as one of dialectical integration. In what follows, where Freire talks of critical consciousness, I invite you to reframe it as *critical planetary consciousness* in preparation for his ecopedagogy introduced below. First, here are four Freirean harmonizing principles relevant to Blue Marble evaluation.

Four Freirean Harmonizing Principles for Blue Marble Evaluation

1. *Harmonize individual and community consciousness.* Consciousness resides in communities of people, not just individuals. The emergence and nurturing of critical consciousness about anything, including the Anthropocene crisis and planetary consciousness, is both a cultural and political activity and is therefore inherently a collective activity: *inquiry together.* Freire's pedagogy involves people together examining issues that are important to them and their situation.

2. *Integrate reflection and action.* Freire was strongly and eloquently critical of the juxtaposition of reflection and action as separate and distinct arenas of human experience. For him, reflection is aimed at action and action is the content of reflection. *Critical dialogue presupposes action* (Freire, 1970, pp. 65–66).

3. *Harmonize the objective and subjective.* For Freire, critical consciousness, reflection, and action must be grounded in objective reality that is subjectively experienced and understood.

One cannot conceive of objectivity without subjectivity. Neither can exist without the other, nor can they be dichotomized. The separation of objectivity from subjectivity, the denial of the latter when analyzing reality or acting upon it, is objectivism. On the other hand, the denial of objectivity in analysis or action, resulting in a subjectivism which leads to solipsistic positions, denies action itself by denying objective reality. (p. 50)

4. *Harmonize thinking and emotion.* Freire (1997) articulated a holistic and humanistic approach to dialogue that valued and integrated reason and emotions. He insisted on connecting our emotions with our reason. Freire spoke of a "reason soaked with emotion."

Ecopedagogy

As the foregoing demonstrates, Freire sought harmony between the individual and community, reflection and action, objectivity and subjectivity, and thinking and emotion. The larger understanding that Freire's work reminds us of is that all evaluation approaches constitute a pedagogy of some kind. *All evaluation teaches something.* What is taught and how it is taught varies, but evaluation is inherently and predominantly a pedagogical interaction.

In his later years, Freire turned to developing *ecopedagogy*, harmonizing and integrating ecology and pedagogy. The ecopedagogy movement emerged in Latin America at the second Earth Summit, held in Rio de Janeiro, Brazil, in 1992. A statement on the interrelationship between society and the environment was ratified as the *Earth Charter* in 2000. The First International Symposium on the Earth Charter from the Perspective of Education was held in 1999 at the Instituto Paulo Freire, Brazil, directed by Moacir Gadotti, in collaboration with the Earth Council and UNESCO. This was followed by the First International Forum on Ecopedagogy, the Ecopedagogy Charter, and ecopedagogy seminars and programs around the world.

Paulo Freire was writing a book on ecopedagogy upon his death in 1997, parts of which are included in his posthumous *Pedagogy of Indignation* (Freire, 2004, edited by his wife, Ana Maria Araújo Freire, from his unpublished notes). Here's a brief excerpt:

> How urgent [it] is that we fight for more fundamental ethical principles, such as respect for the life of human beings, the life of other animals, of birds, and for the life of rivers and forests. I do not believe in loving among women and men, among human beings, if we do not become capable of loving the world. Ecology has gained tremendous importance at the end of the century. It must be present in any educational practice of a radical, critical, and liberating nature. (p. 47)

These were the last words Paulo Freire wrote, dated April 21, 1997, before his death on May 2 (Freire, 2004, pp. 47–48).

Praxis

Praxis is the process by which a theory or idea is enacted, embodied, or realized. As such, praxis harmonizes theory and prac-

Freire tree by Claudius Ceccon (Claudionor). Source: Patton and Guimarães (2018, p. 78). Used with permission.

tice, often treated as opposites. Knight and colleagues (2019) have applied praxis to conservation and sustainability.

> Praxis acknowledges and embraces dualities (i.e., both/and) to promote science and action, knowing and doing. Praxis challenges the notion of dualisms (i.e., either/or) such as the false divides between science and action and between knowing and doing. Dualisms also direct conservation professionals to assign success or failure singularly to outcomes, and focus on the process of planning or implementing action. Instead, embracing dualities endorses the interdependence of different elements, as reflected in notions of science-in-action and adaptive management. As such, practice may precede, and be designed to generate, the knowledge necessary for increasingly effective conservation. (p. 2)

Social Justice and Environmentalism

Paulo Freire was a champion for the poor. He devoted his life to fighting injustice and supporting empowerment of the oppressed. He also became an active environmentalist. Pedagogy of the oppressed and ecopedagogy became deeply intertwined in his later writings. Yet I encounter many working on social justice issues who consider environmentalism a white, middle-class concern or a philosophy relevant primarily to indigenous cultures. In Part III, on global systems transformation principles, I address in more depth the importance of integrating social justice and environmental movements. Perhaps it suffices here to reiterate that those who will be most negatively affected by climate change are those who are poor and vulnerable, especially children. United Nations Children's Fund (UNICEF) executive director Anthony Lake introduced a report on the impact of climate change on children entitled *Unless We Act Now,* with an overview of the threat to poor children worldwide:

> In every crisis, children are the most vulnerable. Climate change is no exception. As escalating droughts and flooding degrade food production, children will bear the greatest burden of hunger and malnutrition. As temperatures increase, together with water scarcity and air pollution, children will feel the deadliest impact of waterborne diseases and dangerous respiratory conditions. As more extreme weather events expand the number of emergencies and humanitarian crises, children will pay the highest price. As the world experiences a steady rise in climate-driven migration, children's lives and futures will be the most disrupted. (UNICEF, 2015, p. 6)

In the field of evaluation, social justice concerns have a long history and dedicated practitioners. Environmental justice lags as an evaluation focus. A challenge of harmonizing opposites is helping social justice and environmental activists come together in common cause. That won't be easy because of the racism and white supremacy that African Americans experience in white-led and white-dominated environmental organizations. Anthony Rogers-Wright (2018), who describes himself as both an Earth Citizen and Black Liberationist, straddles those two worlds and has observed:

> Withdrawal from the challenges associated with climate change and white supremacy is simply untenable at this point in history. The stakes are too high for the climate community and the planet alike. And you have to ask yourself how some of the most ardent climate champions have found the ability to cope with the stress that comes with taking on powerful entities like the fossil fuel industry and political establishments, but not the stress that comes with dismantling racism/white supremacy in their own spaces? Whomever determines the answer to this riddle may be responsible for saving the world. . . .
>   Ironically, if not paradoxically, by not naming white supremacy as a major function of climate change, and by not addressing its

manifestations within "progressive" spaces and their own organizations, the professional environmental non-profit apparatus takes part in their own climate denialism. Discussing climate science may be less uncomfortable than talking about the role racism and white supremacy play in disproportionately impacting Black and Brown folk. And it's certainly less discomforting than discussing the role racism/white supremacy plays in the climate "movement" itself. But embracing this discomfort has become necessary to dismantle the myriad systems of oppression that contribute to the oppressive system of climate change. (p. 1)

Evaluation as a profession suffers this same history of racism and white supremacy. Going blue (Blue Marble) and green (environmental) does not exempt us from dealing with black and white. Quite the contrary. Decolonizing international development evaluation (Chouinard & Hopson, 2016) has to be part of the Blue Marble evaluation commitment and engagement. What Blue Marble principles bring to this divide is the emphasis on crossing boundaries and silos. The theory of boundary critique (Midgley & Pinzon, 2011) offers a model for engaging across divides. Divides must be acknowledged and engaged, not simply ignored or denied, before they can be harmonized around shared concerns like human survival on Earth.

Yin–Yang Graphics

Depicting Tensions and Trade-Offs

I turn now from tough big-picture realities to the mundane—harmonizing conceptual opposites through graphical representations. Over the years in providing feedback to programs, I have often reported on tensions and trade-offs that I found a program or organization faces. I use the word *tension* to characterize how the pursuit of multiple and competing values and goals gives rise to challenges about how to achieve alignment and balance. *Tension* is a descriptive term, not meant to imply judgment. Identifying tensions and making them explicit creates an opportunity to learn about them and become more intentional and effective in managing them. Tensions are largely not resolvable; they come with the territory of engaging multiple people and perspectives. Nor can perfect or even optimal balance be achieved as missions tend to drive organization sentiment around maximizing performance. Furthermore, constrained resourc-

No justice, No peace.
No end to global warming,
No justice, No peace.
No end to hunger,
No justice, No peace.
No end to poverty,
No justice, No peace.

Social justice

Environmental justice

For the love of each other and the Earth

es limit balance and effectiveness. Indeed, what constitutes "balance" can change as conditions and situations change, so too with what constitutes effectiveness. Being alert to tensions and, importantly, their consequences, can enhance effectiveness. Indeed, as I was writing this chapter, I participated in a convening of a large collaboration in which the closing session reviewed tensions that had arisen during the meeting. It was cathartic for the staff and participants to name the tensions and discuss

how to manage rather than resolve them. Negotiating trade-offs is one strategy for dealing with tensions.

Yin–Yang Tensions Embedded in Blue Marble Principles

Exhibits 9.1–9.3 graphically depict Yin–Yang tensions that are embedded in and give rise to Blue Marble principles. Exhibit 9.1 depicts tensions between the dominant nation-state focus in SDGs versus global

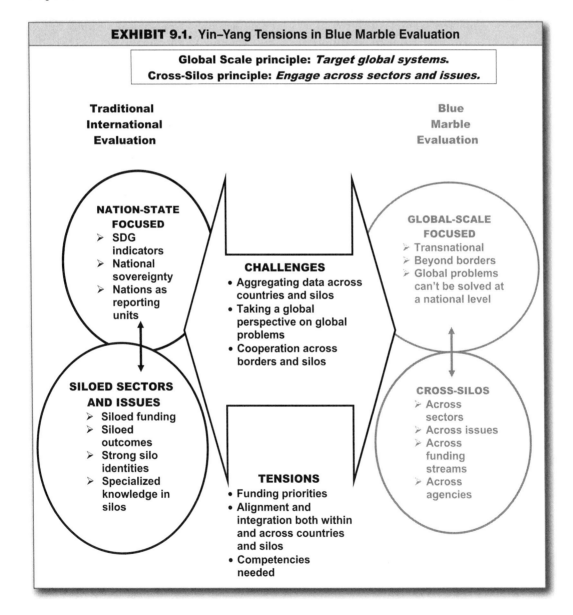

EXHIBIT 9.1. Yin–Yang Tensions in Blue Marble Evaluation

Global Scale principle: *Target global systems.*
Cross-Silos principle: *Engage across sectors and issues.*

Traditional International Evaluation

Blue Marble Evaluation

NATION-STATE FOCUSED
➢ SDG indicators
➢ National sovereignty
➢ Nations as reporting units

GLOBAL-SCALE FOCUSED
➢ Transnational
➢ Beyond borders
➢ Global problems can't be solved at a national level

CHALLENGES
• Aggregating data across countries and silos
• Taking a global perspective on global problems
• Cooperation across borders and silos

SILOED SECTORS AND ISSUES
➢ Siloed funding
➢ Siloed outcomes
➢ Strong silo identities
➢ Specialized knowledge in silos

CROSS-SILOS
➢ Across sectors
➢ Across issues
➢ Across funding streams
➢ Across agencies

TENSIONS
• Funding priorities
• Alignment and integration both within and across countries and silos
• Competencies needed

thinking, as well as the tension between siloed action versus cross-silos integration. Traditional international evaluation approaches are summarized on the left side of the graphic (nation-state and siloed sectors and issues) versus Blue Marble evaluation approaches on the right side (global-scale and cross-silos integration). In the middle are listed some common challenges: aggregating data across countries and silos, taking a global perspective on global problems, and cooperation across borders and silos. Presented at the bottom center of the graphic are examples of operational tensions that arise from these different perspectives and approaches: establishing

funding priorities where the contrasting approaches compete for limited funds, alignment and integration across both countries and silos, and the competencies needed to facilitate and negotiate these tensions and trade-offs.

Exhibit 9.2 presents a similar graphic depiction of the tensions and trade-offs that can emerge in balancing and integrating the local and global (GLOCAL). Exhibit 9.3 depicts tensions between short-term versus long-term thinking, and both in contrast to resilient sustainability. Challenges include employing ecological systems thinking, taking a complexity perspective on global problems and systems, and dealing

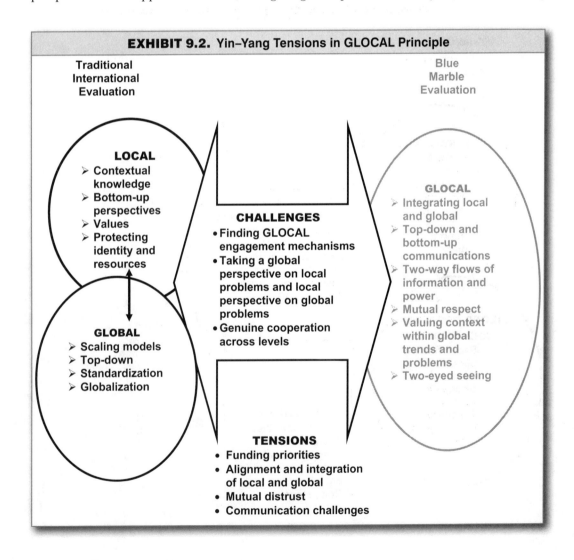

EXHIBIT 9.2. Yin–Yang Tensions in GLOCAL Principle

Traditional International Evaluation

Blue Marble Evaluation

LOCAL
➢ Contextual knowledge
➢ Bottom-up perspectives
➢ Values
➢ Protecting identity and resources

GLOBAL
➢ Scaling models
➢ Top-down
➢ Standardization
➢ Globalization

CHALLENGES
• Finding GLOCAL engagement mechanisms
• Taking a global perspective on local problems and local perspective on global problems
• Genuine cooperation across levels

GLOCAL
➢ Integrating local and global
➢ Top-down and bottom-up communications
➢ Two-way flows of information and power
➢ Mutual respect
➢ Valuing context within global trends and problems
➢ Two-eyed seeing

TENSIONS
• Funding priorities
• Alignment and integration of local and global
• Mutual distrust
• Communication challenges

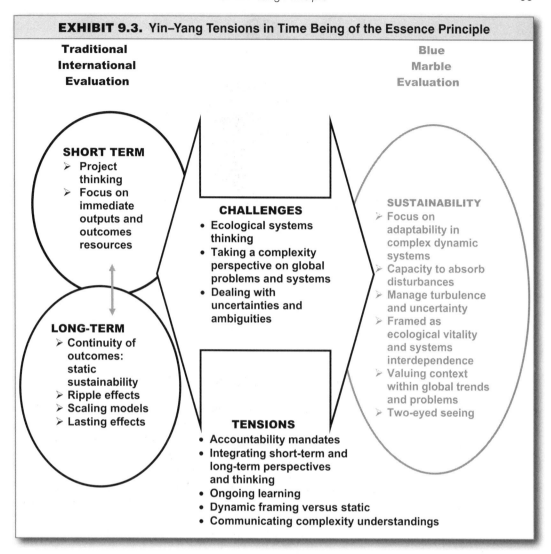

EXHIBIT 9.3. Yin–Yang Tensions in Time Being of the Essence Principle

Traditional International Evaluation

Blue Marble Evaluation

SHORT TERM
➤ Project thinking
➤ Focus on immediate outputs and outcomes resources

LONG-TERM
➤ Continuity of outcomes: static sustainability
➤ Ripple effects
➤ Scaling models
➤ Lasting effects

CHALLENGES
• Ecological systems thinking
• Taking a complexity perspective on global problems and systems
• Dealing with uncertainties and ambiguities

TENSIONS
• Accountability mandates
• Integrating short-term and long-term perspectives and thinking
• Ongoing learning
• Dynamic framing versus static
• Communicating complexity understandings

SUSTAINABILITY
➤ Focus on adaptability in complex dynamic systems
➤ Capacity to absorb disturbances
➤ Manage turbulence and uncertainty
➤ Framed as ecological vitality and systems interdependence
➤ Valuing context within global trends and problems
➤ Two-eyed seeing

with uncertainties and ambiguities. Operational tensions include dealing with narrow accountability mandates that undermine adaptability and flexibility, facilitating ongoing learning, framing evaluation processes and outcomes dynamically instead of as rigidly static, and communicating complexity understandings.

A Blue Marble Vision

Glenn Page, a core member of our Blue Marble evaluation team, has articulated a Blue Marble vision that incorporates Yin–Yang thinking. I close this chapter with his vision.

What we are proposing is a more systematic approach to learning how to respond and adapt in a rapidly changing world. We are using rigorous evaluative thinking, complexity concepts, systems understanding, and principles of co-design and biological diversity to learn how to act in balance with earth systems for current and future generations. The Blue Marble approach builds both individual and collective capacities to lead, design, implement and learn from actions we

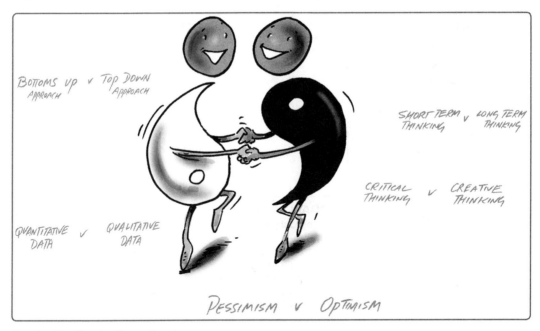

Dancing Yin–Yang by Simon Kneebone.

take toward this bold ambition. This opens a major window of opportunity for innovative evaluative thinking and practice rooted in values and ethics of a more sustainable path than the one we are currently on. It requires finding balance between humans and nature, short term and long term, speed and stability, private and public, women and men, state and religion, north and south, power and poverty, and historical insights informing a new enlightenment for our times and the future.

—GLENN G. PAGE, principal, SustainaMetrix

In Celebration of Harmony

This chapter has barely scratched the surface of conceptual polarities that might be harmonized. We shall have occasion to revisit the *Yin–Yang principle* and harmonize additional opposites in subsequent chapters on Blue Marble methods, competencies, and evaluator stance. For now, I close this chapter with the image of Yin and Yang dancing together *in harmony*.

Bricolage Methods Principle

> There is no scientific method as such, but the vital feature
> of a scientist's procedure has been merely to do his utmost
> with his mind, no holds barred.
> —Percy Williams Bridgman, 1946 Nobel Prize recipient
> in Physics (quoted in Waller, 2004, p. 106)

CONTEXT

I think of the challenge of designing a Blue Marble evaluation as a task of *bricolage*. The term comes from anthropologist Claude Lévi-Strauss (1966), who defined a *bricoleur* as a "jack of all trades or a kind of professional do-it-yourself person" (p. 17). He brought into the world of research the tradition of the French *bricoleur* who traveled the countryside using odds and ends, whatever materials were at hand, to perform fix-it work. The inquirer "as bricoleur or maker of quilts uses the aesthetic and material tools of his or her craft, deploying whatever strategies, methods, or empirical materials are at hand. If new tools or techniques have to be invented, or pieced together, then the researcher will do this" (Denzin & Lincoln, 2000, p. 4). I used this notion of methods bricolage in developmental evaluation (Patton, 2011) and it is even more relevant here because the methodological options and challenges are greater.

Eclecticism

Bricolage is built on a foundation of eclecticism, an open-minded approach that eschews rigidly following recipes about how things ought to be done but instead considers multiple methods, designs, and inquiry possibilities, often combining diverse approaches in creative and situationally appropriate, insightful, and useful ways. Eclecticism originated with ancient Greek and Roman philosophers who resisted settling on any single system of thinking but selected from varied philosophical beliefs those ideas that seemed most reasonable to them. The term *eclecticism* comes from the Greek ἐκλεκτικός (*eklektikos*), literally "choosing the best" and from ἐκλεκτός (*eklektos*), "picked out, selected." Utilization-focused Blue Marble evaluators select appropriate methods to *fit the situation*, which is quite different from following some universally asserted and standardized orthodoxy about what is most valid.

An eclectic approach might seem straightforward, but it was controversial in ancient Greece and Rome, and it is controversial today. Research and evaluation are rife with authoritative methodological hierarchies asserting that certain methods are the "gold standard" and that the preferred designs of the like-minded members of a scientific association or funding institution constitute "best practices." Such claims are unsupportable even within a particular cultural paradigm like Western science. They are utter nonsense in a highly diverse multicultural and multiperspective world. But one of the obstacles to anticipate in designing Blue Marble evaluations is insistence on following methodological recipes designed for projects and programs, but inadequate to address global systems change. And those prescribed recipes are problematic even for evaluating projects and programs. (See Patton, 2008, pp. 419–470; "Fool's Gold: The Widely Touted 'Gold Standard' Is Neither Golden Nor a Standard," Patton, 2015, pp. 93–97, for an in-depth discussion of the logical, philosophical, and methodological fallacies of "gold-standard hierarchies"; see "Best Practices Aren't," Patton, 2015, pp. 191–193, for a rumination on the misnomer "best practices.")

Eclecticism in Practice

This is not a methods book. Although conducting Blue Marble evaluations involve methods, there are no core methods that make up the basic toolbox for Blue Marble evaluation. Being eclectic, any existing tools, methods, or frameworks might be used and new tools, methods, or frameworks may be created for emergent situations based on new technologies. But while this is not a methods text, it would constitute a huge gap not to address methods. So, what I will do is model being the Blue Marble bricoleur and gather an eclectic assortment of methodological options and align them with the Blue Marble principles to demonstrate how to follow the guidance in the Bricolage Methods principle. I'll also offer lessons about using the Blue Marble principles to make Blue Marble methods decisions and share an actual Blue Marble evaluation framework being used by the Global Alliance for the Future of Food (GA).

Bricolage Methods Principle Explicated

> **PREMISE:** The variety of possible Blue Marble evaluation situations is so vast that no predetermined set is adequate. There can be no Blue Marble methods toolbox, a popular metaphor for evaluators offering a limited and definitive set of "tools." Context matters in designing evaluations. Intended purposes and uses matter, as does identifying and working with primary intended users. Standardization is anathema; customization and contextualization rule.

Bricolage Methods Principle

Conduct utilization-focused evaluations incorporating Blue Marble principles to match methods to the evaluation situation.

IMPLICATIONS

- Blue Marble bricoleur teams will likely be needed to access a variety of possible methods, measures, analytical approaches, and methodological specializations.

- Newer technologies like Big Data, geographic information systems (GIS), remote sensing, artificial intelligence (AI), social systems network mapping techniques, and blockchain innovations will likely have Blue Marble evaluation applications.

- Blue Marble evaluation designs may be emergent and adaptive given the diversity

Bricoleur Blue Marble evaluator inventorying eclectic methods to customize a design by Chris Lysy.

of worldwide situations and applications and the dynamic nature of the global environment.

- Qualitative, quantitative, and mixed methods will likely be needed to do justice to the complexity and multidimensional nature of Blue Marble evaluations.

- The GLOCAL principle means that Blue Marble analysis will include national data disaggregated within countries and global data aggregated and synthesized across countries.

- The Time Being of the Essence principle guides evaluation bricoleurs toward longitudinal designs that can capture and assess trajectories toward sustainability and transformation over time.

- Blue Marble evaluations must be utilization focused.

Utilization-Focused Evaluation

Utilization-focused evaluation is a comprehensive decision framework for designing and implementing an evaluation to fit a particular situation and, in that situation, meet the information needs of primary users to enhance their intended use of the evaluation (Patton, 2008, 2015). Utilization-focused evaluation begins with the premise that evaluations should be judged by their utility and actual use—therefore, evaluators should facilitate the evaluation process and design any evaluation with careful consideration for how everything that is done, from beginning to end, will affect use. Use concerns how people in the real world apply evaluation findings and experience the evaluation process. Therefore, utilization-focused evaluation provides systematic, research-based guidance and a set of steps to decide which approach is most appropriate for a particular situation and the users. Utilization-focused evaluation is eclectic in being open to any evaluation option methodologically, conceptually, theoretically, analytically, and procedurally. In essence, utilization-focused evaluation prescribes a process for determining what to focus on based on unwavering attention to intended use. Blue Marble evaluation brings a global perspective to bear within an overarching framework of utilization-focused evaluation.

Blue Marble Evaluation Inquiry Framework

The Blue Marble principles constitute a global systems change design and evaluation inquiry framework. The principles provide guidance on designing systems change initiatives and interventions and a corresponding framework for evaluating such interventions and initiatives. Exhibit 10.1 (pp. 105–107) lists each Blue Marble principle, its design implications, corresponding evaluation criteria, and sample rubrics. This can be used as a checklist or inventory for both design and evaluation.

An Illustrative Example Applying the Principles in an Evaluation

Let me illustrate the logic and process of converting Blue Marble principles into evaluation questions and criteria with the example of evaluating an international conference. There are thousands of such conferences annually dealing with a huge variety of topics, many of which have to do with various aspects of global issues. Let's imagine evaluating such a large, international conference using the Blue Marble principles. The conference is focused on climate change and agriculture. The principles generate questions for conference processes, content, and outcomes. Exhibit 10.2 (pp. 108–109) provides a Blue Marble conference evaluation template.

This generic template could be adapted to evaluate interventions and initiatives of any kind. Additional criteria could be added specific to the theory of change of a particular initiative. For example, a systems change initiative focused on transformations would add principles of and generate evaluation questions relevant to transformations. (See Chapter 14 on evaluating transformations.)

Comprehensive Blue Marble Evaluation Framework: The GA

At various points in this book, I've described the mission, vision, principles, and initiatives of the Global Alliance for the Future of Food. The GA consists of 30 philanthropic foundations working together and with others to transform global food systems now and for future generations. This chapter now features in some detail how the GA is incorporating Blue Marble evaluation principles and methods in their work.

Integrating Blue Marble Evaluation into the GA Monitoring and Evaluation Framework

From the beginning, the GA adopted utilization-focused developmental evaluation as its evaluation approach because the new Alliance was developing and innovating in the complex dynamic systems space of food and agriculture. The evaluation has had two purposes:

1. Document what emerges to facilitate learning, accountability, and future action; and

2. Strengthen action and learning by framing evaluation questions as part of the ongoing developmental process (GA, 2019, p. 1).

One of the milestones in the developmental process of the GA was the adoption of a set of six principles providing common ground for shared action. This brought the

EXHIBIT 10.1. Blue Marble Principles and Corresponding Evaluation Criteria

These evaluation questions can be asked of any systems change initiative or intervention. (See page 107 for guidelines for using the table.)

A. Blue Marble principle	B. Design commentary and explanation	C. Blue Marble evaluation criteria	D. Evaluation rubrics: 4–point scales (specific meanings of points on the scale defined in context)
1a. *Transboundary Engagement principle:* Act at a global scale.	Apply Blue Marble thinking to design, implementation, and evaluation of global systems change.	1. Global-scale evaluation *criterion:* Assess the extent and ways in which an initiative's design, conceptualization, and theory of change are truly global in aspiration and action.	1. Little evidence of global engagement. 2. Some evidence of global engagement. 3. Considerable evidence of global engagement. 4. Great evidence of global engagement.
1b. *Global Thinking principle:* Apply whole–Earth, big-picture thinking to all aspects of systems change.	Types of global engagement vary.	Assess the extent to which each type is present and assess the quality of engagement. a. Global in perspective. b. Global in operations. c. Global in participation. d. Global in knowledge and content. e. Global in collaborative connections and relationships. f. Global in networking. g. Global geographically. h. Global in staffing. i. Global in financing. j. Global evaluation indicators. k. Global in aspiration. l. Global virtually.	Two rubrics applied to each item in Column C: A four-point scale on *degree of engagement* (see scale above) and a four-point scale on *quality of engagement* (quality defined in context). 1. Poor quality. 2. Some quality. 3. Good quality. 4. Excellent quality.

(continued)

105

EXHIBIT 10.1. *(continued)*

A. Blue Marble principle	B. Design commentary and explanation	C. Blue Marble evaluation criteria	D. Evaluation rubrics: 4–point scales (specific meanings of points on the scale defined in context)
2. GLOCAL *principle:* *Integrate complex interconnections across levels.*	Connect global and local perspectives, knowledge, and understandings in support of change. The term that captures this is **GLOCAL**. When designing an intervention or initiative, look at the interactions, interdependencies, and interconnections across levels (micro, meso, macro). Consider how people, information, and resources flow from local to global, and global to local.	2. Multilevel connectivity evaluation criterion: Assess global–local interactions and interconnections. This likely will involve documenting contextual variations locally within a global perspective. *See Demonstrating Outcomes and Impact across Different Scales* (Hall, 2017). *GLOCAL fidelity:* In what ways is an initiative or intervention truly GLOCAL in both processes and results? What are the interactions, interdependencies, and interconnections across levels? How do they intersect for mutually reinforcing systems change? Look for both anticipated and unanticipated interactions, both positive (mutually reinforcing) and negative (disjointed and nonaligned).	*Sample rubric* (points defined in context): 1. Weak global–local interconnection. 2. Moderate global–local interconnection. 3. Good global–local interconnection. 4. Excellent global–local interconnection. *Four-way rubric:* 1. Four-point scale on quality of local (micro) connections. 2. Four-point scale on quality of middle-level connections (national and regional). 3. Four-point scale on quality of global connections. 4. Four-point scale on quality of global–local connections.

Principle		Evaluation criteria	Rubric
3. Cross-Silos principle: *Engage across sectors and issues for systems change.*	Systems issues and problems are interconnected, so effective solutions must cut across traditional program and project sectors. Cross-silos solutions are more sustainable if interconnected and mutually reinforcing.	3. Cross-Silos evaluation *criteria*: Assess the extent and ways in which an initiative addresses multiple interrelated factors (across sectors) and diverse interconnected outcomes. Assess both degree and quality of cross-silos interactions and outcomes.	Intervention operates in (details defined in context): 1. Autonomous, siloed systems. 2. Some positive interconnections. 3. Many positive interconnections. 4. Highly positive interconnections across systems, sectors, and issues.
4. Time Being of the Essence principle: *Act with a sense of urgency in the present, support adaptive sustainability long term, grounding both in understanding the past.*	Blue Marble sustainability is the capacity to absorb turbulence and adapt to changing conditions (not rigid continuation of activities and outcomes already achieved).	4. Time Being of the Essence evaluation *criterion*: Assess short-term results and evidence of resilient capacity built for the longer term.	Four-point scale on evidence of resilient capacity built (scale points defined in context): 1. No or low resilient capacity built. 2. Some resilient capacity built. 3. Considerable resilient capacity built. 4. High resilient capacity built.

Guidance For Using Exhibit 10.1:

1. *Exhibit purpose.* Provide an overview of the nature of the methodological translation from Blue Marble principles to evaluation criteria and rubrics. This table is dense and may come across as difficult to interpret and use at first glance. It is not meant for skimming. It is meant for deep-dive unpacking of the principles, converting them into evaluation criteria, and converting those criteria into rubrics.

2. *Contextual collaboration and specificity.* The general nature of the principles, criteria, and rubrics means that greater operational precision will depend on context and the nature of the intervention or initiative to be designed and evaluated.

3. *Rubric scales.* I have used 4-point scales to illustrate the rubrics. Doing so is not to recommend 4-point scales. Rubrics can also use 3-point, 5-point, and 10-point scales, depending on the distinctions trying to be made in a particular evaluation (see Davidson, 2004, 2012, for guidance on creating rubrics).

4. *Language of the scales.* As with scale size, the terminology of the scales is variable and contextual. The language used in these scales is for illustrative purposes only and should be adapted to what makes sense for a particular evaluation situation and context.

EXHIBIT 10.2. An Illustrative Template for Evaluating an International Conference Using the Blue Marble Principles

These evaluation questions can be asked of any systems change initiative or intervention. (See page 109 for guidelines for using the table.)

Blue Marble principles	Substantive content evaluation questions	Conference process and implementation questions	Conference outcome questions: Follow-up evaluation
1. *Transboundary Engagement* principle: *Act at a global scale.*	To what extent and in what ways did the content of the conference engage participants using a global perspective?	To what extent and in what ways was the conference organized and implemented to facilitate interactions around global issues using a global perspective?	To what extent and in what ways did conference participants increase their knowledge, skills, perspective on, and actions related to taking a global perspective in their work? What will they do with what they learned?
2. *GLOCAL principle:* Integrate complex interconnections across levels.	To what extent and in what ways did the content of the conference focus on interactions, interconnections, and interdependencies from local to global and from global to local?	To what extent and in what ways was the conference organized and implemented to focus on interactions, interconnections, and interdependencies from local to global and from global to local?	To what extent and in what ways did conference participants increase their knowledge, skills, perspective on, and actions related to interactions, interconnections, and interdependencies from local to global and from global to local relevant to their work? What will they do with what they learned?
3. *Cross-Silos principle:* Engage across sectors and issues for systems change.	To what extent and in what ways did the content of the conference engage across sectors and issues?	To what extent and in what ways was the conference organized and implemented to engage participants interactively across sectors and issues?	To what extent and in what ways did conference participants increase their knowledge, skills, perspective on, and actions related to engaging across sectors and issues in their work? What will they do with what they learned?

4. Time Being of the Essence principle: *Act with a sense of urgency in the present, support adaptive sustainability long term, grounding both in understanding the past.*	To what extent and in what ways did the content of the conference engage with the importance, nature, and implications of the Time Being of the Essence principle?	To what extent and in what ways was the conference organized and implemented to facilitate engagement around the importance, nature, and implications of resilient and adaptive sustainability?	To what extent and in what ways did conference participants increase their knowledge, skills, perspective on, and actions related to resilient and adaptive sustainability relevant to their work? What will they do with what they learned?
5. Anthropocene as Context principle: *Know and face the realities of the Anthropocene and act accordingly.*	To what extent and in what ways did the content of the conference engage with the importance, nature, and implications of the Anthropocene?	To what extent and in what ways was the conference organized and implemented to facilitate engagement around the importance, nature, and implications of the Anthropocene?	To what extent and in what ways did conference participants increase their knowledge, skills, perspective on, and actions related to the Anthropocene relevant to their work? What will they do with what they learned?

Guidance for Using Exhibit 10.2:

1. *Template purpose.* Demonstrate the translation of Blue Marble principles into evaluation questions related to substance (content) of an initiative or intervention, processes used, and results attained.

2. *Template adaptation.* This generic template could be adapted to evaluate global systems change interventions and initiatives of any kind. Additional criteria could be added specific to the theory of change of a particular initiative. For example, a systems change initiative focused on transformations would add principles of and generate evaluation questions relevant to transformations (see Chapter 14 on evaluating transformations).

3. *Methods.* Data to answer the template questions can come from surveys, interviews, focus groups, case studies, and feedback at sessions depending on resources availability and the intended uses of the evaluation.

need to integrate the principles into the work of the GA as well as into the monitoring and evaluation (M&E) program through *principles-focused evaluation* (Patton, 2018d). An additional evaluation lens came with the decision to hire the first-ever Blue Marble evaluator, Pablo Vidueira, in March 2017 (see Chapter 1, p. 10, to meet Pablo). This step was taken as a deepened commitment to apply a global systems transformation perspective in developing and evaluating everything that the GA does to foster food systems transformation. This multidimensional, multifaceted approach to evaluation is depicted in Exhibits 10.3 and 10.4.

The GA M&E framework integrates three evaluation approaches—developmental evaluation, principles-focused evaluation, and Blue Marble evaluation—as mutually reinforcing. Together they are intended to support learning, improvement, and accountability toward greater health, equity, renewability, resilience, interconnectedness, and diversity in global food systems.

1. *Developmental evaluation* (Patton, 2011) provides a focus on the GA's development as an alliance: tracking, documenting, assessing, and supporting development, adaptation, and learning about the GA's organization, priority

---

EXHIBIT 10.3. Four Evaluation Pillars of the Global Alliance for the Future of Food

UTILIZATION-FOCUSED EVALUATION	DEVELOPMENTAL EVALUATION	PRINCIPLES-FOCUSED EVALUATION	BLUE MARBLE EVALUATION
• What information and knowledge are needed for whom in order to do what? • How can evaluation support the development, adaptation, learning, and action of the Global Alliance in order to foster its global impact?	• What is emerging in the development of the Global Alliance (as a strategic alliance of philanthropic foundations working together and with others to transform global food systems)? • How and with what consequences is the Global Alliance adapting and responding to these emerging realities in order to foster food systems transformation? • What is being learned from the Global Alliance's development and the development of its work, and what are the consequences?	• To what extent are the Global Alliance principles meaningful—to guide the development and work of the Global Alliance? • If meaningful, to what extent are the principles adhered to in the development and work of the Global Alliance? • If adhered to, to what extent are the principles helping the Global Alliance to advance toward the desired results?	• To what extent and in what ways is the Global Alliance's development and work actually global? • If global, to what extent is it effectively changing global systems toward increased resilience, renewability, equity, diversity, healthfulness, and interconnectedness? • If effective in bringing about desired changes, to what extent are those changes transformative?

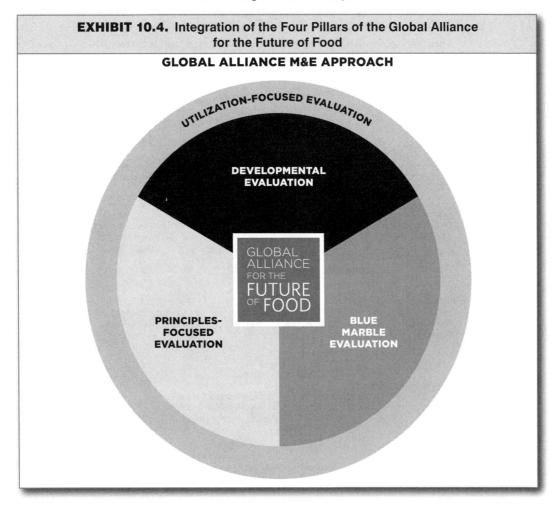

EXHIBIT 10.4. Integration of the Four Pillars of the Global Alliance for the Future of Food

GLOBAL ALLIANCE M&E APPROACH

UTILIZATION-FOCUSED EVALUATION

DEVELOPMENTAL
EVALUATION

GLOBAL
ALLIANCE
FOR THE
FUTURE
OF FOOD

PRINCIPLES-
FOCUSED
EVALUATION

BLUE
MARBLE
EVALUATION

setting, decision making, and emergent and adaptive transformation strategy.

2. *Principles-focused evaluation* provides a focus on how the GA remains aligned with and faithful to its principles.

3. *Blue Marble evaluation* provides a focus on global food systems transformation: tracking, documenting, assessing, and supporting the GA's strategy implementation and contributions to global food systems transformation.

"Each 'evaluation lens' asks different questions that together generate a comprehen-

sive view of what we do and with what consequences" (GA, 2019, p. 2). The evaluation questions are asked of the work in the GA's four impact areas: true cost accounting, agroecology, climate change, and health and well-being. Exhibit 10.5 shows the distinct evaluation questions that flow from each evaluation approach applied to the impact areas. Each evaluation approach yields a detailed set of questions for learning and reflection, and for evaluating the design, implementation, and outcomes for each impact area. The next section offers examples of generic Blue Marble evaluation questions.

EXHIBIT 10.5. Evaluation Questions Generated by Different Evaluation Approaches as Applied to the Global Alliance Impact Areas

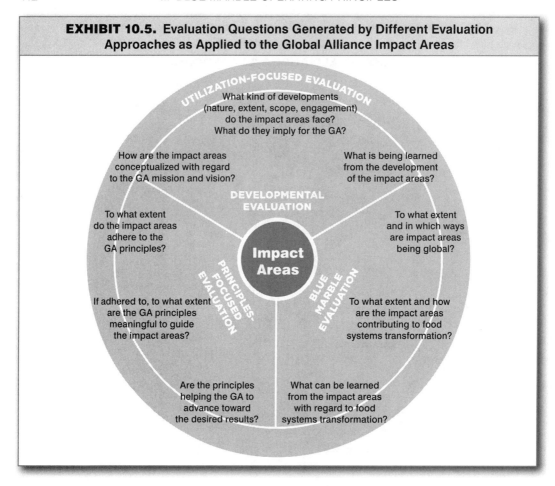

Generic Blue Marble Evaluation Questions

Four interrelated Blue Marble evaluation questions illustrate Blue Marble thinking. The quality and nature of Blue Marble thinking can be evaluated by the questions asked, the design that addresses those questions, and interpretation and use of the findings generated. Blue Marble evaluations, at a minimum, ask these four interrelated questions:

1. ***Blue Marble design thinking.*** To what extent are an initiative's design, conceptualization, and theory of change consistent with, connected to, contextualized by, and framed within Blue Marble thinking? This question involves specifying the theory of change and assessing its likely adequacy for contributing to global systems change results. [Design evaluation]

2. ***Blue Marble implementation.*** To what extent are an initiative's practices consistent with Blue Marble thinking? This is a "walking the talk" question: Is what was conceptualized actually done? To what extent are the principles for global systems change and a particular theory of change followed in practice? [Implementation question]

3. ***Blue Marble sustainable results.*** To what extent and in what ways is sustainable systems change occurring and, if so, to what extent and in what ways has the intervention being evaluated contributed to those changes? This question explicitly connects the results of specific initiatives to

global patterns of sustainable change. [Impact and contribution analysis]

4. ***Blue Marble learning.*** How can the results of the evaluative process be used to learn, adapt, and innovate toward more sustainable, resilient, one-Earth ongoing development? This is the utilization-focused question: How can we more fully use findings and apply what is learned? [Follow-up and utilization question]

While these are classic evaluation questions, asking and answering them from a Blue Marble perspective is quite different from traditional project or program evalua-

tion. Systems change is different from program outcomes. How different? Different in the degree of change, the nature of change, the pace of change, the direction of change, the scale of change, the interconnectedness of change, the magnitude of change, and the implications for sustainability and systems resilience.

Global systems change intervention designs and evaluation must be based on Blue Marble thinking if designers and evaluators are to be part of the solution rather than part of the problem. Conventional planning, design, implementation, and evaluation are all stuck in a project mentality, but closed-system project and program think-

Freire zooming in and out by Claudius Ceccon (Claudionor). Source: Patton and Guimarães (2018). Used with permission.

ing will not suffice to address major systems change on a global scale. And as discussed in Chapter 6, scaling replicable, standardized models is not the pathway to global systems change. Blue Marble methodological bricolage involves an ongoing process of zooming in, zooming out, looking local, looking global, zooming in, zooming out, and adapting, down, out, and up.

Bricolaged Blue Marble Evaluation Methods Lessons

To illustrate utilization-focused Blue Marble evaluation bricolage, here are six eclectic lessons about methodological approaches to Blue Marble evaluation.

1. *Aggregation and disaggregation of data are crucial to thinking globally and evaluating locally, and to understanding locally and evaluating globally.* Blue Marble evaluators need to be able to aggregate and disaggregate data and not just report averages. The 2015 Nobel laureate, economist Angus Deaton, has been lauded for his global perspective. In announcing his award, the Nobel Committee also lauded his integration of macroeconomics and microeconomics by aggregating national data transnationally to see global patterns and disaggregating data at community and household levels to understand local patterns. Then, separating signal from noise, he has been astute and insightful in finding the connections that illuminate global–local (GLOCAL) interdependencies. Deaton (2016) was asked about his commitment to gather and interpret data at the household level when he is trying to understand global trends. He was asked, Why is that so important?

> Well, you know, it's about people in the end, and you have to understand what makes people tick, and you have to understand what they think. And for me, that's always meant trying to understand behavior at the local level.

Disaggregation, for example, is essential for equity-focused evaluations.

> One of the central development objectives of most international development agencies is to promote equity, to ensure that program benefits reach the poorest and most vulnerable groups and to ensure that programs contribute towards the achievement of broader equity goals. However, many evaluations only measure average, aggregated outcomes (e.g., on average a higher proportion of children attend school or that the proportion of the population below the poverty line has been reduced). There is an extensive body of research showing it is quite common to achieve aggregate improvements while the gap between the poorest, for example, 20 per cent and the rest of the population may not have been reduced or may even have increased (Bamberger & Segonem, 2011). To evaluate equity effects, disaggregation of data is critical. (Bamberger, 2016)

2. *Trajectory analysis makes evaluations dynamic rather than static.* The *Time Being of the Essence principle* can be applied in understanding and employing trajectory thinking and analysis at the design, implementation, and analysis stages of evaluation. Trajectory analysis means looking at the likely life cycle of an intervention.

> Program effects can occur over different periods of time and evolve according to different trajectories. While some projects produce steadily increasing outcomes over the project lifetime, in other cases effects may reach a maximum and then gradually decline. This often happens when projects require a high level of maintenance (e.g., irrigation canals and pumps). When funding is no longer available for maintenance, or this ceases to be a priority (e.g., after the completion of donor involvement), it is common for maintenance to deteriorate and the level and quality of services declines. In other cases, most effects may be produced at a particular point in time, for example when a road is completed. Understanding the ex-

pected trajectory of outcomes is critical for determining when the evaluation should be conducted. (Bamberger, 2016)

Trajectory analysis to evaluate resilient sustainability requires follow-up beyond the implementation phase of a project to find out how the intervention unfolds over the long term. Evaluation designs rarely include funding for such follow-up. The evaluation ends when the intervention funding ends. This is because funding agencies require and support evaluation only for the project intervention time period they support and for which they are accountable. For example, the project implementation phase ends when the targeted schools have been constructed, the road or irrigation system has become operational, or the training program model has been finalized. But an end-of-project evaluation is too early to assess whether sufficient capacity for resilient sustainability has been built. Blue Marble evaluation designs need to incorporate and propose resilient sustainability evaluation criteria and follow-up designs if they are to evaluate the longer-term impacts of interventions and initiatives.

3. *Evaluating portfolios of interventions is a powerful way to extract knowledge across silos and geographical boundaries.* The GA commissioned a study of initiatives working toward transformative change in food systems through holistic approaches addressing multiple dimensions of sustainability. They reviewed 128 possible initiatives and through a screening process selected 21 initiatives designated as "Beacons of Hope." The initiatives selected spanned sectors (civil society, private sector, and governmental) and scales that were then further analyzed and profiled in depth. The study provides reflections on how these "Beacons of Hope" have been able to accelerate the transition process to transformed systems and address structural barriers to transitioning (Gemmill-Herren et al., 2018). The 21 case studies show the importance of GLOCAL thinking and action as local

initiatives worked with partners and allies at regional and national levels while paying close attention to overriding global trends and influences.

The Independent Evaluation Group (IEG) of the World Bank evaluated a sample of 20 systems transformation initiatives varying in form, size, the development challenges they addressed, sector, and region, as well as country context. In addition, the IEG reviewed a purposeful and selective sample of country-level engagements. Their comparative and synthesis analysis concluded with five key takeaways:

- Identify the most binding constraints to development in a country, sector, or area by consistently implementing rigorous diagnostic work.

- Enhance the selectivity of assistance programs.

- Build on mechanisms of transformation in program and project design. This includes shaping incentives to effect sustained behavioral change and strengthening institutions to support transformational impact.

- Form broad coalitions through early and wide-ranging interactions with stakeholders. For example, targeted beneficiaries can be involved in an intervention's design and implementation. An increased focus on transformation will also involve exploring new partnerships and managing them effectively and efficiently to ensure interests align.

- Stay the course by undertaking more selective, longer-term, sustained, and programmatic engagements. This involves engaging in fewer, but more focused and long-term engagements (IEG, 2017; see also Heider, 2016; IEG, 2016).

The Climate Investment Funds (CIF) used a similar portfolio analysis to evaluate its investments. With $8 billion contributed since 2008, the CIF was established to scale up finance for climate change mitigation and adaptation, fill urgent financing gaps, and demonstrate the viability of emerging solutions. A cross-portfolio analysis focused on searching for and evaluating "signals of transformational change": evidence indicating that systems transformation is underway. Recognizing that transformational change occurs as a process, and that signals of transformational change become more robust over time, the evaluation identified three stages of signals:

- Early signals are evidence that programs are not only thematically relevant but have been designed and implemented in such a way as to promote transformational impact (e.g., integrating political economy considerations, engaging national support from key champions, and aligning with regional initiatives likely to support change processes).

- Interim signals are those that indicate that external change processes linked to direct program outputs are underway and that these are likely to result in future climate benefits (e.g., greenhouse gas mitigation, improved resilience, sustainable forests), but have not yet been fully realized.

- Advanced signals are those that indicate that climate impact's core to the mandate of the CIF programs are being delivered at scale, with systemic underpinning and in a sustainable manner beyond the CIF program boundary (Itad, 2019, pp. 4–5).

The Blue Marble evaluation toolkit should include cross-portfolio synthesis designs that extract knowledge and lessons from identifying patterns and themes that cut across individual initiatives in a portfolio.

4. *Blue Marble evaluation is a team sport.* The methodological implication of applying a global perspective for evaluation is that most Blue Marble evaluations will need to be done by teams because it is unlikely that any single evaluator is sufficiently globally competent, methodologically eclectic, and world savvy enough to do the job alone. One example is the work that is just getting started in the Gulf of Maine, one of the most rapidly warming bodies of water on the planet. A creative team, led by Glenn Page, a Blue Marble bricoleur, is beginning to take shape and features an engaged set of diverse people, with significant indigenous participation, who are committing to a long-term process of mapping the system together and constructing a baseline for tracking multidimensional systems changes.

As noted in the Preface, this book has been a team effort. While I've done the final writing and editing, and take responsibility for what appears before you, the Blue Marble team, from places around the world, engaged with me chapter by chapter, principle by principle. (See the Acknowledgments in the Preface for details.)

But is conducting evaluations as a team, a method? Isn't that merely a project management and competency issue? From working on teams doing evaluations, I've found the experience altogether different from doing evaluations on my own. It is a methodological approach because it involves interaction processes that determine all aspects of the evaluation, from formulating questions to design and data collection, triangulation of perspectives during analysis, honoring diverse voices and reporting, and generating a methodological and analytical synthesis. Multiple languages, diverse cultural views, evaluators of different ages, gender, and disciplinary background—this combination is methodological. Bottom line: Teaming, especially Blue Marble teaming, is a method.

5. *Systematically mapping the interconnections among SDGs can provide powerful insights into cross-silos evaluation questions, designs, and analytical frameworks.* The International Council for Science (Griffs, Nilsson, Stevance, & McCollum, 2017) has

produced the comprehensive *A Guide to SDG Interactions: From Science to Implementation*. It is based on the premise that "a science-informed analysis of interactions across SDG domains can support more coherent and effective decision-making, and better facilitate follow-up and monitoring of progress."

Understanding possible trade-offs as well as synergistic relations between the different SDGs is crucial for achieving long-lasting sustainable development outcomes. A key objective of the scoring approach described here is to stimulate more science-policy dialogue on the importance of interactions, to provide a starting point for policy-makers and other stakeholders to set their priorities and implementation strategies, and to engage the policy community in further knowledge developments in this field. (p. 7)

Using a 7-point scale, a team of scientists evaluated the key target-level interactions between any one SDG goal and all other goals, and "attributed a score to these interactions based on their expert judgment and as justified through the scientific literature. . . . The assessment identified 316 target-level interactions overall, of which 238 are positive, 66 are negative, and 12 are neutral" (p. 8). Here are three highlights from their findings:

- SDG2 + SDG1: Eradicating poverty cannot be achieved without ensuring food and nutrition security for all.
- SDG2 + SDG3: Health and well-being cannot be achieved without access to a sufficient quantity and quality of food. How the sdg2 targets related to increasing agricultural production and productivity are implemented will have a major influence on soil and water quality, land use, and ecosystem health and functioning, which are key environmental determinants of health. Other factors such as rural income stability from agriculture and related sectors are also important.

Achieving sdg3 supports sdg2, because a healthy population is essential for achieving nutrition and agricultural production targets.

- SDG2 + SDG15: Healthy ecosystems provide vital services, from soil and water quality, to genetic diversity and pollination. Agriculture is a key driver impacting ecosystems. Sustainable agricultural systems and practices contribute to ecosystem health. However, increased agricultural production and productivity, if not sustainable, can result in deforestation and land degradation, jeopardising longterm food security. A careful balance is needed between achieving food for all and conserving and restoring ecosystems. (pp. 10–11)

The Guide provides an assessment framework that can be used in any evaluation to map the interactions among SDGs and implement the Blue Marble Cross-Silos principle.

6. *Relate Blue Marble evaluation narratives to the Anthropocene metanarrative.*

The conservation of natural resources is the fundamental problem. Unless we solve that problem, it will avail us little to solve all others.

—THEODORE ROOSEVELT, in a 1907 speech

Any given Blue Marble evaluation tells the story of an effort to solve a problem or make a difference of some kind. Each Blue Marble evaluation story unfolds in the context of the bigger picture and longer-term story of the Anthropocene. The Anthropocene as Context principle calls on Blue Marble evaluators to understand, adapt to the realities of, and contribute positively to human and ecosystem trajectories in the Anthropocene. The emergence of the Anthropocene is a story of accelerating human impact on Earth, impact that is changing the environment in ways that threaten the future of humanity. So, there are two stories unfolding together: the big-picture long-term story of the Anthropcene and the short-term, real-time story of any given Blue Marble evaluation.

Every evaluation tells a story. There's a beginning (baseline), something happens (the intervention), and results (the story's climax). The context and setting for any Blue Marble evaluation is the Anthropocene story, still emerging. Evaluation bricolage at the analysis stage involves interweaving case studies and statistical data in a creative sense-making enterprise. The methods section of such Blue Marble evaluation reports will also tell a story, a tale of eclectically perusing and selecting methods, creating an appropriate bricolage design, adapting the design and methods to emergent understandings and opportunities to capture the stories of systems change interventions as they unfold, then reporting the results, lessons, and surprises they yield.

Stephen James Purdey (2018) is a political scientist and international relations specialist whose work focuses on the evolution of new forms of governance to meet current socioecological challenges. He has begun a metanarrative project "constructing a new global narrative about planetary sustainability." He writes:

> Given the brute fact that *Homo sapiens* is now a bio-geophysical force fully capable of disrupting long-stable planetary operating systems, it seems illogical for human society to willfully pursue a development agenda which amplifies rather than moderates our extraordinary power. . . .
>
> The new metanarrative we seek isn't a story set in stone. It's a conversation, a dynamic and evolving state of mind which confronts, embraces and shapes our shared future. It begins from the historically exceptional fact that we are the sole creators of, and wholly responsible for, the Anthropocene epoch. The new story we tell will feature self-inflicted danger but it will also offer the opportunity to re-imagine the exceptionalism that ennobles the human animal, to rejoin our

unique endowments to the planet that gave us life, and to meet our destiny with maturity, flexibility, and courage.

Blue Marble Evaluation Quality

In closing this chapter on the Bricolage Methods principle, let us consider the issue of quality. Disciplines have standards for what constitutes methodological quality. Evaluation standards and principles provide overall guidance for what constitutes excellence in evaluation. But what are the characteristics of a high-quality Blue Marble evaluation? Engaging in bricolage and eclecticism is not the prevailing guidance for designing valid evaluations. For that guidance, I turn to Ernest House, one of the profession's distinguished thought leaders.

Evaluating with Validity

In the highly influential classics *The Logic of Evaluative Argument* (1977) and *Evaluating with Validity* (1980), House has insisted that evaluation is not first and foremost about methods but is about making sense of evidence and creating a coherent, logical, and, ultimately, if successful, persuasive argument about what the evidence shows.

> Evaluation is an act of persuasion directed to a specific audience concerning the solution of a problem. The process of evaluation is prescribed by the nature of knowledge—which is generally complex, always uncertain (in varying degrees), and not always propositional—and by the nature of logic, which is always selective. In the process of persuasion one must ascertain who the audience is and find a basis of agreement on premises, both of facts and values, and on presumptions. Two criteria for evaluation are: the most efficient way to a given end, or the most effective use of available resources. . . . Both formulation and interpretation require good intuitive judgment. The evaluator and the audience must employ their reasoning in a

dialogue, and both must assume responsibility, since evaluation is never completely convincing nor entirely arbitrary.

The most significant decisions are those that have long-range implications but defy easy extrapolation, that are so entangled with everything else that they resist precise formal analysis. To those we are forced to apply our intuitive logic, our common sense, it is in the nature of these complex problems that knowledge about them is limited, that it is less than determinate. In the face of uncertain knowledge, the task of entangled decision making becomes less one of absolutely convincing ourselves with proofs than one of persuading ourselves with multiple reasons. The criterion becomes not what is necessary but what is plausible. (1977, p. 2)

Drawing on his roots in philosophy, House (2014) has offered an insightful framework for judging the quality and validity of evaluations: *truth, beauty, and justice.*

If an evaluation is untrue, or incoherent, or unjust, it is invalid. In other words, an evaluation must be true, coherent, and just. All three criteria are necessary [and can be framed as] "truth, beauty, and justice" in evaluation. The underlying concepts were argument, coherence, and politics. Truth is the *attainment* of arguments soundly made, beauty is the *attainment* of coherence well-wrought, and justice is the *attainment* of politics fairly done. (p. 31; original emphasis)

Deciding what is valid is fundamentally a challenge of evaluative thinking. House has provided an inspiring perspective on the core elements of evaluative thinking that go beyond mere logic and reasoning.

Jane Davidson (2014) has added a provocative twist to House's criteria:

True "beauty" in evaluation is a clearly reasoned, well-crafted, coherent evaluation story that weaves all three of these together to unlock both truth and justice with breath-

"We realize we kind of got off to a bad start. How about a second chance on this whole 'we have dominion' over you thing we got into."

Proposing a new Blue Marble storyline by Mark M. Rogers.

taking clarity. . . . Get the social justice priorities right, deliver valid answers relative to those, and then convey it all beautifully and believably.

I'd like to flip House's idea on its head. What if beauty wasn't merely about how well the evaluative story is told? What if the *process* of creating a clear, compelling, and coherent (beautiful) evaluative story was in fact the key to unlocking validity (truth) and fairness (justice)? (p. 43; original emphasis)

So, how ought we to judge the quality of a Blue Marble Bricolage Methods evaluation designed with eclectic elements and adapted to emergent conditions? The Bricolage Methods principle states: *Conduct utilization-focused evaluations incorporating Blue Marble principles to match methods to the evaluation situation.* The principle yields three criteria of quality to which I add the three from House:

1. *Utilization-focused evaluation criterion.* To what extent and in what ways is the evaluation useful?

2. *Blue Marble principles criterion.* To what extent and in what ways does the evaluation adhere to Blue Marble principles (Transboundary Engagement, GLO-CAL, Cross-Silos, and Time Being of the Essence)?

3. *Situational-appropriateness criterion.* To what extent and in ways are the evaluation questions, methods, measures, processes, and reporting appropriate to the evaluation situation?

4. *Truth.* Are the evaluative arguments soundly made?

5. *Beauty.* Is the *attainment* of coherence well wrought?

6. *Justice.* Is the *attainment* of politics fairly done?

CHAPTER 11

World Savvy Principle

As the nature of our most important issues increasingly span national borders and our world becomes more interconnected, high on the list of those new, necessary skills is global competence, the capacity and disposition to understand and act on issues of global significance. As our world becomes more interconnected, the immediacy of issues such as the global economic landscape, climate change, conflict, poverty alleviation, and food security require a new toolkit. Global learning is no longer a luxury, but is essential preparation for a changing world.

—DANA MORTENSON, cofounder and Executive Director, World Savvy (2019)

CONTEXT

The *World Savvy principle* is inspired by the organization that bears that name, a long-time Blue Marble evaluation partner. The idea for creating the World Savvy organization was born in 2001, when Dana Mortenson and Madiha Murshed were in graduate school in New York City. Following the events of 9/11, they observed and experienced what they've described as "alarming levels of xenophobia in New York City, and were deeply struck by how quickly the world was changing, requiring new and different skills, knowledge and dispositions to succeed" (*www.worldsavvy.org/history*).

At the core of World Savvy's mission and programming is global competence. World Savvy has developed several programs for preparing young people to become more globally competent. Over nearly two decades they've worked with some 5,000 teachers and 700,000 students across 26 states and 12 countries. They co-created a program to train and certify teachers as globally competent. The program is both values based and research based, and has had a strong evaluation and learning commitment from its beginning, on which I've consulted. So, when I thought about what competencies are needed to be a Blue Marble evaluator, I turned first to the World Savvy global competency framework.

Global competence is the capacity and disposition to understand and act on issues of global significance. Collectively, global competence represents the *knowledge, attitudes, skills,* and *behaviors* necessary to thrive in today's interconnected world.

As captured by our Global Competence Matrix, globally competent individuals possess and apply these qualities, characteristics, and abilities to learn about and engage with the world. Educators who aspire to help students become globally competent must both develop these attributes in themselves and find ways to foster them in students. (2019; original emphasis)

The *Global Competence Matrix* was developed collaboratively by World Savvy, Teachers College of Columbia University, and the Asia Society for the Global Competence Certificate, an online master's degree-level certificate program for in-service educators (see Exhibit 11.1).

World Savvy Principle Explicated

> **PREMISE:** Being a world savvy evaluator requires a blend of competencies, knowledge, understandings, skills, and sensitivities. Blue Marble evaluators should be globally and cross-culturally competent, as well as competent evaluators and knowledgeable about human and ecosystem interdependencies and stewardship. What competence means and what competencies are valued vary by context.

World Savvy Principle

Engage in ongoing learning relevant to Blue Marble principles and practices.

IMPLICATIONS

- Be thoughtful about what you know, don't know, and need to know; what skills you have, don't have, and need to develop; and your strengths and weaknesses to engage as a Blue Marble evaluator.

- Be intentional and systematic about ongoing learning; have a learning agenda while also being open to emergent learning opportunities.

- Develop capabilities to engage as part of a Blue Marble team since no individual is likely to possess the full range of knowledge, skills, and competencies to engage globally, GLOCALLY, and across silos in diverse contexts on varied initiatives and interventions.

- Be a creative methods bricoleur, astute in matching methods to situations.

- Be savvy about being world savvy.

- Being world savvy is a journey, not a destination.

General Evaluator Competencies

The profession of evaluation is fairly obsessed with competency: a major factor in evaluation use is evaluation credibility, a major factor in evaluation credibility is evaluator credibility, and a major determinant of evaluator credibility is perceived and actual evaluator competency. The American Evaluation Association (AEA) Guiding Principles for Evaluators and the Joint Committee on Standards highlight evaluator competency. AEA endorsed Cultural Competence in Evaluation in 2011 and general evaluator competencies in 2018. Canada, New Zealand, and Japan have been leaders in developing evaluation competency frameworks. The United Nations Evaluation Group has competencies for both evaluators and commissioners of evaluation. These frameworks specify competencies in (1) methods, (2) professional practice, (3) interpersonal skills, (4) project management, and (5) context sensitivity. Blue Marble evaluators are, as professional practitioners, first and foremost evaluators, so attention to evaluator competencies comes with the territory.

The Shadow Side of Competence

In thinking about Blue Marble evaluator competence, it seemed reasonable to integrate global competency, evaluator competency, and cultural competency. I checked in with colleagues involved with the original AEA cultural competence statement and found that they were doing some rethinking. The concept of competence comes with racist, imperialist, colonial, and oppressive baggage. Historically, competen-

EXHIBIT 11.1. World Savvy Matrix

WORLD SAVVY
MATRIX

Global competence is the disposition and capacity to understand and act on issues of global significance. Globally competent individuals possess and apply the following qualities, characteristics, and abilities to learn about and engage with the world. Educators who aspire to help students become globally competent must both develop these attributes in themselves and find ways to foster them in students.

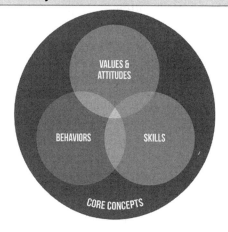

CORE CONCEPTS

- World events and global issues are complex and interdependent
- One's own culture and history is key to understanding one's relationship to others
- Multiple conditions fundamentally affect diverse global forces, events, conditions, and issues
- The current world system is shaped by historical forces

BEHAVIORS

- Seeks out and applies an understanding of different perspectives to problem solving and decision making
- Forms opinions based on exploration and evidence
- Commits to the process of continuous learning and reflection
- Adopts shared responsibility and takes cooperative action
- Shares knowledge and encourages discourse
- Translates ideas, concerns, and findings into appropriate and responsible individual or collaborative actions to improve conditions
- Approaches thinking and problem solving collaboratively

VALUES & ATTITUDES

- Openness to new opportunities, ideas and ways of thinking
- Desire to engage with others
- Self-awareness about identity & culture, & sensitivity and respect for differences
- Valuing multiple perspectives
- Comfort with ambiguity & unfamiliar situations
- Reflection on context and meaning of our lives in relationship to something bigger
- Question prevailing assumptions
- Adaptability and the ability to be cognitively nimble
- Empathy
- Humility

SKILLS

- Investigates the world by framing questions, analyzing and synthesizing relevant evidence, and drawing reasonable conclusions that lead to further enquiry
- Recognizes, articulates, and applies an understanding of different perspectives (including his/her own)
- Selects and applies appropriate tools and strategies to communicate and collaborate effectively
- Listens actively and engages in inclusive dialogue
- Is fluent in 21st century digital technology
- Demonstrates resiliency in new situations
- Applies critical, comparative, and creative thinking and problem solving

This Global Competence matrix was created in collaboration with Teachers College, Columbia University, and the Asia Society for the Global Competence Certification Program (GCC). The GCC program is an online Master's level certificate program for in-service educators.

Learn more at www.worldsavvy.org

cy tests have often been a way of excluding rather than including. Competency tests were administered to blacks in the South by white electoral judges who decided whether blacks were competent to vote. Residential schools that took indigenous children from their communities and cut them off from their families, culture, and language proclaimed that they wanted them to become "competent" to succeed in modern society. Throughout the world, training colonized people to become competent was a way of imposing dominant cultural, political, and educational values on oppressed peoples. Competency tests sometimes continue to play that role. Competency frameworks can lead to exclusion, reinforcing the status and power of the status quo.

Another concern: competency can constitute a fairly low bar as an entry-level, minimum standards construct. I don't want a doctor or lawyer who is just competent, or an evaluator who is just competent. We want people to demonstrate excellence. A criterion of excellence, mutually agreed to, with diverse and contextually appropriate engagement, may be more meaningful and useful than minimum competency standards.

Finally, competency connotes a binary state: competent/incompetent. The concept is static. Get licensed, certified, you are competent. A dynamic view would emphasize ongoing learning and development, not a fixed state of competency.

So, in the end, we are being more circumspect and cautious about the notion of global competency, preferring instead the aspiration to be world savvy. Part of being world savvy is checking out the meaning of competency in different contexts for different stakeholders. That is an example of a commitment to ongoing learning about and engagement with global issues, connecting the global to the local, and connecting social justice with environmental justice. Thus, an unexpected but welcome lesson was reinforced: Being world savvy includes

"Never forget son, successful exclusion systems require reign-enforcing loops."

Reign-enforcing loops by Mark M. Rogers.

being language savvy. Examine old terms in light of new and changed understandings and sensitivities. Concepts are like kaleidoscopes. You have to hold them up to the light and examine them from different perspectives to see their varied shapes and meanings. (More on language below.)

Notions of competency and being savvy in a diverse and divided world point toward the importance of a high degree of self-awareness and self-examination to better understand how our backgrounds and life experiences serve as assets or limitations in the conduct of an evaluation and in helping facilitate understanding of global–local interconnections. This requires reflexivity.

Reflexivity

Know thyself [γνῶθι σεαυτόν in Greek].
—Inscription in the ancient Temple of Apollo at Delphi

The term *reflexivity* has entered the evaluation lexicon as a way of emphasizing the importance of deep introspection, political consciousness, cultural awareness, acknowledging one's position (especially a position of privilege), and ownership of one's perspective. Let me acknowledge immediately that the term *reflexivity* reeks of academic jargon. In everyday conversation we don't say, "I'm in a reflexive mood today. I've set aside time to engage in some serious reflexivity." Such an assertion would likely evoke a profoundly unimpressed and skeptical "Whatever." So why not just use the word *reflection*? Reflexivity encompasses reflection, indeed, mandates reflection, but means to take the reflective process deeper and make it more systematic than is usually implied by the term *reflection*. It may sound pretentious, but the purpose is not pomposity. The term *reflexivity*, in the context of Blue Marble evaluation, is meant to direct us to a particular kind of reflection grounded in the in-depth, experiential, and inter-personal nature of evaluative inquiry from a GLOCAL perspective.

Reflexivity calls on us to consider how we think and inquire into our thinking patterns even as we apply thinking to making sense of the patterns we observe around us. Being reflexive involves self-questioning and self-understanding for "all understanding is self-understanding" (Schwandt, 1997, p. xvi). To be reflexive, then, is to undertake an ongoing examination of what I know and how I know it, "to have an ongoing conversation about experience while simultaneously living in the moment" (Hertz, 1997, p. viii).

Reflexivity reminds those working to bring about change—*and evaluators*—to be attentive to and conscious of the cultural, political, social, linguistic, and economic origins of one's own perspective and voice, as well as the perspectives and voices of those one encounters in doing the work. Research on excellence finds that people who excel in all kinds of things share the quality of being self-aware and using that awareness to adapt to whatever presents itself in the course of taking action (Sweeney & Gosfield, 2013). Taking action, in this case, includes evaluation.

Being world savvy, then, is not a state at which one arrives—rather, it is a process of learning, unlearning, and relearning. It is a sensibility cultivated throughout a lifetime. Being world savvy requires awareness of self, reflection on one's own position in the world, awareness of others' positions, and the ability to interact genuinely and respectfully with others. World savvy evaluators refrain from assuming they fully understand the perspectives of stakeholders whose positions in and experiences of the world differ from their own.

Language and Reflexivity

We think in language and concepts that shape our understanding of the world and ourselves (England, 1994; Gilligan, 1982; Minnich, 2005). One advantage to speaking more than one language is heightened awareness of how language shapes our understandings. A reason that Blue Marble evaluation typically requires a team is to cover multiple language and cultures in the team. One of my favorite reference books is Howard Rheingold's (1988) *They Have a Word for It,* a lexicon of untranslatable words and phrases. For example, he includes the concept of *dharma,* a Sanskrit word that he translates as "each person's unique, ideal path in life, and knowledge of how to find it" (p. 17). He then devotes more than a page to explaining why that is an inadequate translation and the deeper (and sometimes different) meanings of *dharma* in Hindu, Buddhist, and Jack Kerouac's (1958) *The Dharma Bums* frameworks. Blue Marble evaluators have to be savvy about language.

Jeph Mathias, a member of the Blue Marble team from his perch in northern India, and speaker of more than one language, comments insightfully:

> Language is not just different people using different sounds to say the same thing. It is different cultures breaking the world up into different pieces and then finding sounds to signify those shapes. So there are untranslatable words because experiences and context are different. My child's name *Sharhirah* is Mongolian for *the feeling you get at the back of your nose when horses gallop across the plains.* Untranslatable in English but the most romantic word I know. The significance and value of knowing more than one language is that it means you know there are alternative ways to make sense of and understand the world. Not essential for every individual but a very important competency for a Blue Marble evaluation team member. (personal communication, 2019; emphasis added)

What Is Being World Savvy?

No definitive list of world savvy elements is either possible or desirable. The point is to think about what it means for each evaluator in whatever situation is being faced. To stimulate that reflexive process, here are six common Blue Marble evaluation challenges that it helps to become savvy about.

1. ***Ongoing situation and contextual analysis.*** Scholars of decision making and expertise have found that what distinguishes people with great adaptability is not that they have more training and expertise (answers) than others but they are more adept at situational recognition and more intentional about their inquiry processes. The Blue Marble evaluator engages in situational analysis on an ongoing basis—not just at the start of an engagement. Being world savvy includes being situationally savvy as circumstances change.

2. ***Facilitating GLOCAL communications.*** Blue Marble evaluators bring to global and local settings their understandings, perspectives, and experiences that may not be known or appreciated by participants in the evaluation process. World savvy evaluators develop skill at facilitating two-way flows of communication. This applies to everything from generating evaluation questions; incorporating diverse perspectives; understanding context; setting boundaries around the evaluation, identifying important systems interrelationships; and interpreting, reporting, and facilitating engagement with findings.

3. ***Methodological bricolage.*** The Bricolage Methods principle, explicated in Chapter 10, calls for creative eclecticism in matching methods to the situation and evaluation questions. This requires methodological savvy (not just technical competence) about what processes, measures, and data collection approaches are appropriate within the cultural, political, social, and institutional contexts where the Blue Marble evaluation is occurring.

4. ***Astute in detecting significant global–local patterns.*** Some aspects of programs,

services, or products may be globally influenced but not in ways that are visible to those unfamiliar with the global context. Consider the example of an evaluation conducted in a community with one or more identifiable immigrant groups where effective programs are grounded in the values, norms, knowledge, beliefs, practices, experiences, and language that are vital to those groups. In this environment, continued interaction with people and institutions from their countries of origin may be important, even essential to the well-being of those who have left behind families, friends, and familiar places. A world savvy evaluator with a global perspective would include inquiry into such global–local interconnectedness as a part of the evaluation.

5. *Drawing appropriate conclusions.* Blue Marble evaluators have a responsibility to draw valid conclusions from data and facilitate meaningful interpretations by others. The AEA (2011) statement on cultural competence explains:

> To draw valid conclusions, the evaluation must consider important contributors to human behavior, including those related to culture, personal habit, situational limitations, assimilation and acculturation, or the effect of the evaluand. Without attention to the complexity and multiple determinants of behavior, evaluations can arrive at flawed findings with potentially devastating consequences. (p. 2)

In the same vein, without knowledge of and attention to global trends and influences, evaluations may arrive at flawed findings with potentially devastating consequences.

6. *Diplomacy in dealing with controversies.* Blue Marble evaluation departs from and raises questions about a number of traditional and well-established ways of conducting evaluations. Each Blue Marble principle will be controversial in certain contexts. Engaging across nation-state borders and silos may give rise to opposition

that "this is not how we do things here." Methodological bricolage may be questioned, even attacked, as lacking rigor and validity. Thinking globally represents a paradigm shift for many—and paradigm shifts are seldom welcomed by those whose existing paradigm dominance is being threatened. Being world savvy will not necessarily be viewed positively by those who do not share that savviness. In all of these and other controversial matters related to Blue Marble evaluation, diplomacy, respect, and communication skills will be needed. This includes keeping what appear initially to be small disagreements from escalating into major conflicts that can undermine an evaluation—a manifestation of the nonlinear butterfly effect from complexity theory in which something small escalates into something big.

Being world savvy means understanding the butterfly effect from complexity theory by Simon Kneebone. Used with permission of the copyright holder, the Australian Evaluation Society (*aes.asn.au*).

General Evaluator Competencies Related to Being a World Savvy Blue Marble Evaluator

As noted earlier, the AEA adopted a set of evaluator competencies in 2018: professional practice, methodology, context, planning and management, and interpersonal. Exhibit 11.2 takes these five competency domains and identifies what it might mean to be world savvy in each domain. I've limited the comparison to four specific competencies in each of the five domains. Blue Marble evaluators should aspire to excellence in both columns.

Finding the Core

As Exhibit 11.2 illustrates, being a world savvy Blue Marble evaluator is not an easy task. Is there some way to bring focus? Blue Marble evaluation team member John Wilson took a break from gardening in Zimbabwe to offer this insightful synthesis:

> I have this routine when I'm working at home of 45 minutes in front of a thing and then 15 or so minutes in the garden. I was reading the competency documents in my last stint and then went into the garden wondering what is it that we're after. As I sifted compost through a discarded truck air filter-holder that we use, the thought that kept coming to me was that it's all about *making connections*. It's those competencies that we are after, aren't we?
>
> Our current Blue Marble principles are about connecting across and beyond national borders, connecting local to global and vice versa, connecting across disciplines/silos. Ecosystem thinking is about connecting.
>
> Our education systems are all about breaking things down. We specialize, and specialize, and we're pretty good at those things where this works—machines, various technologies, etc., but not good where it's all interconnected: ecological issues, social issues, and so forth. One could say it's about

being holistic. But I don't think "holistic competencies" will work, that it says enough. Seeing the bigger picture, seeing the connections—that's the core competency. (emphasis added)

John's reflection brings powerful focus to the interpersonal dimension of being world savvy about our interconnected world—both biophysical and human systems.

Special World Savvy Issues for Blue Marble Evaluators

This final section explores and elaborates on two issues related to competency that arise in dealing with evaluating global systems change: (1) how much there is to know and how to keep current and (2) facilitating conflicts and evaluating in contested spaces on controversial issues.

What You Need to Know to Be a Blue Marble Evaluator

What you need to know depends on what you already know. Based on the preceding discussion, do an inventory of what you know deeply and are already skilled at, what you are familiar with and have some expertise in, and where you need to further develop as a matter of priority.

Over and over at workshops, in presentations, and from e-mail inquiries, the most common thing I'm told is "I feel overwhelmed." So do I. But we can't let that immobilize us. Early in my career, feeling overwhelmed by how much there was to know, and experiencing an onset of analysis paralysis, I asked a distinguished activist how to begin. She responded as wise women and men have responded throughout the ages:

Begin where you are. Begin with what you already know. Start with yourself and your neighborhood and your network. Begin where you are. Commit. Begin. The path leads forward from there.

EXHIBIT 11.2. General Evaluator Competencies and Ongoing Development as a World Savvy Evaluator	
General evaluator competencies (American Evaluation Association, 2018)	**Ongoing development as a world savvy evaluator**
1. *Professional practice:* Focuses on what makes evaluators distinct as practicing professionals.	
a. Knowing and observing professional norms and values, including evaluation standards and principles. →	a. Knowing global norms and values as expressed in the Universal Declaration of Human Rights, the Rights of the Child, Declaration on the Rights of Indigenous Peoples, and the International Women's Bill of Rights, as examples.
b. Pursues ongoing professional development to deepen reflective practice, stay current, and build connections. →	b. Stays current on issues related to Agenda 2030, SDGs, EvalSDGs, EvalPartners, COP2015, and reports issued on global climate change, pollution, equity, and so forth, and their evaluation implications.
c. Identifies how evaluation practice can promote social justice and the public good. →	c. Understands how evaluation can promote international social and environmental justice, and public and planetary welfare as evaluation criteria, and thereby inform value judgments and support decision making on future designs and actions.
d. Advocates for the field of evaluation and its value. →	d. Can explain and advocate the Blue Marble evaluation niche and principles and ethics.
2. *Methodology:* Focuses on technical aspects of evidence-based, systematic inquiry for valued purposes.	
a. Expertise in the technical aspects of evaluations, such as design, measurement, data analysis, interpretation, and sharing results. →	a. Expertise in aggregating data to detect global patterns and disaggregate data to understand local patterns, and connect the global and local patterns; skill in communicating these interconnections.
b. Uses program logic and program theory as appropriate. →	b. Uses systems thinking and complexity understandings to evaluate systems change; not restricted to project- and program-level thinking.
c. Collects and analyzes data using credible, feasible, and culturally appropriate procedures. →	c. Collects and analyzes data across traditional sector silos and works with specialists in those silos to see cross-silo patterns and their implications. Collects and analyzes data examining local and global interconnections and their implications by using culturally appropriate processes, methods, and procedures.
d. Interprets findings/results in context. →	d. Interprets findings/results in a global context with, as appropriate, engagement around implications for local and global evaluation users.

(continued)

EXHIBIT 11.2. *(continued)*	
General evaluator competencies (American Evaluation Association, 2018)	**Ongoing development as a world savvy evaluator**
3. *Context:* Focuses on understanding the unique circumstances, multiple perspectives, and changing settings of evaluations and their users/stakeholders.	
a. Responds respectfully to the uniqueness of the evaluation context. $\rightarrow$	a. Astute situation analysis skills and thinking. Excellent at asking questions and listening to understand context. Makes local and global patterns, trends, agreements, goals, and indicators part of context for an evaluation; skill in negotiating trade-offs between what is desirable and what is possible.
b. Engages a diverse range of users/ stakeholders throughout the evaluation process. $\rightarrow$	b. Seeks and includes stakeholders affecting and affected by the evaluation and/or the evaluand and primary intended users by embracing diverse perspectives across scales and silos and bringing together local and global perspectives along with short-term and long-term needs and analysis.
c. Describes the program, including its basic purpose, components, and its functioning in broader contexts. $\rightarrow$	c. Maps global system interconnections and the relationships of specific projects, programs, and communities within and across local and global contexts.
d. Clarifies diverse perspectives, stakeholder interests, and cultural assumptions. $\rightarrow$	d. Knows, takes account of, and addresses diverse perspectives, stakeholder interests, and conflicts around global issues and proposed solutions.
4. *Planning and management:* Focuses on determining and monitoring work plans, timelines, resources, and other components needed to complete and deliver an evaluation study.	
a. Coordinates and supervises evaluation processes and products. $\rightarrow$	a. Skills in managing, organizing, and synthesizing the sheer volume of data involved in capturing the dynamic global context, gathering data across silos, and representing GLOCAL interconnections.
b. Teams with others when appropriate. $\rightarrow$	b. Blue Marble evaluations typically require teams that are multinational and diverse in languages, international experience, specialty areas, ethnic backgrounds, and disciplinary expertise.
c. Works with stakeholders to build evaluation capacity when appropriate. $\rightarrow$	c. Every Blue Mable evaluation must include capacity building for GLOCAL thinking and understanding and applying Blue Marble principles.

(continued)

EXHIBIT 11.2. *(continued)*	
General evaluator competencies (American Evaluation Association, 2018)	**Ongoing development as a world savvy evaluator**
4. *Planning and management (continued)*	
d. Plans for evaluation use and influence. $\rightarrow$	d. Blue Marble evaluation feedback is likely to be developmental, ongoing, timely, emergent, and interpersonal; reports must be written with multiple and diverse audiences in mind.
5. *Interpersonal:* Focuses on human relations and social interactions that ground evaluator effectiveness for professional practice throughout the evaluation.	
a. Listens to understand and engage different perspectives. $\rightarrow$	a. Blue Marble evaluation, being utilization focused, is "co-created" with team members interacting with key stakeholders and primary intended users, so it is heavily *relationship focused*: respecting multiple perspectives and building interpersonal relationships as a source of credibility are parallel to methodological rigor in determining the evaluation's relevance and credibility.
b. Attends to the ways power and privilege affect evaluation practice. $\rightarrow$	b. Global power and privilege imbalances and inequities accentuate the importance of dealing with the effects of power and privilege as part of systems transformations.
c. Communicates in meaningful ways that enhance the effectiveness of the evaluation by facilitating constructive and culturally responsive interaction throughout the evaluation. $\rightarrow$	c. Communicating about global issues, patterns, and trends in culturally, politically, and economically diverse arenas with diverse stakeholders comes with the territory of Blue Marble evaluation; also communicating about local trends, perspectives, and effects in diverse global forums.
d. Manages conflicts constructively. $\rightarrow$	d. The global arena is rife with conflict, often intense, because the stakes are so high—the future of Earth and humanity. Blue Marble evaluators must be world savvy about negotiating difference and managing conflict in all aspects of the evaluation process.

Facilitating Conflicts and Evaluating in Contested Spaces on Controversial Issues

In Chapter 9, on the Yin–Yang principle, I wrote that harmonizing does not apply to political polarization. The Yin–Yang principle of harmonization applies to *opposite concepts* like global and local. Opposite political opinions and beliefs (e.g., climate change anti-science deniers vs. climate change scientific advocates) are another matter and may not offer opportunities for finding common ground. As a practical matter, political polarities are distinguishable from conceptual opposites. The World Savvy principle calls for engaging controversies and conflicts knowledgeably, respectfully, diplomatically, and, whenever possible, with good humor.

Everything is contested by someone from some point of view. I'm not just talking about the big, obvious, and ill-informed debate provoked by climate change deniers. Andrew Hoffman (2015) has done a superb analysis of how culture and social class shape the climate change debate. But political and technical disagreements permeate substantive and scientific issues. Here are just three of the debates I've encountered that have shaped evaluation questions, designs, data collection, and interpretation in the global systems change arena.

- Animal production and consumption in relation to global warming, human nutrition, and equity among people with different resources: How much do different kinds of animal production systems contribute to global warming? What additional environmental degradation is caused by large-scale animal production? How do agroecological approaches to animal production support sustainability?

- Fair targets: Given the huge disparity of resources among nations—the historical expropriation of resources from colonized countries by imperialist countries and profiteering companies—who should

bear what proportion of the burden for the economic transformations needed to reverse global warming and reduce pollution? Who sets the targets? How are they to be enforced? How are results to be monitored and evaluated?

- Globalization—its nature, extent, ramifications, meaning, and dimensions—evokes passionately different perspectives, both empirically (what's happening) and attitudinally (how people feel about whatever they think is happening).

What is the role of the Blue Marble evaluator when dealing with such conflicts among key stakeholders? Let me offer an example from participating as an evaluator at gatherings of people with diverse views. My role is to listen closely for the crux of differences and then convert those differences into survey items that participants in the setting can respond to in order to indicate where along a continuum they agree or disagree. Rapid response technology allows for such surveys to be administered in real time in groups—for example, with software accessible through smartphones, or simply on flipcharts. Displaying the results for an entire group helps to decipher how deep the conflicts are (or are not) and overcome the domination of one or two voices in a group. Such feedback also helps the group move from debate to action by bringing closure to elucidation of conflicts in transition to where the group finds common ground for action. Moving forward, that process then yields evaluation questions and data collection options for initiatives that emerge from the group. Such a data gathering and reporting role must be tightly coordinated with group facilitators and leaders who come to understand the role that an evaluator can play in managing conflict.

The larger point is to be prepared to be immersed in settings where conflict is in high gear without, as the evaluator, taking sides on the contentious issues, but playing a data-gathering role to clarify the nature, depth, and implications of divisions. In a convening of diverse stakeholders from around the world assembled to review a draft report for a major evaluation, discussions about how to interpret the data and what recommendations were supported by the data became quite intense, at times argumentative. Stakeholders had high stakes in the evaluation and were determined to represent those stakes, which is why they were there. The purpose of the meeting was to clarify findings, generate feedback, and build interest. As the evaluator, I had to be open and attentive, without becoming defensive or argumentative myself, but reiterating that I valued hearing the diverse perspectives and that, in the end, it would be my responsibility as the evaluator to draw conclusions and determine recommendations. Periodic role clarification, calm but firm, kept the heated discourse from escalating into damaging and irresolvable conflict.

Personal Engagement

Being world savvy is a principle, not a job description. In the end, being world savvy can't be reduced to a definitive list of competencies. It is a mindset, a way of thinking and a way of being in the world as both an evaluator and a person. All the Blue Marble principles become personal in the end: thinking globally and GLOCALLY, acknowledging and facing the realities of the Anthropocene, transformative engagement across borders and boundaries, staying grounded in the implications of the Time Being of the Essence principle, harmonizing opposites, and designing evaluations as a methodological bricoleur. Integrating those overarching and operating principles is ultimately both personal and interpersonal.

To illustrate the personal and interpersonal nature of being world savvy, I asked two Blue Marble evaluators to reflect on

global competence and being world savvy. One is a wily veteran with years of experience, the other relatively new to evaluation.

The Perspective of an Emerging Blue Marble Evaluator

Charmagne Campbell-Patton came to evaluation through World Savvy, the organization featured at the beginning of this chapter. She is also my daughter and has joined me in Utilization-Focused Evaluation as Director of Organizational Learning. I asked her to reflect on how she came to be involved with World Savvy, how she thinks about *being world savvy,* as both a person and an evaluator, and her current thoughts about global competence.

> I first learned about World Savvy while sitting in a closet just outside Glacier National Park in Montana. It was memorable for many reasons. There I was in one of the most beautiful (and now threatened) places on earth with a phone cord stretched from the staff lounge of the restaurant where I was working into the utility closet. I was interviewing with the founder, Dana Mortenson, for an internship. Dana had founded World Savvy the previous year and was looking for interns. I had recently graduated from college with a liberal arts degree in Political Science and French, but no real practical skills or much of a plan for my future. Hence the waitressing job. But when I read World Savvy's mission—to educate and engage youth in community and world affairs—something resonated in me. I was not really interested in living abroad or working in international development, but was deeply committed to global citizenship. Working for World Savvy seemed like a great way to combine global and local—or glocal, as it's called now in the BME principles.
>
> Fast forward fifteen years and World Savvy has grown from serving 90 students and 10 teachers in the San Francisco Bay Area to reaching nearly 700,000 youth and over 5,000 educators, from three offices, including the one I helped to open in my home

state of Minnesota. I got that internship in 2004 and it set me on a path first of promoting global citizenship among students and teachers, to defining and evaluating global competence. As World Savvy's work grew and developed, so did our understanding of the knowledge, skills and dispositions required for informed global citizenship.

If I've learned anything since sitting in that utility closet talking with Dana about World Savvy for the first time, it's that global competence is dynamic, emergent, and difficult to define or measure. Yet it remains critically important not only for personal success in our globalized world, but for our planet's salvation. That may sound a little dramatic, but if you've gotten this far in the book, you can see that the stakes are high. If we're going to save those glaciers I love so much, we need to understand the systems that are causing them to melt rapidly and transform them. Remember, time is of the essence.

For me, the most critical aspects of global competence are empathy, humility and courage. Seeking multiple perspectives by getting outside of your comfort zone is also critical. Knowing that you will never know everything, but not letting that stop you from engaging, staying curious, asking hard questions, and pushing the boundaries of your own understanding and comfort are key. And for white folks especially, being aware of how much space we take up, privileging the experience of people of color and indigenous people, working on our fragility to allow us to recognize and learn when we make a mistake.

As for being globally competent, I like to say, as soon as you think you're globally competent, you're probably not anymore. Because feeling globally competent means continuing to learn, question, adapt, grow and change. Hence the importance of humility and courage.

I asked Charmagne what Blue Marble evaluators ought to know.

The biggest thing is to always be aware of what you might not know (again that humil-

ity piece). You will never know everything. But that doesn't let you off the hook—you should have a basic understanding of how the current world system came to be. Pay particular attention to different cultural groups' understandings of history and globalization. And as I said before, also get to know yourself—where do you come from? What do you bring to the table? I am currently working with an indigenous immersion school that is getting some pushback for trying to develop a culturally relevant reading assessment using the current reading standards as a starting point. Several community members would prefer they start completely from scratch rather than within the Wašícu (white) framework of standards. They asked me to come in and help move the process along. I inquired whether my being white was going to help or hinder the process, to which the director replied—"You just have to get in touch with your own indigenous heritage." When I told her my family hails from Ireland, she asked if I spoke any Gaelic. Unfortunately I do not, but she helped me to identify a place where I can deepen my own understanding of myself and my culture so that I can better connect with and support evaluation in indigenous communities.

The Perspective of a Seasoned Veteran

Deborah Rugg is former director of the UN Evaluation Group, the UN Inspection and Evaluation Division (New York), Monitoring and Evaluation Guidance at UNAIDS (Geneva), and Monitoring and Evaluation in the Global AIDS Program at the Centers for Disease Control and Prevention. She has worked in over 100 countries and has more than 35 years' experience in various international evaluation efforts. I asked her what it takes to be a competent Blue Marble evaluator.

I would say to be a genuine Blue Marble evaluator means having the prerequisite *fundamental technical skills* in whichever type of evaluation you are drawn to, and then work-

Action, reflection by Claudius Ceccon (Claudionor). Source: Patton and Guimarães (2018). Used with permission.

ing to become a *pioneer,* which means you have to be brave and strong; persistent; have a true *passion* for the work and know why you are doing it; and are comfortable being *humble, listening and always, always learning,* because you will never know enough. By definition you will be *interdependent* on so many levels and people to be able to conduct these systemic Blue Marble evaluations. You will need others strategically placed, to help your contributions make a real difference, like I found when evaluating the UN Peacekeeping operations. People in high places helped the process work. Yet others *will look up to you to lead the way,* so you will need to nurture your *vision and clarity and communication skills* so that you may help *to guide the troops on the best pathway for impact.*

And finally, you also have to have a healthy *daily sense of your own humanity* as you work with diversity of all kinds. Serving humanity is truly where deep satisfaction comes from. (original emphasis)

Contributing as a Blue Marble Evaluator

There's important work to be done in transforming global systems toward sustainability and equity. Blue Marble evaluators can contribute. To do so, they will need, and we all will need, to apply the World Savvy principle *Engage in ongoing learning relevant to Blue Marble principles and practices.*

CHAPTER 12

Skin in the Game Principle

How much you truly "believe" in something can be manifested only through what you are willing to risk for it.
—NASSIM NICHOLAS TALEB (2018)

CONTEXT

Having skin in the game means you have a stake in the outcome. It means you are a stakeholder. The origin of the phrase is unknown and, of course, contested (Safire, 2006), but the phrase is most widely used in the financial investing world as a version of "put your money where your mouth is." In that spirit, global financial expert Nassam Nicholas Taleb (2018) exhorts: "Don't tell me what you 'think' [is a good stock to buy], just tell me what's in your portfolio" (p. 4). Taleb has written a best-selling book entitled *Skin in the Game* in which he warns us to be leery of advice in any field from anyone who doesn't have skin in the game. I'll share more insights and provocations from Taleb below. But first, what does this have to do with Blue Marble evaluation?

are not outside looking in. We are part of the global system and there's a good chance that we are each, in our own way, part of the problem. This gives us a quite different stance from what is typically expected. Evaluators are virtually always outside the programs or projects they evaluate. Acknowledging and facing the realities of the Anthropocene transforms the stance of evaluators from external observers of change to internal participants in change.

Skin in the Game Principle

Acknowledge and act on your stake in how the Anthropocene unfolds.

IMPLICATIONS

- A shift in evaluator stance from independence to interdependence.
- Making the evaluators' values explicit and transparent.
- Identifying your stake, whatever role you play—evaluator, designer, implementer,

Skin in the Game Principle Explicated

PREMISE: When it comes to the survival of humanity and the planet, we all have skin in the game—we and our loved ones are in the world that is under threat. We funder, commissioner of evaluations, intended user, policy maker—then sharing how you view your stake and the implications of that view for how you engage and fulfill your role. As a utilization-focused evaluator, I always have a stake in whether and how an evaluation is used.

- Reality test for yourself to be valuable as a reality tester for others. So, how good are you at reality testing for yourself? For example, to what extent are you practicing in your life the things you know you ought to be doing (exercising, eating right, getting enough sleep . . .)?

Independence and Interdependence

The overwhelmingly predominant view of evaluation is that credibility depends on independence, impartiality, and neutrality, which means not having skin in the game. Even "internal evaluators"—those internal to the organization running a program—have not traditionally been involved or viewed as a participant in the program being evaluated. Evaluator independence is asserted as a fundamental principle. Let's examine that premise from a Blue Marble perspective.

In the spirit of the Yin–Yang principle, instead of treating independence and interdependence as conflicting opposites and mutually exclusive positions, let's look at their interconnection. First, it's helpful to understand that these are culturally learned predispositions.

Some cultures value individual independence more than interdependence with other people, while other cultures cherish interdependence instead of independence. Geert Hofstede has not only identified this cultural parameter, but also researched how residents of particular countries tend to vary on it. People from Great Britain and its former colonies in the United States, Australia, Canada and New Zealand generally value independence, as do Germans, Belgians, Swedes, Italians, Danes, the Dutch, and the French, for example. Countries that generally value interdependence include some countries in Central and South America (Mexico, Brazil, Venezuela, Peru, and Chile, for example), as well as people from China, South Korea, Pakistan, Portugal, and Greece, among others. (Augustin, 2010, p. 1)

This cultural preference extends to evaluation and evaluator credibility. In Western (Global North) professional, institutional, and bureaucratic settings, independence and autonomy are prerequisites for credibility. But if an unknown and independent evaluator enters most indigenous communities and is not known to or championed by people in the community, that evaluator has no credibility. Being an outsider doesn't ensure credibility—instead, it can bring suspicion.

The Yin–Yang harmonization of opposites can emerge from transparently expressing interdependence and connection around shared values and interests, but independence of judgment as an evaluator resides in being neutral about the effectiveness of any particular intervention based on those shared values until that intervention has been evaluated. I share with advocates of sustainability the vision of a more just and equitable future in the face of a rapidly changing planet. My value to those implementing interventions and initiatives aimed at sustainability is my neutrality about their effectiveness and independence of judgment about the merit, worth, and significance of what they are doing and accomplishing. We each have our responsibilities and contributions to make. Implementers implement. Evaluators evaluate. Where their interests intersect and overlap is around shared values about what constitutes the greater good—and knowledge that each has skin in the game.

How Far Dare an Evaluator Go Toward Saving the World?

Robert Stake (2004) is one of the great pioneering thought leaders of evaluation. He yields to none in his commitment to rigorous inquiry. He is a distinguished methodologist. He has used his inquiries and methods to understand and expose social injustices. In an article published in the *American Journal of Evaluation,* he asked this provocative question in the title, "How Far Dare an Evaluator Go Toward Saving the World?"

Most evaluators claim to make dispassionate searches for quality and dysfunction. They speak disdainfully of advocacy and promotion. Yet it is clear that most of us evaluators have strong feelings about certain matters which we promote in our work. Here are six advocacies common in evaluation studies:

1. *We care about the evaluand, the object being evaluated.* Often we believe in it. . . . Barry MacDonald once said, "One should not evaluate a program if one does not support its goals." Occasionally we have a conflict of interest; more often a confluence of interest. . . .

2. *We care about evaluation.* We want to see others care about it. We want to encourage them to do it. We promote evaluation services, our own and those of our profession. We favor methods that evaluate well, and encourage others to use them too. It is an advocacy we flaunt.

3. *We advocate rationality.* We would like our clients and other stakeholders, our colleagues and heads of department to explicate and be logical and even-handed. We often pause in our data gathering or reporting to point out a way that the evaluand could have been run more rationally.

4. *We care to be heard.* We are troubled if our studies are not used. We feel evaluation is more useful if program participants take some ownership of the evaluation.

5. *We are distressed by under-privilege.* We see gaps among privileged patrons and managers and staff and underprivileged participants and communities. We aim some of the evaluation at studying issues of privilege,

conceptualizing issues that might illuminate or alleviate under-privilege, and assuring distribution of findings to those often excluded.

6. *We are advocates of a democratic society.* We see democracies depending on the exchange of good information, which our studies can provide. But also, we see democracies needing the exercise of public expression, dialogue, and collective action. Most evaluators try to create reports that stimulate action. (pp. 103–104; emphasis added)

Beyond Neutrality: What Blue Marble Evaluators Care About

Stake's list of things evaluators care about is a good start, but it's more than 15 years old. I propose to update his list with the Blue Marble principles, both overarching and operational. Here goes.

- The Global Thinking principle—*Apply whole-Earth, big-picture thinking to all aspects of systems change*—means we care about how problems and issues are conceptualized and understand the implications of thinking, acting, and evaluating globally.
- The Anthropocene as Context principle—*Know and face the realities of the Anthropocene and act accordingly*—means we care about humanity taking responsibility for our collective impacts on Earth and one another and want to be part of the solution and not part of the problem.
- The Transformative Engagement principle—*Engage consistent with the magnitude, direction, and speed of transformations needed and envisioned*—means we care about and understand the need for transformative change both in systems change initiatives and evaluation of those initiatives.
- The Overarching Integration principle—*Integrate the Blue Marble principles in the design, engagement with, and evaluation of systems change and transformation initiatives*—means we value coherence and

understand how coherence enhances effectiveness.

- The Transboundary Engagement principle—*Act at a global scale*—means we care about the future sustainability of the planet and humanity more than preserving national autonomy and sovereignty.

- The GLOCAL principle—*Integrate complex interconnections across levels*—means we care about our families, neighbors, communities, and networks of relationships, and because we care about those close to us, we think and act globally because global trends affect them and each of us.

- The Cross-Silos principle—*Engage across sectors and issues for systems change*—means we care about meaningful knowledge and useful information, not protecting disciplinary territoriality, arbitrary program categories, university departments, and SDG silos.

- The Time Being of the Essence principle—*Act with a sense of urgency in the present, support adaptive sustainability long term, grounding both in understanding the past*—means we care about future capacity to continuously adapt and not rigid continuation of short-term activities and outcomes.

- The Yin–Yang principle—*Harmonize conceptual opposites*—means we work toward and see value in understanding interrelationships and interconnections, and take a holistic perspective, not promulgating artificial divisions that separate, isolate, and divide rather than integrate.

- The Bricolage Methods principle—*Conduct utilization-focused evaluations incorporating Blue Marble principles to match methods to the evaluation situation*—means taking responsibility for finding the right eclectic design to answer the priority Blue Marble evaluation questions.

- The World Savvy principle—*Engage in ongoing learning relevant to Blue Marble principles and practices*—means we want to be effective and make a difference, which requires having the appropriate knowledge, skills, mindsets, behaviors, tools, and frameworks to engage many different global contexts with a high level of competence.

- The Skin in the Game principle—*Acknowledge and act on your stake in how the Anthropocene unfolds*—means we acknowledge we care, make our values and caring transparent, and act with integrity and professionalism to advance our own stake, the stakes of those we care about, and our common human stakes as members of the global village.

Reframing Caring and Credibility

To repeat the opening context, the predominant view of evaluation is that evaluator credibility depends on independence, impartiality, and neutrality, which means not having skin in the game. So, if I care about the future sustainability of the planet, does that mean I can't be a credible evaluator of interventions aimed at enhancing sustainability? Or might it be the case that I will not only be more credible but do a better job because I do care about whether the intervention is effective? I care enough to not cut those implementing the intervention any slack.

My younger brother died early in the acquired immunodeficiency syndrome (AIDS) epidemic. When I evaluate AIDS programs, I tell them about my family's loss and say, "Preventing AIDS matters to me. It's personal. If your program isn't effective, I'm going to be on you like a fly on feces. If your program is effective, I'll help you make it even better. Let's do this."

Confusing Caring with Bias

Researchers and evaluators are admonished to stay rational. The third item in Stake's (2004) list of things evaluators care about is *We advocate rationality.* Another framing of opposites: emotion versus reason. Don't get emotional. Feelings are the enemy of rationality and objectivity. Emotions and feelings lead to caring—and caring is a primary source of bias. Stay distant and unfeeling. Caring emerges from connecting to people, an empathic sense of interdependence rather than independence. So, avoid connection and caring, eschew empathy, maintain rationality and independence, and you can avoid bias, the greatest of scientific failings. In other words, deny that you have skin in the game, even to yourself. Act like you're on another planet, Planet *X*, watching the inhabitants of Earth, Planet *Y*, approach the apocalypse. That would be fine, perhaps, if there was a Planet *X*.

Brian Knutson (2014), a professor of psychology and neuroscience at Stanford University, makes the case that scientific inquiry should incorporate emotions as a source of data and insight into the nature of the human experience.

> The absence of emotion pervades modern scientific models of the mind. In the most popular mental metaphors of social science, mind as reflex (from behaviorism) explicitly omits emotion and mind as computer (from cognitivism) all but ignores it. Even when emotion appears in later theories, it is usually as an afterthought. . . . But over the past decade, the rising field of affective science has revealed that emotions can precede and motivate thought and behavior.
>
> Emerging physiological, behavioral, and neuroimaging evidence suggests that emotions are proactive as well as reactive. Emotional signals from the brain now yield predictions about choice and mental health symptoms, and may soon guide scientists to specific circuits that confer more precise control over thought and behavior. . . . Literally and figuratively, we should stop relegating emotion to the periphery, and move emotion to the center—where it belongs. (p. 1)

Having Skin in the Game Is Emotional

Caring, having a stake in what happens, having skin in the game—these human experiences evoke emotions, not out-of-control, over-the-top emotions but feelings about what matters. When I was in graduate school, we were constantly warned that emotion was the enemy of reason. Now, based on the latest research on how we as humans make decisions, brain science, and cognitive science, we know that emotion is not opposed to reason; our emotions assign value to things and are the basis of reason (Brooks, 2011; Patton, 2014). "Emotive traits," like "empathetic sensitivity," are not barriers to scientific inquiry about the human experience—rather, the capacity for empathy enhances, enriches, and deepens human understanding (Brooks, 2011).

Blue Marble thinking invites analysis based on values about what matters for the future sustainability of Earth and the well-being of humanity. Blue Marble thinking, then, is not only analytical but inspirational—and thereby, emotional. The Blue Marble perspective integrates analysis and caring. Analysis involves thoughtfully examining reality. Caring is manifest in values and emotions. As discussed in Chapter 9, on the Yin–Yang principle, world-renowned Brazilian philosopher, educator, and activist Paulo Freire (1997) articulated a holistic and humanistic approach to critical consciousness and dialogue that valued and integrated reason and emotions. Freire spoke of "reason soaked with emotion."

When we engage with one another as whole human beings, both thinking and feeling come into play. We think about things and we care about things—ideally, we think about the things we care about and care about the things we think about. Research in brain science, decision sciences, and behavioral economics (Patton, 2014), to name but a few examples, have revealed the deep interconnections between thought and feeling, cognition and emotion.

Distinguishing Bias from Caring

Michael Scriven (1993), the distinguished philosopher of science and evaluation research pioneer, concluded his influential volume *Hard-Won Lessons in Program Evaluation* with astute observations about both empathy and bias. First, empathy:

> The most difficult problems with program evaluation are not methodological or political but psychological. . . . What is lacking is the ability to see the point of view of those on the receiving end of the evaluation [intended users]. . . . (p. 87)

Scriven also commented on the common fallacy of defining bias as a lack of belief in or concern about something:

> Preference and commitment do not entail bias. It is crucial to begin with a clear idea of the difference between bias in the sense of prejudice, which means a tendency to error, and bias in the . . . sense of preference, support, endorsement, acceptance, or favoring of one side of an issue. Only the first of these senses is derogatory, and in the legal context the term bias is restricted to the first sense. From none of the synonyms for the second sense can one infer prejudice, because the preference, support, and so on may be justified. It is insulting, and never tolerated in a court of law where these matters are of the essence, to treat someone who has preferences as if they are thereby biased (and hence not a fair witness). It is especially absurd in the science, mathematics, engineering, and technology areas to act as if belief in [something] shows bias. Bias must be shown, either by demonstrating a pattern of error or by demonstrating the presence of an attitude that definitely and regularly produces error. . . . People with knowledge about an area are typically people with views about it; the way to avoid panels of ignoramuses or compulsive fence sitters is to go for a balance of views, not an absence of views. (pp. 79–80)

Evaluator Responsibilities

In Chapter 11, on the World Savvy principle, I cited the statements on standards, principles, and competencies that have been adopted by evaluation professional associations. When we're talking about what we care about, the AEA's Guiding Principles for Evaluators indicate that as a matter of professional excellence, we are far from values neutral.

> Common Good and Equity: Evaluators strive to contribute to the common good and advancement of an equitable and just society. (2018)

Is not the future viability and sustainability of Earth and humanity a matter of the common good and equity? Our professional obligation is to contribute to that common good and equity. The stakes for doing so have gone up given the realities of the Anthropocene, for there are general evaluator responsibilities as expressed in the general guiding principles, but in addition there are specific evaluator responsibilities that rise from living and working in the Anthropocene. It is to those responsibilities I now turn.

Evaluator Responsibilities in the Epoch of the Anthropocene

Where there is great power there is great responsibility, where there is less power there is less responsibility, and where there is no power there can, I think, be no responsibility.
—WINSTON CHURCHILL, in a 1906 speech to the House of Commons

Evaluators do have power, not great power, but not no power. So, asked Zenda Ofir (2018) in a blog posting, "What is the responsibility of evaluators in the era in which we live today?" Here is part of her rumination. (The full post, online, is worth reading.) She expresses powerfully the responsibility taken on by Blue Marble evaluators in adhering to the Anthropocene as Context principle and having *skin in the game*.

We live in the era of the Anthropocene—an era that is being defined by the intersection of the ambition and idealism of the Sustainable Development Goals with the Fourth Industrial Revolution, human-induced climate change, activism for a return to a more humane economy, and extremely powerful multinational monopolies that control vast swathes of global supply chains and international investments amidst vicious geopolitical jostling for power and resources.

In such an era, how can we keep ourselves so intensively busy with "project" or "programme" evaluation—and then mostly without engaging with or even understanding the larger frameworks, contexts and systems in which they play out?

Very high on the list of the responsibilities of evaluation professionals today should be support for the fostering and acceleration of positive development trajectories—of societies, countries, regions, ecosystems—but most importantly, within planetary boundaries. This requires not only positive outcomes that sustain in the long term, but deep engagement with frameworks, models and practices that enable resilience and transformational change in society. Such a focus will ensure that we attend to deep causes of problems, to underlying systems and the interconnectedness of the world, and appropriate solutions that sustain.

We will stop focusing on band-aids that often exacerbate under-development and exploitation, and even more often waste resources and energies. This means that evaluation professionals will have the responsibility to look far beyond our narrow technocratic endeavors. We will have to engage with those who are busy challenging dominant dogma and development paradigms . . . such as China's highly impressive escape from the poverty trap. We have to grapple with some of the "big picture" issues affecting our societies. We have to be openminded, informed and critical—including of dominant narratives around evaluation and development; of development indicators and global indexes that compare countries; of the extent to which evaluation is helping to resolve key challenges faced by the world; and fully cognizant of the implications of systems and complexity concepts and insights.

Most importantly, we have to understand how we define and judge "success," and why. (p. 1)

Reframing the Game

The game is real, complex, high stakes, and with people who are not just passionate, but feel deeply responsible for the future of the planet. Evaluators' mission-critical contribution to the game is wildly good reality-testing.
　　—MARK CABAJ, Canadian evaluator

Success is different depending on the nature of the "game." When we say, "skin in the game," what is the game? Game theory distinguishes zero-sum versus non-zero-sum games. In zero-sum games, resources are finite, no new resources are created during the game, and winners take all, losers get nothing. Games are competitive. Non-zero-sum games generate win–win possibilities and create new resources, or new ways of thinking about and sharing resources through cooperation rather than competition. Blue Marble team member Jeph Mathias, highly knowledgeable about game theory, suggests reframing the Blue Marble game this way. He sees the zero-sum history of much human "success" and "progress" having involved a competition between humans and nature in which humans "win" by exploiting nature. Those who play the game only for economic profit seek unconstrained exploitation of nature. Environmental stewards are driven singlemindedly to protect ecosystems. Here's his reframing from a zero-sum to a non-zero-sum game:

We are ecosystem stewards *and* humanity stewards at the same time. With globalization and the expansion of humanity, we have every human system nested in an ecological system and every natural system nested in a human system. Somehow Blue Marble evaluators have to understand and work with that koan—like a paradox. What we have at present is human development creating a tension between human and natural systems. What we need is evaluators who are not so much stewards of the natural world alone or the human world alone but who can find synergies between the two systems which our present development trajectory puts in conflict.

In game theory we at present have a zero-sum game—either humanity or the environment. Blue Marble thinkers, including but not limited to evaluators, have to be *game changers*. We change the zero-sum game into a dynamic non-zero-sum game at local and global levels. (personal communication, 2019; emphasis added)

Taking a Stand: Promoting and Making Common Cause with Science

Robert Picciotto (2019), former director of the Independent Evaluation Group of the World Bank and international thought leader on evaluation, has asked, "Is evaluation obsolete in a posttruth world?" He concludes that the contemporary posttruth phenomenon threatens liberal democracy and that evaluation is more needed than ever but needs reform.

The contemporary post-truth phenomenon is characterised by denial of facts and tolerance of politicians' lies. It has enhanced the appeal of authoritarian and nationalist leaders as a populist reaction to policy failures. While emerging market countries hugely benefited from globalization, the hourly wages of working people in high-income countries have stagnated while inequality has surged, and environmental stresses have escalated. Post-truth dispositions are distorting decision making in the public sphere and they have increased public distrust of knowledge professionals. This is likely to aggravate the very problems that gave rise to the post-truth phenomenon. Evaluation can help reverse the trends that underlie voters' anxieties, amplification of tribal prejudices and appeals to national pride through sound advice, transparency and public education. This will require new evaluation policy directions. Evaluation internationalization, diversification, democratization and professionalization will have to take place simultaneously. (p. 88)

Let me join with my good colleague Bob Picciotto in warning that the anti-truth, posttruth phenomenon is real, serious, and global. Evaluators have skin in the game when science is attacked, facts are treated as mere opinion and perspective that anyone can make up, and the president of the United States makes outright lying and distorting reality a matter of presidential prerogative and public policy. Culturally and politically, the anti-science trends include "alternative facts," "fake news," and a "posttruth" world. In November 2016, the year Donald Trump was elected president of the United States, *Oxford Dictionaries* announced *posttruth* as its international Word of the Year, defining it as "relating to or denoting circumstances in which objective facts are less influential in shaping public opinion than appeals to emotion and personal belief." Casper Grathwohl, president of Oxford University Press's Dictionary Division, explained, "Given that usage of the term hasn't shown any signs of slowing down, I wouldn't be surprised if posttruth becomes one of the defining words of our time."

The implication of living in a posttruth political culture is that science becomes just another perspective. Scientific evidence is no more valid than personal opinion. Every political persuasion advocates not just values but promulgates its own "facts." The distinction between evidence and opinion becomes blurred. This, by extension, has a corrosive and delegitimizing effect on evaluation. Evaluation findings become just another kind of opinion. Truth, finding and speaking it, is devalued and disputed.

Having skin in the game means taking action to support one's interest and values. On April 22, 2017, millions marched for science in 600 cities worldwide. The AEA was one of the 270 partner organizations that supported the March for Science. I joined more than 40,000 in Washington, DC, marching with my son, daughter-in-law, and granddaughter. The questions of the day were, naturally enough: What brings you to the march? Are you a scientist? What kind? If not, what's your connection to science?

The first time I had this conversation was with a stranger after she successfully elicited a smile from my 9-month-old granddaughter. My daughter-in-law, a cell biologist at Yale, shared her identity without a moment's hesitation. I paused. I've been an evaluator for 45 years. I haven't identified myself as a sociologist in years. Saying I was a social scientist seemed vague and would naturally invite the follow-up query: What kind? So, I tried on a new identity. "I'm an evaluation scientist," I said. "I do evaluation science."

At first the phrase felt strange, awkward, even alien. I expect that I sounded tentative. And, of course, I had to explain what evaluation science is, which I got better at as the march progressed. But the real surprise was that, after several hours and multiple repetitions, I realized that the label resonated. I liked proclaiming myself an evaluation scientist. I reveled in explaining evaluation science. I even formulated an "elevator speech" to explain evaluation science:

Science is systematic inquiry into how the world works. Evaluation science is systematic inquiry into how, and how well, interventions aimed at changing the world work.

I wrote an article about *evaluation science* in which I recounted that experience (Patton, 2018a). I argued that *both* science in general and evaluation in particular are evidence-based processes with conclusions derived from systematic inquiry to understand and explain how some aspect of the world works. The credibility of scientific evidence is under attack. Guilt by association, the credibility of evaluation evidence is diminished. To defend the value of scientific evidence, then, is to defend the value of evaluation evidence. It is in our interest as evaluators to make common cause with those who support science. We have skin in the game.

As a Blue Marble evaluator, I find presenting myself as an evaluation scientist has added value. The professional world dealing with climate change, pollution, and other Anthropocenic crises is populated by scientists of all kinds, including the new field of sustainability science. Evaluation has historically been treated as an administrative and management function, but what we do qualifies as science in every definition of the term I've found. Based on common understandings, perceptions, wisdom about, and definitions of science and evaluation, I proffered a working definition of evaluation science that incorporates the explanation I had the opportunity to field test during the March for Science.

Science is systematic inquiry into how the world works. Evaluation science is systematic inquiry into how, and how well, interventions aimed at changing the world work. Evaluation science involves systematic inquiry into the merit, worth, utility, and significance of whatever is being evaluated by adhering to scientific norms that include employing logic, using transparent methods, subjecting findings to review, and providing evidence and explicit rationales to support reason-based interpretation, valuing, and judgment. (Patton, 2018a, p. 187)

A huge variety of new fields have emerged that take on the moniker of science:

- Complexity science
- Cognitive science
- Improvement science
- Implementation science
- Translational science
- Urban science
- Management science
- Service science
- Design science
- Developmental science
- Community science
- Big Data science

This is just a beginning inventory. Add evaluation science to the list. I now proudly introduce myself as a Blue Marble evaluation scientist. And, so positioned, I have skin in the game—which comes with the responsibility to combat posttruth, anti-science forces wherever they appear, locally or globally. It also carries the responsibility to use science as an intervention toward global systems transformation.

Science as Intervention

In an important article in the journal *Energy Research and Social Science* on transformations and climate change research, 48 researchers from institutions around the world published a manifesto that included the importance of positioning science as not just producing knowledge but contributing to change. They assert that "for an unprecedented issue like climate change where urgent action is required," research must be focused on solving the problem and not just generating knowledge about the problem.

Researchers are inevitably embedded within, and not separate from, the systems they seek to observe. Researchers are also arguably always interveners. Intervention is the "purposeful action by a human agent to create change," where action is influenced by knowledge, including perceptions, implicit understandings, conscious and unconscious motivations, as well as values, morals, ethics and norms and behavioral habits. . . . Science can thus be understood as an active process of intervention, either directly in practice or more indirectly through the generation of knowledge. . . . Focusing on gaining a better understanding of the climate problem on the assumption that this will lead to formation of policy and change may be laudable, but in the context of constrained research budgets and value-driven budget allocations, a focus on problems may be at the expense of arguably more urgent "how to" questions that can no longer be ignored. Acknowledging that science is essentially a choice about focusing on a particular kind of intervention thus frees up possibilities for new questions, domains of application and different ways of learning about, and influencing change. (Fazey et al., 2018, p. 56)

Approach Research as Occurring from Within

The manifesto goes on to make the case for conceptualizing research as being conducted from within the system being studied.

Developing practical knowledge requires a shift from researchers viewing themselves as being "apart from the universe," such as looking as if through a peephole upon the unfolding universe, to viewing themselves as "a part of the universe," implying that when they act, they are also changing themselves and the world around them. These different ways of conceptualizing science have significant implications. Importantly, moving towards conceptualizing science as being from within allows for a powerful widening of the scope of research processes and for a shift towards explicitly acknowledging research as being an actor that is part of the process of promoting change. (Fazey et al., 2018, p. 62)

Individuals Matter

Stake (2004) concluded his article "How Far Dare an Evaluator Go Toward Saving the World?" with the observation that no two evaluators would likely produce the exact same evaluation design and report. He then suggests a new standard for the field.

One of the guiding principles should say something like: It should be expected that any two competent evaluators, working together or apart, will seldom agree fully on criteria and standards, critical incidents and experience, and on the appropriateness of the evidence of merit and worth. The full use of validation, triangulation, and meta-evaluation is essential but it will not eliminate uncertainty in the evaluation findings. Evaluators should be encouraged to "have a life" and to "have a dream" so their interpretations are enriched by personal experience. Comprehensive, idiosyncratic interpretations are small steps toward saving the world. (p. 107)

Institutions, networks, and agencies can have skin in the game, but formal organizations do not have feelings. People do. What it feels like to have skin in the game, to make a commitment, to take a risk, resides in individuals. The prestigious journal *Science* published an article by a young laboratory scientist working on research related to climate change. To do so authentically, he had to connect his professional and personal lives.

Just as I came to see my research as part of a larger scientific ecosystem, today I understand that scientific advancements are just one part of the needed response to climate change. I reduced my environmental impact by taking public transportation to work, significantly cutting my meat intake, and resist-

ing my consumerist impulses. My lifestyle changes will not single-handedly reverse climate change, and neither will my individual scientific contributions. But we all need to work together to address such challenges, each of us contributing in the best way we can. (Rogge, 2018, p. 706)

This is precisely the position that climate change activists Auden Schendler and Andrew Jones (2018) took in a *New York Times* op-ed article titled "Stopping Climate Change Is Hopeless. Let's Do It." They outline the many lifestyle changes needed from retrofitting light bulbs and reducing (eliminating) meat consumption to political actions like running for office, marching in protest, writing letters, and "uncomfortable but respectful conversations with fathers-in-law." Such work, they argue, must be "habitual," must become a way of life, "a practice."

We know what happens when enough people take up a cause as practice: Cultural norms change. Think gay marriage. Think the sharp decline in smoking in the United States.

There should be no shortage of motivation. Solving climate change presents humanity with the opportunity to save civilization from collapse. . . . The work would endow our lives with some of the oldest and most numinous aspirations of humankind: leading a good life; treating our neighbors well; imbuing our short existence with timeless ideas like grace, dignity, respect, tolerance and love. The climate struggle embodies the essence of what it means to be human, which is that we strive for the divine. (p. SR10)

Connecting the Personal, Professional, and Global

Million Belay is coordinator of the Alliance for Food Sovereignty in Africa (AFSA), a broad alliance of different civil society actors that are advocating for and working toward food sovereignty and agroecology in

Africa. I introduced Belay in Chapter 3, on the Transformative Engagement principle. I bring him back here to talk about the linkage to personal transformation.

> I globe trot from one meeting to another. Some of us are caught up in this cycle and there seems to be no way out of it. Anyway, this year (2017), I participated in nine international meetings. I was active in all of them either as part of the organizing group or as a presenter. There is one thread connecting all of them: "*transformation.*"
>
> At last there is a realization that change, fundamental change in the way we are living, is needed. . . . I think that the majority of us are all caught up in this paradox of deeply understanding the kind of transformation that is needed but being part of perpetuating the same system that we hate so much. . . .
>
> Transformation of global systems includes, and may even begin with, individual transformation. Each of us is called to change our lifestyles. If we are to become part of the movement for global systems transformation, individual mindsets, knowledge, and behavior are part of the larger global systems transformation process. Small local programs to large global programs are all part of transformation. (original emphasis)

John Colvin, based in the United Kingdom, is director of the Emerald Network and has been involved extensively in evaluating global transformation initiatives and participating in transformation conferenc-

"I don't know, Zeus. Athena suggested we watch it for a few eons instead of breaking up this mess."

Zeus by Mark M. Rogers.

es. He wrote to me about the personal dimension of the GLOCAL principle.

> It might be useful to extend the GLOCAL principle to include an intrapersonal element: "Transformation of our internal world" (caring for ourselves). I have in mind a framework that recognizes the interconnections between caring for all beings, for our social movements, for others, and for ourselves. This is important given the intense intellectual, emotional, and spiritual challenges of the transformational work we are seeking to co-lead. (personal communication, 2018)

Know What's at Stake

This chapter has focused on acknowledging and acting on your stake in how the Anthropocene unfolds. I close with an observation by Taleb (2018), author of *Skin in the Game,* with which I opened this chapter. Humanity must evolve if the needed global transformations are to occur. But Taleb asserts:

> Evolution can only happen if risk of extinction is present. Further, *there is no evolution without skin in the game.* (p. 14; original emphasis)

PART III

Global Systems Transformation Principles

Part I presented four overarching Blue Marble evaluation principles.

Overarching Blue Marble Principles
1. *Global Thinking principle*
2. *Anthropocene as Context principle*
3. *Transformative Engagement principle*
4. *Integration principle*

Part I challenged evaluators to think globally in the face of the realities of the Anthropocene and support, through evaluation, the global systems transformations necessary to create a more sustainable and equitable future for humanity. The overarching Blue Marble principles are interrelated and mutually reinforcing and, in accordance with the Integration principle, are meant to be integrated with the more specific operating principles explicated in Part II.

Blue Marble Operating Principles

- CHAPTER 5. Transboundary Engagement Principle
- CHAPTER 6. GLOCAL Principle
- CHAPTER 7. Cross-Silos Principle
- CHAPTER 8. Time Being of the Essence Principle

Global Systems Transformation Principles

Overarching Transformative Engagement Principle

Engage and evaluate consistent with the magnitude, direction, and speed of transformations needed and envisioned.

Introduction and Context

I live on nine acres in the Northwoods of Minnesota where we are working to transform abandoned, weedy farmland into pollinator habitat. When I think of transformation, I think of bees and butterflies. Bees transform nectar into honey. Butterflies epitomize transformation for me, from egg to caterpillar to pupa to majestic monarch.

The transformation represented by global warming can be captured in photographs of melting glaciers, satellite images of barren, brown land once covered in ice, and graphs of annual temperature increases. The transformation of plastic into ocean pollution is represented by the Great Pacific Garbage Patch, 80,000 tons of discarded plastic covering an area of about 617,800 square miles (1.6 million square kilometers), a vortex of micro-particles swirling in a gyre of marine debris. The process of transforming the lush Amazon rain forest, the Earth's biodiversity-rich lung, into a massive despoiled and degraded landscape is visible in large fires and denuded land. The Anthropocene is a geologic epoch defined by the theory that the human species has transformed the ecosystem function of planet Earth in ways that are unsustainable. That transformation has accelerated dramatically in just one human generation—ours!

A Michael Quinn Patton / Mark M. Rogers collaboration

"Mother Earth, we want to make peace with you. We promise we'll take better care of you from now on."

Make peace with Mother Earth by Mark M. Rogers.

CHAPTER 13

Theory of Transformation Principle

All the World's a Stage for Theory

Tony Kushner's Pulitzer Prize–winning play *Angels in America, Part Two,* opens in the Hall of Deputies, the Kremlin, where Aleksii Antedilluvianovich Prelapsarianov, the world's oldest living Bolshevik, speaks with sudden, violent passion, grieving a world without theory.

How are we to proceed without Theory? What System of Thought have these Reformers to present to this mad swirling planetary disorganization, to the Inevident Welter of fact, event, phenomenon, calamity? Do they have, as we did, a beautiful Theory, as bold, as Grand, as comprehensive a construct . . . ? You can't imagine when we first read the Classic Texts, when in the dark vexed night of our ignorance and terror the seed-words sprouted and shoved incomprehension aside, when the incredible bloodied vegetable struggled up and through into Red Blooming gave us Praxis, True Praxis, True Theory married to Actual Life. Period. . . . You who live in this Sour Little Age cannot imagine the grandeur of the prospect we gazed upon: like standing atop the highest peak in the mighty Caucasus, and viewing in one all-knowing glance the mountainous, granite order of creation. You cannot imagine it. I weep for you.

And what have you to offer now, children of this Theory? What have you to offer in its place? Market Incentives? American Cheeseburgers? Watered-down Bukharinite stopgap Capitalism? NEPmen! Pygmy children of a gigantic race!

Change? Yes, we must change, only show me the Theory, and I will be at the barricades, show me the next Beautiful Theory, and I promise you these blind eyes will see again, just to read it, to devour that text. Show me the words that will reorder the world, or else keep silent.

—TONY KUSHNER, *Angels in America, Part Two: Perestroika* (1994, pp. 13–14)*

Chapter 2 reviewed the evidence that humanity has entered the epoch of the Anthropocene. Chapter 3 presented the case for transformation. This chapter follows with a pathway for transformative engagement toward greater sustainability and equity: a theory of transformation. I'll both explain what a theory of transformation is and present such a theory for global transformation toward adaptive sustainability and greater equity.

Theory of Transformation Principle Explicated

> **PREMISE:** A theory of change specifies how a project or program attains desired outcomes. Transformation is not a project. It is multidimensional, multifaceted, and multilevel, cutting across national borders and intervention silos, across sectors and specialized interests, connecting local and global, and sustaining across time. A theory of transformation incorporates and integrates multiple theories of change operating at many levels that, knitted together, explain how major systems transformation occurs.

Theory of Transformation Principle

Design and evaluate transformation based on an evidence-supported theory of transformation.

IMPLICATIONS

- Systems transformation is the focus for both design and evaluation.
- Systems transcend projects and programs, though they may be thought of as subsystems.
- Transformation transcends project- and program-level changes while building on and integrating them for greater momentum and cumulative impact.

- Complexity theory and systems thinking inform and permeate transformative theory.
- No one, no organization, no entity, and no network is in charge of, controls, or manages transformation, but synergistic interactions can propel and accelerate transformation.
- Transformational engagement and momentum will generate opposition and resistance from those who benefit from the status quo.
- Transformation frames the nature, scope, and magnitude of change desired and needed, but values, stakes, and perspectives inform judgments about the desirability of the direction of transformation—that is, *transformation* is a descriptive term. Whether any particular transformation is viewed as positive or negative, as desirable or undesirable, depends on where one is positioned in the current and projected systems and the perceived costs and benefits of the transformation.

Theory

Theories explain how the world works. Einstein's theory of relativity changed our understanding of the whole universe. Quantum theory changed our understanding of nature at the smallest scales—energy levels of atoms and subatomic particles. Traditional physics theories described nature at an ordinary scale. In *Breakfast with Einstein: The Exotic Physics of Everyday Objects,* Union College physicist Chad Orzel (2019) shows how quantum physics is a part of our everyday lives, and that there is *quantum magic* in the mundane activities and objects of daily life. Which brings us to the daily activities of programs and why they are what they are and do what they do, which is explained by program theory, to which I now turn as a foundation for presenting a theory of transformation.

Program Theories of Change

Program theory aims to explain why a particular program approach should work to achieve desired results. This involves making explicit and testing a program's theory of change (Funnell & Rogers, 2011; Ringhofer & Kohlweg, 2019; Rogers 2000a, 2000b). In 1995, Carol H. Weiss, an applied sociologist and pioneering evaluation theorist who helped create the field of evaluation, wrote an article for the Aspen Institute about the importance of basing community interventions on a solid theory of change. Her article was entitled "Nothing as Practical as Good Theory." She was reacting to the emergence of large-scale community initiatives funded by philanthropic foundations and government agencies that poured millions of dollars into community change efforts with no knowledge of the relevant social science research that should have been informing such efforts. Her article became one of the most influential, if not the most influential, article in the history of program evaluation. Today, we would say, it went viral.

To be credible, useful, relevant, and meaningful, a theory of change must be theoretically sound, empirically based, and substantively relevant. Theories of change identify and hypothesize the causal linkages that will lead to desired results. The influence of Weiss (1995) can be found in the fact that virtually every philanthropic foundation, major government agency, nonprofit, and international development organization now requires that a theory of change be included in funding proposals and development initiatives. The difficulty is that these funding institutions miss the part about having research-based and theoretically coherent theories of change. Instead, what has emerged is a cottage industry of communication facilitators who take foundation and nonprofit staff through a retreat process of formulating something called a "theory of change" with no knowledge of what theory is, what a theory of change should do, or the underlying research findings that would inform a viable and meaningful theory of change. The idea was never to just get a bunch of people together to share ignorance and biases, and fabricate a theory of change out of thin air, though in my experience, that's often what happens.

I review a great many of these so-called theories of change every year, and I feel certain that Carol Weiss, were she still with us, would be aghast at the poor quality of thinking and research that have emerged in response to her brilliant articulation of the importance of having verified theory to inform action. She was especially articulate about the theory–practice connection. She wrote:

> It is sometimes said that there are two kinds of people in the world: thinkers and doers. And, of course, the third type: those who neither think nor do, but we won't worry about them just now. Thinkers are the world theoreticians. They love ideas, many of which have yet to be tested and may prove quite impractical. Doers, on the other hand, are too busy doing to worry about theory. But ultimately, theory and practice ought to connect. Practice is the test of theory. Theory is the explanation of practice.
>
> The evaluator's job is to challenge both practitioners and theoreticians. With the latter we ask, "So, it works in theory, but does it work in practice?" And with practitioners we ask, smiling diabolically, "Yes, it works in practice, but does it work in theory?" (1995, p. 1)

Evaluating the theory–practice interconnection is especially important at the global level where the crisis posed by the Anthropocene has spawned a large number of initiatives, conferences, and strategic plans aimed at nothing short of *transforming* global economic, political, social, environmental, and institutional systems. I've seen a great many of these transformational proposals. The analysis of the global challenges tends to be well-informed and frightening, for the trends are dismal. But the proposed solutions are the same-old repackaged projects mired in ineffective and outdated project thinking. *How are we to proceed without theory?*

Theory of Transformation

As explicated at the beginning of this chapter, but worth reiterating, transformation involves a different order of magnitude and speed than project-bounded changes. The language of transformation suggests major systems change and rapid reform at a global level. A transformational trajectory would cut across nation-states, across SDG and sector silos, and connect the local with the global (Blue Marble principles). The language of transformation has emerged across the globe wherever people convene to contemplate and initiate collective action to deal with global issues. A vision of transformation has become central to international dialogues about the future of Earth and sustainable development. (See Chapter 3.)

In what follows, I show how Blue Marble principles contribute to a theory of transformation and what else is needed for a comprehensive theory of transformation. This has implications for design and implementation of initiatives that seek to enable transformation as well as for evaluating transformation.

Constructing a Theory of Transformation

What follows is my attempt to make sense of how transformation occurs. I set out to write about evaluating transformation and realized that to do so, I needed to present some sketch of what transformation might

look like and how it could occur. Trying to pull together what I've observed and learned over 50 years of evaluating projects, programs, and interventions of all kinds at all levels, doing my best to keep up with the vast literature addressing how sustainable change occurs (yet failing to keep up), and working to make practical sense of historical and interdisciplinary evidence (Sisyphus rolling a boulder uphill), I arrive at a landscape that I can only characterize as networked *theories of change and frameworks interrelated and mutually reinforcing that, together, constitute one version of a possible comprehensive theory of transformation.*

Theory Knitting, Layering Theories, Theory Ladders

Leeuw and Donaldson (2015) have done a masterful job of reviewing approaches to integrating multiple theories.

> Theory knitting is integrating parts of (at first sight non-related or loosely coupled) theories and by doing so not only reduce "theoretical segregation" but also increase the chances of accumulation. . . . In theory knitting, one attempts to integrate previous theories into a single higher order theory, rather than to segregate a new theory from previous ones. But, they caution, not all the types of theory can be knitted together, only "those that are more or less similar, in terms of their type of content and orientation." (p. 474)

I remain unconvinced of this restriction, but in deference to their argument on this point, *I propose to network theories and frameworks.* In so doing, I aim to loosen their restriction on what theories and theoretical frameworks can be knitted together.

Leeuw and Donaldson (2015) also examined layering theories and theory ladders, based on Westhorp (2012), to address a

> well-known problem in evaluation: that interventions work for some but not for others, or work for some for a long time and for oth-

ers for only a very short time. . . . The very concept of *theory layering* not only makes it possible to understand complex phenomena and to predict what will work for whom, but it also helps the evaluator to find variables that are in need of measurement at different system levels. (p. 475; original emphasis)

Again, however, Leeuw and Donaldson caution that "As is the case with regard to theory knitting, layering theories can only apply to theories of a similar orientation and type of content" (p. 475). They also mention the strategy of nesting systems and subsystems of "mechanism based explanations" into a theory hierarchy (Liberman, 2005; Marra, 2011).

Lemire, Christie, Donaldson, and Kwako (2019) claimed that "Theory knitting is the explicit and purposeful integration of social science theory in program design and program theories." The unit of analysis for theory knitting is a program or project. Transdisciplinary theory is generated when members of different disciplines use "a shared conceptual framework drawing together discipline-specific theories, concepts, and approaches to address a common problem" (Slatin, Galizzi, Melillo, & Mawn, 2004, p. 62). The focus (evaluand) for Blue Marble evaluation is global systems transformation—the relevant set of integrated theories must all relate to transformation. To that end, I propose designating the integration of multiple theories that combine to explain transformation as a *theory of transformation* rather than a theory of change.

Toward a Theory of Transformation

A theory of transformation emerges from studying major transformations of the past and examining current challenges and patterns that portend future possibilities. Transformations that are instructive include the end of colonialism, the end of apartheid, the fall of the Berlin Wall and communism, turning back the AIDS epidemic, the Internet, and, today, social media. It is instructive to understand how these systems emerged into dominance in the first place, for none of these transformations occurred due to a centrally conceptualized, controlled, and implemented strategic plan or massive coordinated initiative. These transformations occurred when multiple and diverse initiatives intersected and synergized to create momentum, critical mass, and ultimately, tipping points.

In identifying potential theories and frameworks that together constitute a theory of transformation, I have drawn on my own limited knowledge, experiences, predilections, and, let me call them what they are, biases. By theory I mean an explanatory framework that explicates some aspect of how the world works and tells us what to pay attention to in efforts to bring about change. For example, complexity theory contributes to our understanding of how dynamic interactions in turbulent and emergent systems result in transformation, and that such transformations emerge from diverse and multilayered innovations and cross-system interconnections and interactions. Considering elements of this theory of transformation allows me to illustrate how to evaluate a theory of transformation in the next chapter. I suggest two theories that could contribute substantively to a theory of transformation: network theory and innovation theory. That will give us enough to work with to turn to evaluating based on a theory of transformation.

The Contribution of Network Theory to a Theory of Transformation

Networks as a means of mobilizing for transformation has gained significant attention in recent years. I now cite three examples of major books addressing global networks. In a scholarly research-based book on networks entitled *Organizations Working Together,* Alter and Hage (1993) open with this observation:

New mechanisms for coordinating and controlling different sectors of the economy are emerging, and it is the systemic network that offers the greatest competitive advantage in a global economy. . . . Systemic networks—clusters of organizations that make decisions jointly and integrate their efforts to produce a product or service—adjust more rapidly to changing technologies and market conditions [and] develop new products and services in a shorter time period and provide more creative solutions in the process. (pp. 1–2)

They predict that interorganizational networks

are the future institution . . . , that this new institutional form will increasingly replace both markets and hierarchies as a governance mechanism, and that networks are as fundamentally different as were the multidivision corporation and its predecessor the large bureaucracy. (p. 13)

They conclude as follows:

By concentrating attention on a discrete problem, such as global warming, acid rain, or the ozone layer, the world can move into a new stage of history. In this stage, the importance of single nations declines just as the importance of single corporations and agencies has declined as networks become the dominant institutional arrangement for producing products and providing services. (p. 297)

Three highly experienced network specialists and activists—Peter Plastrik, Madeleine Taylor, and John Cleveland (2014)—state their premise in their book's title *Connecting to Change the World: Harnessing the Power of Networks for Social Impact*. They offer insights about network building that emphasize the dynamic, evolutionary, and adaptive characteristics of networks. The implication for evaluating networks is that evaluation must also be dynamic, evolution-

ary, and adaptive. Fixed, static designs will distort and not illuminate.

The third example is Steve Waddell's (2011) *Global Action Networks: Creating Our Future Together*. He offers a vision of interacting, highly participatory global action networks as "a world where globalization works for all" (p. 238). He identifies four trends that support interacting networks as a pathway to global transformation:

1. *Continuing globalization.* "Globalization—the process of developing transnational inter-connectedness socially, politically, and economically—is increasing. . . . Globalization presents opportunities to create a much more equitable, healthy world of connections. History suggests that these opportunities have an irresistible allure" (p. 225).

2. *Inability of traditional strategies to address globalization.* "We are in the midst of a 'global governance' crisis. . . . We need to invent new ways to approach the challenges and opportunities, and global action networks represent one of those inventions" (pp. 225–226).

3. *Disruptive impact of new technologies.* "Our transformed ability to gather, manage, produce, and exchange goods and information. . . . We must find new ways of asserting the common good. . . . Global action networks can be an important part of the solution" (p. 226).

4. *Shifting assumptions about the way the world works.* "Perhaps the most important impact of these first three trends [above] is that they are changing the way we see and think about the world" (p. 226). These new ways of seeing and thinking about the world include the following paradigm-level transitions:

- From addressing issues in parts to whole systems thinking.

- From international structures for addressing global issues to multistakeholder ones.

- From assuming the natural environment to nurturing it.

- From change that can be addressed by linear approaches to complex system strategies.

- From negotiating our way to solutions to envisioning futures.

- From an enforcement focus to a collective value focus (pp. 224–236).

Waddell concludes that global action networks are "critical for bending the curve into the future in the direction of [a] flourishing world for all" (p. 238).

Much of the network literature focuses on building and engaging through individual networks. For example, June Holley's (2012) *Network Weaver Handbook* is subtitled *A Guide to Transformational Networks*. The guide supports transformation aimed at the shared interests of the network members.

Networks take a variety of forms. Networks can connect individuals, organizations, communities, communities of practice, collaborations, businesses, schools—indeed, all kinds of entities, including networks. The global transformation theory moves to that next level: *networks of*

networks. Exhibit 13.1 graphically depicts a variety of interlocking types of networks.

The Knowledge Base for a Networked Theory of Transformation

I've had the privilege while writing this book to read a *magnum opus* that integrates centuries of philosophy, historical analysis, scholarly inquiries, empirical research, social science theory, extensive case studies, and practical applications. A magnum opus doesn't come along every day. When it does, it is worth paying attention. But first, a bit of context.

My background is in sociology. In graduate school I studied the classics, wrote papers on the various schools of sociological thought, and have continued to read sociology and other social science journals. While my main identity is as an evaluator, I think of myself as an applied social scientist. I tell you all this because I think I have some modest basis for recognizing a major scholarly achievement. Jerald Hage is director of the Center of Innovation in

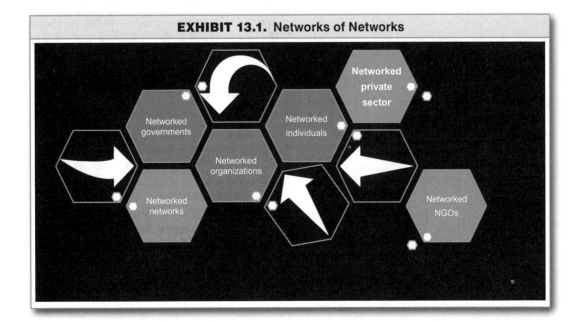

EXHIBIT 13.1. Networks of Networks

Social network analysts by Chris Lysy.

the Department of Sociology at the University of Maryland. His book *Techniques and Problems of Theory Construction in Sociology* (1972) remains, in my judgment, the best book there is on explaining the importance of theory for making sense of the world and what constitutes meaningful and useful theory. Hage has synthesized a lifetime of knowledge into a forthcoming book titled *Knowledge Creation and Social Change: New Minds, Adaptive Problems, Institutional Solutions and Novel Ideologies*. As of this writing it is not yet published, but I've had the privilege of reading the draft manuscript and discussing it with the author, who has given me permission to share an overview with you. I've followed Hage's work since he was my dissertation adviser at the University of Wisconsin, Madison (see Alter & Hage, 1993; Hage, 1972, 1980, 1988, 2011; Hage & Aiken, 1970; Hage & Finsterbusch, 1987; Hage & Meeus, 2006). The issues he addresses include how human beings and societal institutions deal with global inequality, changing dimensions and meanings of economic prosperity, climate change, new technologies, threats to human health, nuclear brinksmanship, ongoing innovation, future knowledge creation, and the host of

problems facing humanity together under the umbrella of the *Anthropocene*. He characterizes his overall stance as one of "postmodern conservatism" (markets are not the only solution) and "postmodern liberalism" (governments are not the only solution). This is but one example of how Hage integrates perspectives in supporting the key idea of the book, creating knowledge relevant to effectiveness in adapting to social problems. That is his orientation to social evaluation.

The Hage Hypothesis

Hage has generated a comprehensive, conceptually coherent, theoretically rigorous, and empirically tested theory of social evolution and societal transformation. This is all synthesized in what I've come to call the *Hage hypothesis*.

The Hage Hypothesis on Social Evolution and Transformation: Successful evolution and institutional transformation require increased diversity in innovative technologies and skill sets that are integrated into strongly connected and systemically coordinated networks.

Let's look at the elements of this hypothesis. (What follows is based on my personal interactions with Hage as this book was being completed.)

- *Transformation* means major systems change through radical innovation.

- *Diversity* means multiple and varied stakeholders, organizations, networks, resources, capacities, connections, perspectives, and niches across sectors and arenas of action (private sector, public sector, nongovernmental organizations [NGOs], social movements, and formal and informal networks).

- *Innovative technologies and skill sets* refers to postmodern thinking, ongoing innovation, and team-based capacities attuned to the challenges, opportunities, and imperatives of the Anthropocene, including global networks and virtual communications. Hage views innovation as problem solving and radical innovation as solving radical problems. This is one of the main reasons to support networks; they are problem-solving mechanisms designed for very complex, even intractable problems.

- *Integrated* means interconnections, interactions, and mutually reinforcing feedback loops of the diverse stakeholders, organizations, and networks.

- *Strongly connected and coordinated* refers to enlightened, risk-taking, transformational leadership engaged strategically, not just laissez faire, ad hoc interactions but rather repeated and scheduled interactions in a decentralized mode at both administrative and operational levels, and globally through a diffusion network that connects localities, including across national boundaries. Coordination, Hage emphasizes, includes being able to control and discipline disruptive behavior. Also, coordination has to occur on multiple levels, which is the idea of networks of networks.

- *Systemic network* means that a scarce relational resource is being provided that

develops in stages (if successful) such that the whole becomes greater than the sum of the parts, interactions across levels are systematized (micro, meso, macro), and dynamic feedback loops deepen integration and adaptation.

Innovation, for Hage, is the pathway to transformation. Diversity of cross-sector organizations symbiotically networked into a production/service delivery/idea development system generates innovation. Moreover, his extensive review of evolutionary systems transitions historically shows that as the complexity of the goals increases, network coordination has to be increasingly decentralized. If it is not, then not only does conflict increase but intended goals are less likely to be achieved. He shows that diversity may incorporate a considerable range of perspectives and expertise and that interorganizational systems may vary in size and composition. Coordination involves the active and mutual collaboration of the participant organizations, networks, leaders, and change agents. These interactions both build and draw on social capital.

Hage examines the explosion of studies about social networks that have centered on Facebook, Twitter, LinkedIn, and other social networking sites, as distinct from various kinds of interorganizational linkages. He concludes that this social media focus has missed the most interesting transformation that has occurred as a consequence of a postmodern wave of knowledge creation—the construction of systemically coordinated products, services, and research networks that are designed to solve complex problems by means of collaborative cohesion across diverse organizational boundaries.

Hage also concludes that the greater the task complexity, the more power must be shared. Since knowledge growth drives the complexity of tasks—not just in research but everywhere—even people without postmodern minds will have to learn to share power. He then shows how such sharing can be accomplished, including solving adaptive problems that are created by knowledge growth.

A cumulative body of research and knowledge expressed succinctly in the Hage hypothesis points to systemic networking, shared learning, co-creation, collective action, and ongoing adaptation as mutually reinforcing pathways to transformation in complex dynamic systems, especially globally. Examples of research, theory, and practice supporting the Hage hypothesis include Arena (2018); Cahill and Spitz (2017); Houle (2012); Pelling (2011); Plastrik et al. (2014), Waddell (2011); Westley, McGowan, and Tjornbo (2017); and Westley and colleagues (2007).

Using the Hage Hypothesis to Generate a Theory of Transformation for the GA

As described in earlier chapters, the Global Alliance for the Future of Food consists of 30 philanthropic foundations working together toward a shared vision of transforming food systems now and for future generations (*https://futureoffood.org*). The GA's strategy has three pillars:

1. Forge new insights and strengthen evidence for global systems change.

2. Convene key food-system actors, facilitate meaningful dialogue, and strengthen interconnections.

3. Stimulate local and global action and interaction for transformational change in collaboration with other committed stakeholders to realize healthy, equitable, renewable, resilient, and culturally diverse food systems.

Based on the GA's vision and strategy, we used the Hage hypothesis to draft a theory of transformation. Exhibit 13.2 presents the result.

A theory of transformation can inform and validate the GA's engagement strategy. It also provides evaluation criteria for judging the quality of the GA's structures, processes, and results and learning for adaptation. Embedded in the Hage hypothesis is the premise that innovations generated by network interactions and processes produce the content of transformation—thus, to network theory I now add innovation theory to the emergent theory of transformation.

Innovation Theory

My graduate studies in sociology focused on innovation. My master's degree in rural sociology took me deeply into the diffusion of innovations literature and the pioneering work of Everett Rogers (1962, 2003). Rogers identified and validated four core criteria that influence the spread of new products and ideas: (1) characteristics of the innovation itself—for example, understandability and relevance, (2) communication channels through which word of the innovation passes (Rogers & Shoemaker, 1971), (3) time for an innovation to spread, and (4) characteristics of the social system in which the innovation is diffused. He found that an innovation must be widely adopted in order to be sustained and he was among the first to hypothesize and verify that as adoption of an innovation increases, a tipping point of critical mass is reached in which there are more who have adopted the innovation than haven't. That means the system has tipped in favor of the innovation. Resisters and laggards eventually join the adoption trajectory or become obsolete outliers of the former practice, production, or way of doing things. His distinctions of types of innovation adopters remain relevant today: early adopters, early majority, late majority, and laggards (Rogers, 1962, p. 150).

Diffusion of innovations theory emphasizes focusing on early adopters, supporting them rather than trying to overcome resistance. Those who resist innovation are very good at what they do. Enormous resources can be wasted trying to overcome resistance; resources better used engaged early adopters to influence secondary adopters

EXHIBIT 13.2. Draft Theory of Transformation for the Global Alliance for the Future of Food

Create, nurture, and sustain an alliance of diverse philanthropic foundations that includes diverse people, perspectives, and resources that share a common vision and strategy (integrated diversity).

↓

Connect and engage with other networks, collaborations, alliances, and movements committed to and engaged in transforming diverse systems (strong connections).

↓

Support and facilitate convergence of multiple diverse networks and initiatives around shared values, principles, and strong local actions related to transforming global food systems.

↓

Help coordinate and integrate networked actions systemically toward transformation.

↓

Successful and sustainable transformation follows from the integration of diverse, multilevel, cross-system strong connections and coordinated systemic action.

In narrative form, this theory of transformational change would read as follows:

Narrative Theory of Sustainable Transformation

Given that successful and sustainable transformation follows from the integrated strategic action of diverse, multilevel, cross-system strong connections and coordinated systemic action, any given alliance aimed at global systems change must be organized and engaged as a committed alliance of diverse change makers that share a vision of and principles guiding work toward global systems transformation. Such an alliance strategically creates, supports, participates in, and catalyzes as appropriate and possible networks and initiatives of diverse organizations, people, perspectives, networks, and resources (integrated diversity). Such multiple intersecting alliances and collaborations can convene and facilitate convergence around shared values and strong niche-specific actions, thereby supporting and enhancing coordinated and integrated actions across networks, *ensuring through evaluation, learning, and adaptation* that those actions are systemically and systematically geared toward resiliently sustainable transformation of targeted global systems.

and reached the early majority to then attain critical mass where the tidal wave of change overwhelms resistance. This theory of change is consistent with the Hage hypothesis that transformation can be accelerated by connecting early adopters across sectors, geographical regions, and levels of engagement (local to global).

My doctoral studies in organizational sociology and social change focused on organizational innovation under the direction of Professor Hage. I mention this personal history again by way of disclosing where my engagement with innovation originated and to acknowledge that anyone integrating theories of change to explain a major phenomenon like transformation will bring to that enterprise his or her background knowledge, experiences, and relationships that will influence what is included in the theory of transformation. That is all the more reason to have teams of diverse people create a theory of transformation for a collective impact initiative.

Networks connecting globally by Simon Kneebone.

Following my graduate studies and over the course of my career I have worked with agricultural and cooperative extension programs in the United States and internationally, the mission of extension services being to diffuse knowledge. For 3 years I edited the *Journal of Extension*—thus, attention to innovation theories, research, and practices has been an ongoing focus informing my approaches to evaluation and has a prominent niche in my theory of transformation.

In directing the Center of Innovation in the Department of Sociology at the University of Maryland, Hage has been engaged in international research on innovation across many sectors through many years. Understanding innovation has been at the center of his distinguished career. The Hage hypothesis on the transformative potential of coordinated networks, discussed above, posits that diversity of cross-sector organizations symbiotically networked into a production/service delivery/idea development system generates innovation (Hage, personal communications, 2019). In his book *Restoring the Innovative Edge,* Hage (2011) identified, based on research, that transformational leadership is not limited to transforming a team or organization, though that may occur, but the distinctive difference is leading the team to transform their environment (p. 160). His overarching finding about generating innovation, expressed as a narrative equation (Hage, 2011, p. 259; Hage & Meeus, 2006, p. 551), is that

Knowledge sharing through diversity of paradigms + cross-fertilized collective learning = innovation and new knowledge

This narrative formula for innovation summarizes a great deal of scholarship on innovation in sociology and management: "Given a diversity of perspectives (complexity) that is integrated (organic structure), and provided that leadership takes a high-risk strategy, radical innovation (transformation) is more likely" (Hage & Meeus, 2006, p. 547). This formulation involves dynamic perspectives on complexity, integration, high-risk strategies, collective learning, knowledge, and innovation. Let me now extend my network of influence on innovation theory.

My long-time colleague and friend Frances Westley holds the J. W. McConnell Chair in Social Innovation in the Waterloo Institute for Social Innovation and Resilience at the University of Waterloo. She has devoted a distinguished career to not only studying social innovation but conducting programs to train leaders and teams in how to generate social innovation, and consulting with organizations and initiatives involved in social innovation initiatives. She and her colleagues define social innovation as "a new program, policy, procedure, product, process and/or design that seeks to address a social problem and to ultimately shift resource and authority flows, social routines and cultural values of the social system that created the problem in the first place" (Westley et al., 2007, 2011, 2017).

Westley and colleagues (2017) have examined the connection between technological innovation and social innovation. They have drawn on research and theory about how combinations of existing technologies within or between innovative hot spots can create new technologies to look for similar innovative breakthroughs in social innovation. That led them to study how new social or political mindsets can have catalytic effects. They asked, "How does the researcher interested in the transformation of social institutions determine which novel ideas, designs or initiatives, identified in the early stages of their development, are most likely to have transformative impact?" (p. 5). They examined historical examples, such as the history of national parks in the United States, the global derivatives market, and Native American residential schools, in order to trace the entire process of successful transformation back to the emergence of innovative phenomena. This work is also unique in that they apply a common theory, the multilevel perspective developed by Frank Geels, across all the case examples, and use a common software to visualize the change over time with common symbology. Their work and that of others are opening "new frontiers in social innovation research" (Nicolls, Simon, & Gabriel, 2015).

Social Innovation and Transformation

Just as I am attempting to interconnect diverse theories into a theory of transformation, Westley and colleagues (2013) have been integrating theory on "leadership in linked social–ecological systems" combined with the theory on "institutional entrepreneurship in complex adaptive systems to develop a new theory of transformative agency in linked social–ecological systems."

> Although there is evidence of the importance of strategic agency in introducing innovation and transforming approaches to management and governance of such systems, there is no coherent theory to explain the wide diversity of strategies identified. Using Holling's adaptive cycle as a model of phases present in innovation and transformation of resilient social–ecological systems, overlaid by Dorado's model of opportunity context (opaque, hazy, transparent) in complex adaptive systems, we propose a more coherent theory of strategic agency, which links particular strategies, on the part of transformative agents, to phases of system change. (Westley et al., 2013; see also Walker, Holling, Carpenter, & Kinzig, 2004; Westley et al., 2017)

Scaling Innovations

Sustainable transformation occurs when major innovations at the organization and societal levels become integrated and widely diffused. Indeed, a major issue in innovation theory concerns scaling (deep, up, and out), how innovations at one place, one level, and one time expand to more places, other levels, and future times—the continuation of Rogers's pioneering work on diffusion of innovations. "The failure of social innovations to have a lasting impact is common. . . . [The key question is] how and why some social innovations do in fact result in the transformations to which they aspire" (Westley et al., 2017, p. 5).

I discussed adaptive scaling in Chapter 6, on the GLOCAL principle. Here I have subsumed the issue of scaling—and theories of scaling—under innovation as a practical matter of not adding more theories to the transformation theory. But scaling would be a candidate for an additional identifiable node and niche, as would transformational leadership (see Cahill & Spitz, 2017, chap. 10; Hall, 2017; Harnish, 2014; Kaiser & Budinich, 2015; Patton, 2011; Riddell & Moore, 2015; Schorr, 1989, 2009, 2012; Sutton & Rao, 2014; Westley & Antadze, 2010; and Chapter 6, in this book, for more on scaling).

Exhibit 13.3 depicts innovation theory as consisting of several related areas of knowledge.

Network theory, the Hage hypothesis, and innovation theory could constitute distinct contributions to a theory of transformation.

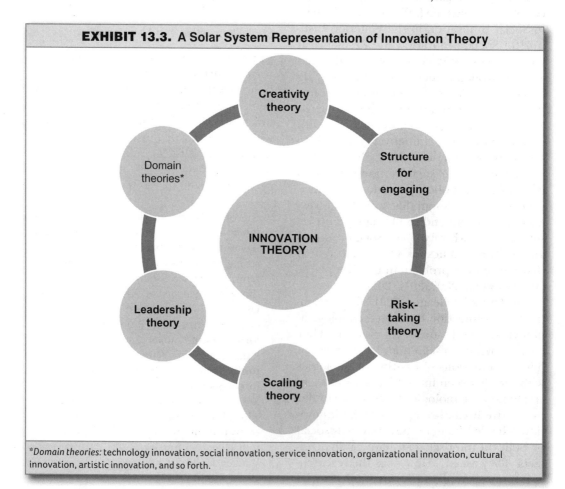

EXHIBIT 13.3. A Solar System Representation of Innovation Theory

Creativity theory

Domain theories*

Structure for engaging

INNOVATION THEORY

Leadership theory

Risk-taking theory

Scaling theory

*Domain theories: technology innovation, social innovation, service innovation, organizational innovation, cultural innovation, artistic innovation, and so forth.

Systems and complexity theory are embedded in and integral to both. I could continue to add supporting theories of change that amplify and accelerate the trajectory toward transformation and more meta-theories (big-picture theories) that strike me as especially relevant. There are any number of other such theories that might be added based on what you and those you are working with consider relevant and informative. I considered theories of learning, positive psychology, economic development theories, integration, complexity, leadership, communications, functionalism, conflict, resilience, knowledge, cybernetics, decision sciences, sustainability science, ecosystems, social constructivism, cultural responsiveness, and philosophy of science, to name but a few possibilities. In the end, any and all theories and knowledge frameworks are relevant to global systems transformation. The trick is to figure out within your own context and among those with whom you engage, what set of theories, knitted together, nested, networked, and/or integrated in a transformation theory will guide in a meaningful and useful way what you, and those with whom you engage, actually do. Then use that framework as a basis for strategizing, implementation, evaluation, learning, and adaptation. I'll save my own additional notions of what theories to add

for another time and place, except for one addition: Blue Marble evaluation theory.

Blue Marble Evaluation Theory

Chapter 9, on the Yin–Yang principle, discussed the roots of Blue Marble evaluation in utilization-focused, developmental, and principles-focused evaluation. The Blue Marble principles presented in this book constitute a conceptual framework for designing and evaluating global systems transformation initiatives and interventions: thinking globally and GLOCALLY, looking beyond nation-state borders and across silos, and engaging with consciousness, intentionality, and a sense of urgency, knowing that *time is of the essence*. Blue Marble evaluation theory includes facing the realities of the Anthropocene, harmonizing opposite concepts (the Yin–Yang principle), and being both *world savvy* and *evaluation savvy*. The role and function of Blue Marble evaluation in the theory of transformation is to monitor and provide feedback about the meaningfulness of, adherence to, and results of acting on each of the theories in their own niches, and their interactions and interconnections toward a whole, offering a coherent trajectory toward global systems transformation.

Transformative Evaluation for Social Justice

Donna M. Mertens, a distinguished international evaluation thought leader, has developed an approach she calls *transformative evaluation*, a framework for making methodological decisions and conducting research and evaluations that promote social justice. The "transformative paradigm" (Mertens, 2007) focuses on communities that have been pushed to the margins, such as ethnic, racial, and sexual minority group members and children and adults with disabilities. She shows how to formulate evaluation questions based on community needs, develop evaluator–community partnerships grounded in trust and respect, and how to skillfully apply quantitative, qualitative, and mixed-methods data collection strategies.

Transformative evaluation would be a natural fit and fill an important niche in a comprehensive theory of transformation.

Enlarging or Reconceptualizing a Theory of Transformation

New kinds of initiatives and new forms of intervention will be needed that can respond to the challenges of global problems, including designing and evaluating systems transformations. This chapter has asserted that transforming systems must be multifaceted, multidimensional, multisectoral, multinational, and multiplicative. Transformation flows from an understanding that the status quo is not a viable path forward and that networked action on multiple fronts using diverse change strategies across multiple landscapes will be needed to overcome the resistance from those who benefit from the status quo. Multiple interventions are needed to multiply effects, creating streams of diverse interventions flowing together to generate critical mass tipping points and mammoth change in global systems. Thus, transformation is simultaneously and interactively global and local at the same time, contextually sensitive and rooted while being globally manifest and sustainable. Tracking these new, transformational initiatives requires a complex global systems change approach to evaluation, which is what Blue Marble evaluation aspires to be.

In preparation for Chapter 15, Transforming Evaluation to Evaluate Transformation, let me revisit a core premise of this book—*that evaluation theory and practice must be further developed and adapted if, together, they are to be part of the solution rather than part of the problem.* Traditional project and

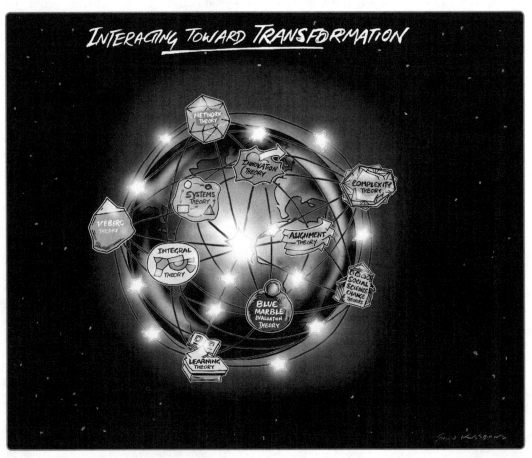

Global theories by Simon Kneebone.

program evaluation will not suffice to address systems change on a global scale. Indeed, traditional approaches to project and program evaluation can create barriers to systems change and reinforce the patterns that accelerate global instability. Innovations in evaluation include multifaceted, multidimensional, and methodologically mixed approaches, a many-splendored, diverse tapestry of knowledge-generating and learning-oriented processes that can be applied in designing and implementing meaningful, effective, and sustainable global systems transformations. To that set of evaluation challenges we now turn—with a closing reminder of the options we face—to filmmaker and humorist Woody Allen, who is not altogether joking:

> More than any other time in history, mankind faces a crossroads. One path leads to despair and utter hopelessness. The other, to total extinction. Let us pray we have the wisdom to choose correctly.

CHAPTER 14

Transformation Fidelity Principle
Evaluating Transformation

A central principle of development theory: Those development programs
that are most precisely and easily measured are the least transformational,
and those programs that are most transformational are the least measured.
—ANDREW NATSIOS (2010, p. 1), Agency Head, U.S. Agency
for International Development, 2001–2006

CONTEXT

Transformation should mean transformation, but, alas, things are not always what they are said to be. "Free" comes with hidden costs and obligations. "Guaranteed" comes with lots of fine-print exceptions. The parameters and characteristics of transformation are inherent in the word itself and its nature is conceptually clear in the dictionary definition:

1. Transformation: a thorough or dramatic change in form or appearance; the act or process of changing completely; a complete change (Google Online, 2019).

2. There is a secondary definition given by the *Merriam-Webster Dictionary* (*www. merriam-webster.com/dictionary/transformation*) that need not concern us (well, most of us), though its meaning is also dramatic, visible change: "false hair worn . . . to replace or supplement natural hair."

Chapter 4 reviewed the ascendance of calls for transformation on the world stage. Transformation conferences, reports, speeches, headlines, documentaries, research, and proposals are everywhere, multiplying like invasive species in an ecosystem without resistance. The scope, scale, and acceleration of challenges and crises of the Anthropocene are beyond piecemeal projects and Band-Aid solutions that treat system symptoms rather than change system dynamics. Evaluation's contribution now, as ever, begins with reality testing: To what extent does reality match rhetoric? In what ways, if at all, are visions being realized in the real world? How does the evidence of change align with claims about transformation? In Chapter 6, I quoted the observation by Taleb (2018, p. 12), author of *Skin in the Game,* that "It is easier to macrobullshit than to microbullshit." One job of evaluators is to detect and expose the bullshit—whether micro or macro—but there's so much, that it's hard to keep up, as it's piling deeper and higher.

Transformation Fidelity Principle Explicated

PREMISE: Transformational change, by its very definition, must be major, must be big, and therefore must be observable and/or measurable. The end of apartheid: observable. The fall of the Berlin Wall: observable. Significant reduction in new cases of HIV and AIDS: measurable. Significantly reduced smoking in a population: measurable. Huge increase in opioid deaths: measurable. Major reduction in soil erosion: observable and measurable. Transformed system reactions to sexual harassment or racial discrimination: documentable. People glued to their devices, checking for messages and news: observable.

The challenge is not evaluating transformation, not when it actually happens. True transformations are hard to miss and pretty easy to document. The challenge is bringing about transformation. That's hard. Very hard. But if it has happened, it can be observed.

Transformation Fidelity Principle

Ensure that what is called transformation constitutes transformation.

IMPLICATIONS

1. Not all programming is transformational in intent, not all Blue Marble initiatives have a transformation vision, so not all Blue Marble evaluations are transformational in focus. Most interventions aspire to make a significant difference on some problem, but few have the capacity to aspire to

transformational impact. The World Savvy global competency program described in Chapter 11, on the World Savvy principle, has a global perspective but does not have the capacity to be transformational, at least not yet, though the vision is there. The Blue Marble evaluation principles and practices in the first two parts of this book do not presume a transformational agenda. This final part assumes that agenda and applies Blue Marble evaluation principles to the challenge of evaluating transformation. However, I want to emphasize that a focus on transformation is not an essential dimension of Blue Marble evaluation.

2. Where an initiative does have a transformational vision and aspiration, the concept of transformation means it is taking on major structural and systems change. The results expected should be transformational. If you need a significance test to tell whether or not transformation change has happened, *it hasn't*. Transformation can be judged by *interocular significance*. Fred Mosteller, the great applied statistician, was fond of saying that he did not much care for statistically significant differences. He was more interested in the differences that hit us between the eyes—interocular significance (Scriven, 1993, p. 71).

3. It is important to distinguish genuine transformations from hype. Compare these examples:

- Transformation claims put forward by the Independent Evaluation Group (IEG) of the World Bank:
  - Six million Kenyans accessing electric power for the very first time.
  - More than 1.3 million poor Argentineans obtaining health coverage and services.
  - Forty million Vietnamese being lifted out of extreme poverty (2016, p. 1).
- Transformation headlines in the popular media:
  - Why brand name is essential to business transformation (Badr, 2019).
  - *Total transformation*: a garage into a living room (Payne, 2019). (This is the equivalent of wearing a wig as transformational.)
  - Grocery store finance director takes on new title of *transformation director*: "Part of the cultural change that's underway in business to celebrate hard work" (Farrell, 2019).
  - Breaking news: Transforming the customer experience by putting the customer first (Miller, 2019).

You get the point. Many claims of *transformation,* like "best-practice" claims, can be more hype than substance. Which affirms the importance of the Transformation Fidelity Principle: *Ensure that what is called transformation constitutes transformation.* Exhibit 14.1 provides some examples of transformation to reinforce the point about what the term means.

4. The fourth implication is that the Transformation Fidelity principle epitomizes evaluation's reality-testing function. As the term *transformation* has grown in popularity and attained widespread use, the first

EXHIBIT 14.1. Examples of Transformations		
System	**System before transformation**	**System after transformation**
1. Agricultural system: smallholder farmers in developing countries (see Exhibit 14.2)	a. Food insecurity b. Soil degradation c. Economic insecurity d. Lack of access to research e. Low productivity f. Gender inequity	a. Food security b. Improved soil health c. Secure livelihood d. Access to research e. Increased productivity f. Gender equity
2. Women's health and demographic transition	High child marriage and pregnancy rate; high infant death rate; large proportion of low birth weight babies.	No child marriage; low child pregnancy rate; low infant death rate; low proportion of low birth weight babies.
3. Global warming	Trajectory exceeding 1.5°C increase by 2030.	Trajectory to stay below 1.5°C increase by 2030.
4. Status of homosexual couples	Gay relations are stigmatized and pathologized; gay sex is illegal; gays are discriminated against in every aspect of life.	Gays have equal rights under the law; gay marriage is legal; gays are accepted in society.
5. Girls' education	Girls lack access to secondary school.	Girls have genuine access to and attend secondary school.

level of evaluation is bringing some degree of rigor to the very notion of transformation. Begin by simply applying a face validity criterion, meaning, *on the face of it,* just by examining the logic and merits of the proposition being made, is what is being envisioned transformational? In what sense? Here are four common examples where I find people confuse the possibility of transformation with transformation having already occurred.

a. *Signing an agreement to do something is not a transformation.* The thing to be done, *if done,* may constitute transformation. The Paris Agreement on Climate Change (2015) requires all national signatories to put forward their best efforts on climate change through nationally determined contributions and to strengthen those efforts in the years ahead. The existence of a voluntary agreement with no enforcement mechanisms and no penalties for noncompliance is business as usual, not transformation. By the way, a nation withdrawing from an agreement that it had no intention of complying with is also not transformational. It is unusual. The usual case is to stay a signatory to the agreement and do nothing to comply. Don't get me wrong. COP2015 was an important event and may play a role in turning back global warming. But the agreement itself, on the face of it, did not transform global warming, as evidenced by the subsequent reports on the accelerating trajectory of global warming.

b. *Setting goals and targets is not transformation.* The SDGs have 169 goals and 232 indicators. The global indicator framework was adopted by the United Nations General Assembly on July 6, 2017. The SDG framework may be a stimulus for global transformation. It expresses a transformational vision. But this is not a case of what gets measured gets done. It's more likely a case of what gets measured gets reported and explained away. Aspirational indicators are not, by themselves, transformational. Actually achieving aspirational targets may be. Whether such achievements are transformational is the evaluation question. The two-degree safety barrier for avoiding climate change disaster makes for a powerful rally-around target, "yet there is nothing natural or immutable about the existence of such a safety barrier, or that it should be set at two degrees. Rather, like previous green limits, this is socially and politically constructed, and has a history," and is a matter of considerable contention with the climate change community of scientists, activists, and policymakers (Leach, 2015, p. 28).

c. *Issuing reports is not transformation.* Hardly a week goes by that some major report is issued about the climate change crisis. Such data are important. When well done, scientifically credible, and evaluative, they can stimulate action. But they do not constitute action. I believe it's safe to say that reports transform nothing. A plethora of reports may actually have the unintended effect of generating report fatigue and people stop paying attention.

d. *Silver bullet narratives about transformation can oversimplify and distort.* In the book *Science That Changed Our Lives: Five Scientific Revolutions That Changed the Way We Live and Understand the World,* Martin Gellender (2017) names the following:

- Invention of the airplane and the air transport revolution.
- Breakthrough brought on by harnessing nuclear energy.
- Paradigm shift brought about by the theory of relativity that redefined the nature of time and space.
- Electricity, electronics, and digital revolutions.
- Innovations in architecture, materials, design, and construction that have

revolutionized the structural limits of what can be built.

Mobile (cell) phones are also often granted silver bullet status as a transformational revolutionary technology. These are all major breakthroughs, but each occurred within a larger dynamic context of political, economic, social, cultural, political, educational, commercial, military, international, governmental, and technological changes that were recursively and iteratively interdependent, interactive, and mutually influential. These are spider web complex human and nature transformational narratives, and not single-cause silver bullet stories. By the way, the silver bullet metaphor is derived from the legend that *only* a silver bullet could kill a werewolf, the ultimate necessary and sufficient causal model.

I'm not being cynical. The need for transformation is too great to be confused about what it entails or to water down what it means. That's why the Transformation Fidelity principle is important: Ensure that what is called transformation constitutes *transformation*.

So, then, what constitutes transformation? The answer is not hard, it's just not one thing. It's contextual, because transformation is not a standardized concept. It's a sensitizing concept, and that determines how it is evaluated.

Transformation as a Sensitizing Concept

Let me explain sensitizing concepts with a metaphor. Dark matter is a hypothetical form of matter that is thought to account for approximately 27% of the matter in the universe. Dark energy makes up approximately 68% of the universe and appears to be associated with the vacuum in space. Dark matter does not absorb, reflect,

or emit light, making it extremely hard to spot. Astronomers have inferred the existence of dark matter from observations of the gravitational effect it seems to have on visible matter. "Dark matter seems to outweigh visible matter roughly six to one. . . . The matter we know and that makes up all stars and galaxies only accounts for 5% of the content of the universe!" (CERN, 2019).

Dark matter is thought to be a nonluminous material postulated to consist of some as yet undiscovered subatomic particles that could take any of several forms, including weakly interacting particles (*cold dark matter*) or high-energy randomly moving particles created soon after the Big Bang (*hot dark matter*). The primary evidence for dark matter is that calculations show that many galaxies would fly apart instead of rotating, or would not have formed or move as they do, if they did not contain a large amount of unseen matter. Dark matter, dark energy, and black holes—all unseeable, known yet unknown (Davis, 2015; Fletcher, 2019). Dark matter is a *sensitizing concept*, a way of talking about something that is not yet well understood, precisely defined, or operationally measured.

Sociologist Herbert Blumer (1954) is credited with originating the idea of a "sensitizing concept" to orient fieldwork. Sensitizing concepts include notions like victim, stress, stigma, and learning organizations to provide some initial direction to a study as one looks into how the concept is given meaning in a particular place or set of circumstances (Schwandt, 2001). The observer moves between the sensitizing concept and the real world of social experience, giving shape and substance to the concept and elaborating the conceptual framework with varied manifestations of the concept. Such an approach recognizes that while the specific manifestations of social phenomena vary by time, space, and circumstance, the sensitizing concept is a container for capturing, holding, and examining these manifestations to better understand patterns and implications.

Evaluators commonly use sensitizing concepts to inform their understanding of situations and context-specific outcomes. Consider the very notion of *context*. Any particular evaluation is designed within some *context* and we are admonished to take context into account, be sensitive to context, and watch out for changes in context. But what is context? Systems thinkers posit that system boundaries are inherently arbitrary, so defining what is within the immediate scope of an evaluation versus what is within its surrounding context will inevitably be arbitrary, but the distinction is still useful. Indeed, being intentional about deciding what is in the immediate realm of action of an evaluation and what is in the enveloping context can be an illuminating exercise—and different stakeholders might well provide different perspectives. In that sense, the idea of context is a sensitizing concept. Those seeking an operational definition of *context* will be frustrated by the ambiguity, vagueness, and diverse meanings of the term. Yet, attention to context as a sensitizing concept is paramount for Blue Marble bricoleurs.

Understanding Transformation as a Sensitizing Concept

A sensitizing concept raises consciousness about something and alerts us to watch out for it within a specific context. That's what the concept of transformation does. It says that things are happening to people and changes are taking place through initiatives that aspire to bring about major, rapid systems change. Find out what people mean by "transformation." Pay attention to various meanings offered. Help the people in the situation pay attention to what's going on and determine whether what is happening meets criteria, even their own criteria, for "transformation."

Don't judge the maturity and utility of the concept by whether it has "achieved" a standardized and universally accepted operational definition. Judge it instead by its utility in sensitizing us to contextual meaningfulness and utility. This means that specific evaluations of transformation will generate their own operational definitions as appropriate. Over time, many empirical studies may use the same or similar definitions. Periodically, syntheses and comparisons will be undertaken. We can learn a great deal from how different initiatives define transformation, whether operationally (deductively and quantitatively), nominally (as a sensitizing concept), or inductively (exploring emergent meanings and manifestations). Blue Marble evaluators will track, share, and interpret these various approaches to transformation and their implications for evaluation. Over time, an *options by context framework* can be constructed to portray the variations in meanings, processes, and results. Blue Marble evaluation uses the principles as the basis for generating transformation options by context, as I illustrate below.

I start with observations about dark matter and dark energy. Let me conclude with this observation about concepts from 1946 Nobel Prize–winning physicist Percy Bridgman, who wrote extensively about the philosophy of science and the scientific method.

We have here no esoteric theory of the ultimate nature of concepts, nor a philosophical championing of the primacy of the "operation." We have merely a pragmatic matter, namely that we have observed after much experience that . . . what we always find when we push our analysis to the limit; operations are not ultimately sharp or irreducible any more than any other sort of creature. We always run into a haze eventually, and all our concepts are describable only in spiraling approximation. (quoted in Waller, 2004, p. 106)

Blue Marble Evaluation and Transformation: Taking Transformation Seriously

In discussing implications of the Transformation Fidelity principle above, I noted that a focus on transformation is not an essential dimension of Blue Marble evaluation. Not every Blue Marble initiative will have a transformational vision. With that reminder, let's continue with evaluating transformation when that is the vision and aspiration.

THE COMMUNITY COLLEGE TRANSFORMATIVE CHANGE INITIATIVE

Started in 2012, the Transformative Change Initiative (TCI) is dedicated to assisting community colleges to scale-up innovation in the form of guided pathways, programs of study, and evidence-based strategies to improve student outcomes and program, organization, and system performance.

Transformative change refers to implementing, sustaining, and scaling change that produces unprecedented results without sacrificing the historic commitment of community colleges to access, opportunity, and equitable outcomes.

Community colleges that engage in TCI are committed to innovations that are as effective for underserved learners as they are for student groups that have traditionally enrolled in college. Pushing performance to new levels is not just an axiom for TCI, it is TCI's fundamental mission. (Bragg et al., 2014, p. 1; original emphasis)

The transformations envisioned include transformational leadership in community colleges, technological innovations, changes in teaching practices and relationships between students and teachers, transformed curricula, and other contextually specific transformations chosen by a particular community college. I am convinced that I could spend a day observing classrooms; interviewing teachers, students, and administrators; reviewing documents; and examining records—and I would know, as you would, whether transformation had occurred. It's not that hard. The TCI has an evaluation process and that evaluation reporting finds some hot spots of innovation. There's a TCI network advocating transformation, a community of practice, and a book entitled *13 Ideas That Are Transforming the Community College World* (O'Banion, 2019). There are examples of specific colleges and programs within colleges engaging in transformational initiatives with some success. But I'm prepared to go out on a limb and assure you that the community college *system* has not been *transformed* in any U.S. state, much less the entire United States.

From Transformation to Transformational Engagement

I have positioned transformation as a sensitizing concept. It can't be operationally defined and measured in a standardized way applicable to any context. Rather, it is a concept that has to be given meaning and specificity within the context where transformation is targeted.

I also asserted in opening this chapter that transformation is not hard to evaluate—if it has actually happened. Nor is it hard to evaluate if it has not happened. But it is hard to achieve transformation of systems. It is largely impossible to attribute causality, though contribution pathways can be identified. But here is the bigger evaluation challenge and the question we have to address as evaluation's contribution to transformation: Is an initiative, or more likely a set of initiatives and interventions, *on a trajectory toward transformation*? That's a much harder question to answer than whether transformation has occurred. Asking the trajectory question changes the evaluation criterion from transformation having occurred (or not) to *transformational engagement*. That is the reframing formulated by the influential IEG of the World Bank. Assessing the trajectory toward transformation is what most funders, decision makers, and implementers of initiatives are looking for from evaluation.

What Is a Transformational Engagement?

Transformational engagement is an intervention or a series of interventions that helps achieve deep, systemic, and sustainable change with large-scale impact in an area of a major development challenge. These engagements help clients remove critical constraints to development; cause or support fundamental change in a system; have large-scale national or global impact; and are economically, financially, and environmentally sustainable. (IEG, 2016, p. 1)

The transformational engagement criteria suggest a corollary to the Transformation Fidelity principle.

> **Corollary to the Transformation Fidelity Principle**
>
> *Evaluate whether and how what is called transformational engagement constitutes a trajectory toward transformation.*

Exhibit 14.2 presents the four IEG dimensions defining transformatonal engagements.

Lessons for Transformational Engagement

The IEG evaluated a sample of 20 transformational engagements varying in form, size, the development challenges they address, sector, and region, as well as country context. In addition, the IEG reviewed a purposeful and selective sample of country-level engagements. Their comparative and synthesis analysis concluded with five key takeaways:

EXHIBIT 14.2. The Four Dimensions Defining Transformational Engagements

Dimension	Description	Criteria
Relevance	Addresses a major developmental challenge such as poverty, equity, or climate change.	The constraint or problem addressed is of critical importance to development.
Depth of change	Causes or supports fundamental change in a system or market; addresses a root cause; supports a change in trajectory.	Market change, systemic change, or behavioral change.
Scale of change	Causes large-scale impact at a national or global level.	Scale-up of approaches and innovations in the replication; catalytic effects; demonstration effects; positive spillovers and externalities; acceleration or discontinuity in a development indicator.
Sustainability	Impact is economically, financially, and environmentally sustainable in the long term.	Financial, economic, and environmental sustainability of results after engagement ends.

Source: Independent Evaluation Group (2017, p. 2).

1. Identify the most binding constraints to development in a country, sector, or area by consistently implementing rigorous diagnostic work.

2. Enhance the selectivity of assistance programs.

3. Build on mechanisms of transformation in program and project design. This includes shaping incentives to effect sustained behavioral change and strengthening institutions to support transformational impact.

4. Form broad coalitions through early and wide-ranging interactions with stakeholders. For example, targeted beneficiaries can be involved in an intervention's design and implementation. An increased focus on transformation will also involve exploring new partnerships and managing them effectively and efficiently to ensure interests align.

5. Stay the course by undertaking more selective, longer-term, sustained, and programmatic engagements. This involves engaging in fewer, but more focused and long-term engagements. (IEG, 2017; see also Heider, 2016; IEG, 2016)

The Utilization-Focused Approach to Evaluating Transformation

Utilization-focused evaluation focuses on intended use by intended users. That means the evaluator identifies and works with primary intended users to frame evaluation questions, select appropriate methods, interpret findings, and support use (Patton, 2008, 2012). I reiterate this at this point because the frameworks reviewed here are illustrations of what can be and might be, but are not meant to be off-the-shelf, ready-to-use, standardized, context-free resources. They are meant to suggest a direction an evaluator might take in working with primary intended users. The same is true for the theory of transformation. I'm not positing its universality. I'm offering it as a framework to stimulate and guide contextual adaptation.

Evaluation Criteria for Transformational Engagement

I've had occasion to work with groups engaged in transformation initiatives. Exhibit 14.3 offers additional criteria for evaluating transformational engagement that came from those groups. The exhibit includes examples of shorter-term and longer-term evidence of progress and sample rubrics for rendering judgments about progress. Exhibit 14.3 could be used by a Blue Marble evaluation team as a starting point in working with primary intended users to generate their own criteria, milestones toward transformation, and rubrics for judging how well the transformational process is unfolding along the way.

Evaluating Transformation with the Theory of Transformation

Let me review the transformation principles we're working with so far.

Blue Marble Evaluation Questions about Transformation

Overarching Transformative Engagement Principle

Engage and evaluate consistent with the magnitude, direction, and speed of transformations needed and envisioned.

Theory of Transformation Principle

Design and evaluate transformation based on an evidence-supported theory of transformation.

Transformation Fidelity Principle

Ensure that what is called transformation constitutes transformation.

Corollary to the Transformation Fidelity Principle

Evaluate whether and how what is called transformational engagement constitutes a trajectory toward transformation.

EXHIBIT 14.3. Ten Illustrative Criteria for Evaluating Transformational Engagement with Rubrics

Criteria for transformational engagement	Current situation	Demonstrated short-term actual results on a trajectory toward potential transformation	Sustainable long-term transformation vision	Evaluation rubric 4-point scales (specific meanings of points on the scales defined in context)
1. Alignment among pathways of change.	Institutions, policies, markets, technologies, education, capacity building, behavior change, and other pathways of change are treated in isolation from one another. Some or many pathways not engaged at all.	Engaging in change across several pathways; coordinated engagement.	High degree of alignment among all relevant pathways and trajectories in ways that collectively support transformation.	Strength of alignment (specifics defined in context): 1. Little or no alignment. 2. Weak alignment. 3. Moderately effective alignment among several pathways but not all. 4. Excellent, high-quality alignment.
2. Capacity for transformational engagement.	People within a particular social-ecological system are relatively uninformed about climate change, its potential effects within their context, low carbon economic options, and practices within their context that support adaptability.	Capacity-building engagement increases peoples' understanding of climate change effects and how to organize, engage, collaborate, and adapt to generate and support a healthier system for all.	Demonstrated capacity among people to adapt and sustain a healthy human system and subsystems in the face of climate change trends, and other shocks to the system.	Capacity (defined in context): 1. Low across the board. 2. Spotty, some capacity, but only among a few. 3. Moderate capacity, improving. 4. High and broad capacity for transformational engagement.
3. Positively interlocking systems.	Systems (e.g., water, energy, agriculture, soils, and market system) are siloed, interconnections and interdependencies ignored or inadequately managed.	Systems changes are becoming explicitly interconnected, interdependent, and mutually reinforcing.	Tightly interlocked and overlapping systems in which the healthy functioning of each system or subsystem positively aligns with and supports the healthy functioning of other systems or subsystems.	Systems (details defined in context): 1. Autonomous, siloed systems. 2. Some positive interconnections. 3. Many positive interconnections. 4. Highly positive interconnections across systems.

(continued)

EXHIBIT 14.3. *(continued)*

Criteria for transformational engagement	Current situation	Demonstrated short-term actual results on a trajectory toward potential transformation	Sustainable long-term transformation vision	Evaluation rubric 4-point scales (specific meanings of points on the scales defined in context)
4. Integrated levels of change (micro, meso, and macro); local to global interactions.	Local, community, regional, national, and global systems viewed and engaged with separately. No attention to cross-level scaling.	Multiple levels of change being undertaken in ways that are mutually reinforcing and have cumulative and broadening impact *at scale*.	Multiple levels of transformation are interconnected and mutually reinforcing, maintaining scaled impact.	Levels of engagement and impact: 1. No working across levels. 2. Modest cross-level interactions. 3. Significant cross-level interactions. 4. High-quality interconnections across levels.
5. Depth, strength, and breadth of change.	Change efforts characterized by bounded projects; history of incremental, small-scale changes; relatively small number of targeted beneficiaries benefit.	Scope and scale expanded from projects to broad multisector initiatives that impact a significantly larger number of people and/or territory.	Tipping points reached so that the transformation encompasses and benefits most people.	Results rubric: 1. No or narrow project outcomes achieved. 2. Multiple interdependent project outcomes achieved. 3. Some system impacts. 4. System transformed.
6. Speed.	Lack of a sense of urgency; lack of attention to accelerating climate change effects.	Strategic, collaborative community and institutional engagement organized to act expeditiously with timeline targets to propel action and results quickly.	Real-time adaptive action is embedded in governance, financial, institutional, and community-based collective action initiatives.	Speed levels (defined in context): 1. Slow pace. 2. Moderate pace. 3. Strong momentum. 4. Rapid changes.

7. Significant positive effects on people's lives and well-being.	Climate change threatens the well-being of people living in (a) threatened and/or deteriorating ecosystems, and (b) environmentally destructive human systems.	People's lives improving or deleterious effects prevented so that things do not get worse.	People are better off long term, and/or worsening effects are reversed.	Effects on people (defined in context): 1. No or few positive effects on people's lives. 2. Some effects. 3. Significant effects. 4. Transformative effects.
8. Aware of and adapting to larger societal and global forces.	Larger societal and global forces are ignored, misunderstood, or underanalyzed.	Climate change-related initiatives are strategized to build momentum by connecting to larger societal, ecological, and/or global trends.	Highly developed sensing systems for ongoing monitoring of larger and broader trends to strategically adapt, connect, or protect as appropriate.	Global awareness and thinking (defined in context): 1. Provincial and insular in perspective. 2. Some global tracking, little adaptation. 3. Major global tracking, significant responsiveness. 4. Embedded, ongoing, high-quality global tracking and adaptation.
9. Quality of intentionality.	Poor planning mechanisms; low or no engaging people in systematic change together; passive, reactive (if active at all).	Planning undertaken with attention to the dimensions of transformational change and engaging people to participate in change.	High capacity for ongoing planning, responsiveness, adaptation, and engagement across all dimensions of transformational change.	Intentionality (defined in context): 1. Low-quality planning and engagement. 2. Moderate quality. 3. High quality. 4. Ongoing, systematic, highly intentional and adaptive intentionality.
10. Ecosystem resilience.	Ecosystem threatened or deteriorating due to climate change.	Immediate threats being mitigated and/or adaptations reversing deterioration.	Healthy, resilient ecosystem with ongoing adaptive capacity.	Resilience (defined in context): 1. No to low resilience. 2. Moderate resilience. 3. High resilience. 4. Transformative resilience.

Based on the overarching and operating principles above, Blue Marble evaluation asks three interrelated questions:

1. To what extent and in what ways is a transformative initiative conceptualized as truly transformative?

2. To what extent are engagement and implementation processes consistent with transformational change?

3. To what extent and in what ways is systems transformation occurring and, if so, to what extent and in what ways has the intervention contributed to documented transformation?

The first question involves specifying the theory of transformation and assessing its likely adequacy for contributing to systems transformation results. The second question is a "walking the talk" question: Is what was conceptualized actually done? To what extent are the principles for global systems transformation and a particular theory of transformation followed in practice? The third question is the results question: What systems transformations can be documented, and what was the contribution of the intervention or initiative to any observed changes?

While these are classic evaluation questions, asking and answering them about global systems transformation initiatives is quite different from traditional project or program evaluation. As I've said throughout this book, systems transformation is different from program outcomes. How different? Different in the degree of change, the nature of change, the pace of change, the direction of change, the scale of change, the interconnectedness of change, the magnitude of change, and the implications for sustainability and transformed systems resilience. Exhibit 14.4 takes the Blue Marble principles already presented in this book, the theory of transformation elements, and a few additions, and converts them into principles and evaluation criteria.

The IEG four-dimensions framework (relevance, depth of change, scale of change, and sustainability) represents a *criteria-based approach to evaluating transformation*. The same is true of the more elaborate set of criteria generated from practitioners, evaluators, and the literature in Exhibit 14.4. These different sets of criteria are derived from the definition of transformation being used, which is appropriate—thus, they are definition based and not theory based. That is not a criticism, but an observation. What I want to offer now is an evaluation inquiry framework based on the theory of transformation. The purpose of developing the theory of transformation (see Chapter 13) was to get to the point where we are now: *using the theory of transformation to evaluate transformation*.

Evaluating Capacity to Collaborate across Networks

The theory of transformation hypothesizes networks collaborating together toward a shared vision with common values as a mechanism for global systems change. The theory of transformation in the previous chapter discussed the centrality of synergies among networks. The Center for International Private Enterprise (CIPE) has developed a Capacity to Collaborate Tool built around "the five C's." These five core capabilities are (1) commit and act, (2) relate and attract, (3) balance diversity and coherence, (4) create results, and (5) adapt and self-renew. Each is necessary but none is sufficient by itself. Without strengths in all five capabilities, organizations risk getting stuck in a situation of "low commitment, low capacity, low performance" (Baser & Morgan, 2008, p. 28).

The Capacity to Collaborate Tool draws upon 14 functional areas of collaboration, eight stages of collaboration maturity, and the five C's, and outlines 10 dimensions of coalition capacity built around three basic collective action steps: establishing a coalition, building support, and making the

EXHIBIT 14.4. Blue Marble Transformational Sustainability Design Principles and Evaluation Criteria

Design principles aimed at sustainable transformation	Commentary and explanation	Blue Marble evaluation criteria
1. **Transformational Sustainability principle**: *Design and implement interventions for adaptive resilience.*	Design for sustainability that is adaptive and resilient in complex, dynamic systems, and developmental in formulation and evaluation.	E1. *Resilient sustainability criterion:* Within the context of the evaluation, define and assess sustainability over time focused on capacity for adaptive resilience.
2. **Cross-Sector principle:** *Integrate and coordinate interventions across sectors and traditional program areas (cutting across silos).*	Transformational interventions work across sector divisions and program specializations.	E2. *Cross-silos criterion:* Assess the extent to which the initiative addresses multiple interrelated factors (across silos) and diverse interconnected outcomes.
3. **Global–Local Dynamic Interconnection principle:** *Connect global and local perspectives, knowledge, and understandings in support of change.*	Global systems change must be contextually sensitive and grounded in the interactions between local and global processes and scales of change. The term that captures this is **GLOCAL.**	E3. *Multilevel connectivity criterion:* Assess global–local interactions and interconnections. This likely will involve documenting contextual variations locally within a global perspective. See *Demonstrating Outcomes and Impact across Different Scales* (Hall, 2017).
4. **Systems Thinking principle:** *Apply systems thinking in formulating and implementing transformational engagements.*	Design interventions with attention to interrelationships, perspectives, boundaries, and dynamics.	E4. *Systems criterion:* Systematically monitor and evaluate interrelationships, perspectives, boundaries, and dynamics.
5. **Complexity Theory principle:** *Apply complexity understandings to design and implementation of transformational engagements.*	Design interventions with sensitivity to nonlinearities, emergence, uncertainties, turbulence, and adaptive capacity.	E5. *Complexity criterion:* Apply complexity theory in all aspects of the evaluation. Document responses to and effects of nonlinearities, emergence, uncertainties, turbulence, and adaptive capacity.

(continued)

EXHIBIT 14.4. *(continued)*		
Design principles aimed at sustainable transformation	**Commentary and explanation**	**Blue Marble evaluation criteria**
6. *Iceberg Framework principle:* *Design and implement transformational initiatives with attention to both formal and informal relationships, cutting across social, political, economic, and environmental arenas of action.*	Formal relationships include, for example, treaties, contracts, public commitments, structured collaborations, formal alliances, and explicit financial arrangements. Informal relationships include network interactions, working groups, behind-the-scenes conversations, verbal understandings, shared interests, and informal cooperative endeavors.	E6. *Iceberg criterion:* Document the extent to which, and how, formal and informal structures and processes are targets of change, and the interactions and interconnections between the formal and the informal. Examine underlying structures and processes that inform the visible and nonvisible. Make the invisible visible.
7. *Contextual Adaptation principle:* *Direct change at both standardized global outcomes (SDGs) and contextual variations in desired and important impacts.*	Quantitative indicators are standardized across the world and within sectors. Contextual variation analysis delves into uncommon and unique dimensions of change and portrays the nuanced dynamics of situational variation.	E7. *Bricolage eclectic methods and measures criterion:* Capture both standardized patterns and contextual variations of transformation, both quantitative and qualitative data.
8. *Innovation Theory principle:* *Facilitate creative and innovative opportunities among diverse people with diverse expertise and perspectives.*	Innovation drives transformation; multiple mutually reinforcing innovations lead to transformation (not silver bullets).	E8. *Innovation criterion:* Document, interpret, and extract lessons from innovation efforts. Use developmental evaluation to support innovation.
9. *Network Theory principle:* *Build and nurture networks of transformative engagement.*	The Hage hypothesis guides transformation: Successful evolution and institutional transformation require increased diversity in innovative technologies and skill sets that are integrated into strongly connected and systemically coordinated networks. Network theory is one theory in the nested theory of transformation.	E9. *Theory of transformation criterion:* Test the Hage hypothesis and dimensions of the theory of transformation in context. Put muscle and flesh on the bones of the Hage hypothesis with documented details of network interactions aimed at transformational engagement.

change. The results are calculated interactively based on the self-ratings of coalition members and their confidence in the scores they give themselves. An external facilitator guides the process.

> To pilot the tool, we took on the facilitator role ourselves. In Albania, where CIPE worked with a coalition of 11 reform-minded business support organizations (the National Business Forum) to develop a common platform for economic reform through public–private participation, the implementation of the tool sparked a vivid discussion on [the] coalition's sustainability. In Armenia, we employed the tool with the Business Advocacy Network, a coalition of 18 organizations that advocates on behalf of 3,000 Armenian companies. As a result, the Network identified three priority areas for internal capacity building, which later formed the basis of a strategic plan. In both pilot cases, we were able to assist CIPE's partners in developing comprehensive roadmaps for successful coalitions while preserving local ownership, fostering sustainable democratic participation and impact. (Hrvolova & Jedwab, 2019)

Another collaboration framework that is useful for Blue Marble evaluators focuses on entry points for enhancing the quality of collaboration across networks and communities of practice (Woodland & Hutton, 2012). They found that an increased quantity of collaboration can get in the way of quality.

Working Pragmatically with Primary Intended Users in Support of Transformational Engagement

Jonathan Tepperman (2016) spent several years traveling the world looking for success stories, people, and initiatives overcoming major obstacles under difficult conditions but ultimately achieving success in changing systems. He called his published collection of "good news stories" *The Fix* and concludes that the characteristic shared by all the change makers he encountered was pragmatism: "the dogged refusal to let party, tribe, philosophy, or custom stand in the way of the search for solutions. . . . [Pragmatism] offers the single best explanation for their outsize accomplishments" (p. 220). Exhibit 14.5 offers questions to address in designing and evaluating transformational engagement initiatives. It should be applied with pragmatism and not dogmatism. It is a menu of options, not a mandatory checklist that must be followed strictly item by item. These are principles, not rules or recipes. Nor is there one right way to go about engaging primary intended users in evaluating transformation. That's why this chapter offers a variety of tools.

Narrative Dimensions of Transformative Change

The very language of transformation and transformational engagement implies a story. There's a beginning point (the baseline, the status quo system, the situation that is the target of change) and then the action begins (intervention designed, initiative formed). Implementation and adaptation unfold, things emerge—forward movement, setbacks, plot twists—and then some temporary ending point where transformation has occurred, or not occurred, or the trajectory is identifiable. Evaluating transformation must involve capturing the story, communicating the process and results, interpreting meanings, making values-based judgments about what occurred, extracting lessons, and facilitating visioning the way forward both short term and long term. Telling the transformation story will involve mixed methods. The World Bank and Climate Investment Funds (CIF) synthesis reports on transformation involve presenting case study data and identifying cross-cutting themes and lessons. That requires knowledge and skill in collecting and analyzing qualitative data (Patton, 2015). Exhibit 14.6 provides a suggestive framework for reporting a transformation narrative.

EXHIBIT 14.5. Sample Questions to Address in Designing and Evaluating Transformational Engagement Initiatives

1. What is to be transformed?

2. What is the nature of the system to be changed?

3. What is the nature of the change sought?

4. How does transformation occur?

5. What action arenas and processes support complex dynamic transformational change?

6. How and when are diverse change strategies employed and made mutually reinforcing?

7. How does the group learn, adapt, and become more effective in moving toward the vision of transformation?

8. How is innovation generated?

9. What are the levels, scope, and types of transformative engagement?

10. What observations does the evaluator make systematically?

11. How are problems solved?

12. How are diverse arenas of action, multiple subnetworks, and different degrees of engagement by key stakeholders coordinated and integrated?

13. How can these distinct elements of theories of change be integrated?

14. What barriers must be overcome?

15. How can evaluation support transformation?

Evaluation bus by Simon Kneebone. Used with permission of the copyright holder, the Australian Evaluation Society (*aes.asn.au*).

EXHIBIT 14.6. Elements of a Transformation Narrative

Factors to monitor and address in order to elucidate and *tell the story* of the nature, scope, and momentum of transformational change intervention and initiatives:

1. Actual speed and pace of change, starts and stops, acceleration periods and lulls: speed of change dynamics.

2. Catalytic effects on other changes.

3. Momentum among diverse arenas of change.

4. Direction of change.

5. Challenges faced, barriers overcome (or not), degrees and nature of resistance.

6. Winners and losers.

7. Durability (degree of irreversibility).

8. Cumulative change, ongoing dynamics.

9. Nature and implications of financial instruments/investments.

10. Situation analysis.

11. Larger societal and global trends, events, and patterns.

12. Contextual factors.

13. Knowledge contributions.

14. Learnings.

15. Partners, collective impact.

16. Appropriate monitoring and evaluation processes.

Note. This is a suggestive and evocative list, neither exhaustive nor is every element required.

Transforming Evaluation to Evaluation Transformation

The question this chapter has addressed is how to evaluate global systems transformation. The conclusion that emerges for the Blue Marble evaluation team from contemplating how to evaluate transformation is *that evaluation must be transformed if it is to be part of the solution rather than part of the problem*. The next and final chapter takes up transforming evaluation to evaluate transformation.

CHAPTER 15

Transformational Alignment Principle
Transforming Evaluation to Evaluate Transformation

> We are the first generation to know we are destroying our planet and the last one that can do anything about it.
> —WORLD WILDLIFE FUND (November 2018)

CONTEXT

Blue Marble evaluation begins with the iconic image of Earth from space, one planet, one humanity. That image of wholeness and ideal of unity invites us to think globally. When we do so, we immediately encounter the realities of the Anthropocene epoch in which humans are using Earth's resources at levels and scales that are changing Earth's systems, and, in so doing, warming, polluting, and degrading the environment at a level that threatens the future survival of humanity. Along the way, humanity has become divided politically, economically, socially, and culturally. Critically examining how we got into this situation, evaluation emerges as part of the problem, too often focusing only on projects and programs that function within larger systems—but examining those larger system connections and implications would be outside the "scope" of the evaluator's terms of reference. This would manifest in inadequate, ineffective, and ultimately damaging ways of judging what matters and what works by ignoring critical systems issues. New initiatives and large-scale interventions are underway and more are emerging aimed at transforming global systems to make them more equitable and sustainable. This provides new opportunities for Blue Marble evaluators to contribute to those transformational processes and trajectories.

Chapter 3 reviewed the emergence of and need for *transformation* as the clarion call on the global stage of the Anthropocene. That led in Chapter 13 to conceptualizing what transformation means and offering the beginning of a theory of transformation to guide both transformational initiatives and evaluation of those initiatives. Chapter 14 offered ways of evaluating transformation. Each of those chapters was framed around a Blue Marble principle. Here they are together.

Overarching Transformative Engagement Principle

Engage and evaluate consistent with the magnitude, direction, and speed of transformations needed and envisioned.

Transformational Alignment Principle Explicated

PREMISE: Current evaluation practices, adequate for program and project evaluation, are inadequate for evaluating transformation. For evaluation to contribute to transformational engagements and become part of the solution rather than part of the problem, evaluation must be transformed in alignment with the thrust and trajectory of systems transformations globally. Alignment provides coherence. Picciotto (2005) has eloquently advocated evaluating the policy coherence of development aid by ascertaining "the impact of rich countries' policies on the economic and social prospects of poor countries" . . . and examining "the combined impact of aid and non-aid policies on poor countries" (p. 311). Likewise, we need to evaluate the coherence of evaluation practices, approaches, models, and methods for evaluating transformation. Blue Marble principles provide guidance for that alignment, coherence, and transformation.

IMPLICATIONS

Applying the Transformational Alignment principle to evaluation means ensuring that what is called transformation constitutes transformation, and that what aspires to movement along a trajectory toward transformational engagement is on such a trajectory. This means applying the Transformation Fidelity principle—ensuring that what is called transformation constitutes transformation—not just to initiatives but to evaluation itself. Here, then, based on the Blue Marble principles, is my vision and agenda for transforming evaluation to evaluate transformational engagements results.

Transforming Evaluation Vision and Agenda

1. Move from a project mindset to global (Blue Marble) thinking.
2. Treat global systems, even the whole Earth, as the evaluand.
3. Treat all evaluations at whatever level as open systems affected by global trends.
4. Connect the global and the local.
5. Integrate design, engagement, implementation, and evaluation.
6. Engage across silos, sectors, and issues.
7. Examine the interactions among SDGs.
8. Aggregate and disaggregate data beyond nation-state averages to highlight and better understand variations within and across countries.
9. Move from theory of change to theory of transformation for developing and evaluating transformations.
10. Advocate for conceptual fidelity: Ensure that what is called global is in fact global; ensure that what is called transformational actually constitutes transformation.
11. Move from an external, independent stance to a skin in the game stance.
12. Design and implement evaluation as a transformative intervention—contributing to transformation.
13. Move beyond ending evaluations at the

end of projects and programs; instead, encourage support for follow-up evaluations that address resilient sustainability (not just rigid continuity of what has already been accomplished).

14. Connect evaluators through transformational evaluation networks.

15. Move beyond evaluator competence to being *world savvy* through ongoing learning.

16. Make contributions to equity and global sustainability universal criteria in evaluations.

17. Make the complex challenges of the Anthropocene the context for and narrative of evaluation.

18. Adopt and adapt new technologies to serve Blue Marble evaluations.

19. Engage and evaluate with a sense of urgency, knowing that time is of the essence.

20. Connect the ecological and human domains as the essence of Blue Marble Evaluation, knowing that the planet's capacity to support humanity and therefore the future of humanity are at stake.

Exhibit 15.1 systematically lists each transformation and the principle that informs that transformation.

From Here to There: Evaluation's Trajectory

Calls for global systems transformation arise from the realities of the Anthropocene. What is the parallel analysis that leads to a call for transforming evaluation? Let me review and summarize the arguments made throughout this book.

The profession of evaluation is roughly 50 years old, give or take the arguments about when it began, maturing at the same time as the "great acceleration" of the Anthropocene. Over those five decades, evalu-

ators have become very good at program and project evaluation, specifying SMART (specific, measurable, achievable, relevant, time-bound) goals, and developing performance indicators. We've become skilled at developing logic models and theories of change. We know the importance of distinguishing monitoring from evaluation and how to do so. We have identified many different types of evaluations, diverse uses of evaluation (accountability, learning, decision making, enlightenment, etc.), and how to work with diverse stakeholders. We have standards for what constitutes evaluation quality and checklists for what should be included in an evaluation. We have a variety of ways of reporting findings and facilitating evaluation use. We have worked across disciplines and blended theory with practice. We have become good at creating networks across the globe and engaging in high-quality collaborations. This is by no means a comprehensive or exhaustive list, but hopefully, it provides a sense that we've learned a lot, know how to do a lot, and merit the designation of being a knowledge-based profession and transdiscipline, an umbrella discipline like philosophy and statistics that is essential and foundational for all other disciplines (Scriven, 2008).

We've largely moved beyond the qualitative–quantitative paradigm debate and come to value mixed methods. But evaluation reports remain largely siloed, with separate qualitative and quantitative sections, rather than integrating methods to provide triangulated data on common core questions. The evaluation profession has recognized the importance of being competent at more than methods, even though methods remain the focus of most training. We're still figuring out how to provide training for other professional competencies like interpersonal skills, reflective practice, project management, adherence to standards and guiding principles, and building capacity for cultural competence and responsiveness.

EXHIBIT 15.1. Transformations Linked to Blue Marble Principles

Issue	Current dominant evaluation practice	Transforming evaluation to evaluate transformation	Relevant Blue Marble evaluation principle
1. Mindset	Program mentality, program boundaries make a closed system; program as the evaluand; control mindset.	Global systems thinking, understanding complex dynamic environments, open systems, unpredictable, turbulent, no one in control.	***Global Thinking principle:*** *Apply whole-Earth, big-picture thinking to all aspects of systems change.*
2. What is evaluated?	The evaluand (thing evaluated) is a project, program, or policy.	Treat global systems, even the whole Earth, as the evaluand.	***Global Thinking principle:*** *Apply whole-Earth, big-picture thinking to all aspects of systems change.*
3. Magnitude of change	Program and project outcomes and impacts.	Transformed systems.	***Transformative Engagement principle:*** *Engage and evaluate consistent with the magnitude, direction, and speed of transformations needed and envisioned.*
4. Scale	Focusing often at one scale.	Multiscalar.	***Transboundary Engagement principle:*** *Act at a global scale.*
5. Focus	Local or national or international: one arena of action.	Local–global interactions: interconnections and interdependencies; two-way flows of influence.	***GLOCAL principle:*** *Integrate complex interconnections across levels.*
6. Scope	Programs and evaluations operate in mission silos; SDGs siloed.	Problems and issues conceptualized and engaged across sectors, issues, and SDGs.	***Cross-Silos principle:*** *Engage across sectors and issues for systems change.*
7. Time frame	Monitoring done during program and evaluation completed at the end of the program. Sustainability means continuity of processes and outcomes achieved.	Ongoing, timely, developmental evaluation during transformational engagement. Follow up to emphasize, support, and evaluate long-term, adaptive capacity for resilient sustainability.	***Time Being of the Essence principle:*** *Act with a sense of urgency in the present, support adaptive sustainability long term, grounding both in understanding the past.*

(continued)

EXHIBIT 15.1. *(continued)*			
Issue	**Current dominant evaluation practice**	**Transforming evaluation to evaluate transformation**	**Relevant Blue Marble evaluation principle**
8. Evaluation criteria	Evaluating program* effectiveness: merit, worth, and significance of goal attainment.	Contributing to equity and resilient sustainability of transformational engagements in the Anthropocene epoch.	***Anthropocene as Context principle***: *Know and face the realities of the Anthropocene and act accordingly.*
9. Knowledge paradigm	Human and ecological systems are separate domains of knowledge, action, and evaluation; disciplinary autonomy and specialization rule.	Integrate human and ecological systems; interdisciplinary engagement across social and natural sciences, across humanities and arts, across thinking and doing, across knowledge and action, knowing and applying.	***Yin–Yang principle***: *Harmonize conceptual opposites.*
10. Evaluator competence and credibility	General evaluator competency standards; professional practice, methods, context, planning and management, interpersonal skills, and cultural competence.	Being world savvy through global thinking, world systems knowledge, cultural sensitivity, and bringing Blue Marble principles and practices to bear in accordance with general evaluation principles, competencies, and standards. Ongoing learning in aspiring for excellence.	***World Savvy principle***: *Engage in ongoing learning relevant to Blue Marble principles and practices.*
11. Methods	Methodological hierarchies establishing gold-standard and best-practice preferences; evaluator disciplinary training determines methods used; qualitative and quantitative silos.	Blue Marble evaluation teams bring together evaluators with diverse methodological capabilities to design evaluations appropriate to the nature of the transformational initiative or intervention. All options are on the design table. No context-free hierarchy of methodological preferences. Genuinely mixed methods.	***Bricolage Methods principle***: *Conduct utilization-focused evaluations incorporating Blue Marble principles to match methods to the evaluation situation.*

(continued)

EXHIBIT 15.1. *(continued)*			
Issue	**Current dominant evaluation practice**	**Transforming evaluation to evaluate transformation**	**Relevant Blue Marble evaluation principle**
12. Evaluator stance	Credibility flows from being independent, external, and neutral.	Credibility flows from shared values, transparent acknowledgment of the stakes involved for each actor, including the evaluator. Interdependence in relationships with commitment to represent the data and evidence, however it unfolds.	***Skin in the Game principle:*** *Acknowledge and act on your stake in how the Anthropocene unfolds.*
13. Position of the evaluation function	The evaluation function is isolated from other functions like design, implementation, intervention development, and program decision making.	Blue Marble design, implementation, and evaluation are integrated as mutually interconnected functions requiring alignment and integration.	***Integration principle:*** *Integrate the Blue Marble principles in the design, engagement with, and evaluation of systems change and transformation initiatives.*
14. Intervention	Program or project logic model; single theory of change.	Theory of transformation consisting of multiple, integrated theories of change; networks of innovators striving for convergence to generate critical mass tipping points.	***Theory of Transformation principle:*** *Design and evaluate transformation based on an evidence-supported theory of transformation.*
15. Evaluation influence and use	Focus on findings use. The evaluation should be conducted so as not to affect the program's effectiveness during the evaluation. Measurement is independent of the thing measured. Minimize reactivity.	Blue Marble evaluation is designed, implemented, and conducted to contribute to global sustainability and transformation. Evaluation becomes part of the intervention through process use, feedback, and transformational engagement.	***Evaluation as Intervention principle:*** *Integrate and network evaluations to inform and energize transformation.*
16. Fidelity concerns	Fidelity to evaluation models (realist evaluation, theory-driven evaluation, empowerment evaluation, etc.).	Fidelity to the face validity meaning of language to ensure authentic actions and claims. Take seriously the terms *global* and *transfor-*	***Transformation Fidelity principle:*** *Ensure that what is called transformation constitutes transformation.*
			(continued)

		EXHIBIT 15.1. *(continued)*	
Issue	**Current dominant evaluation practice**	**Transforming evaluation to evaluate transformation**	**Relevant Blue Marble evaluation principle**
16. Fidelity concerns *(continued)*	Insistence on standardized operational definitions of key terms and variables.	*mation.* Treat transformation and global as sensitizing concepts where results are made meaningful within the context where the engagement is occurring.	***Corollary:*** *Evaluate whether and how what is called transformational engagement constitutes a trajectory toward transformation.*
17. Coherence	The linear logic of logic models and program goal attainment.	Anthropocene narrative: The complex story of the nature, momentum, and scope of transformational interventions and initiatives.	***Integration principle:*** *Integrate the Blue Marble principles.*
18. Approach to innovation	Preference for known, established, proven, credible, and accepted designs, methods, measures, and reports.	Innovation to evaluate transformation. Open to new technologies and approaches like Big Data, artificial intelligence (AI), remote sensing, geographic information systems (GIS), robotics, animation, and blockchain technology. Blue Marble evaluation involves ongoing learning, adaptation, innovation, and networking.	***Transformational Alignment principle:*** *Transform evaluation to evaluate transformation.*
19. Evaluator commitment	Evaluators meet commitments of and are responsible to those who commission evaluations and to adhere to general professional standards.	Evaluators add commitments to the general welfare and connect with each other to build and engage with each other through transformational evaluation networks.	***Skin in the Game principle:*** *Acknowledge and act on your stake in how the Anthropocene unfolds.*
20. Vision	Quality evaluations that are useful and used.	Connect the ecological and human domains as the essence of Blue Marble Evaluation, knowing that the planet's capacity to support humanity and therefore the future of humanity are at stake.	***Global Thinking principle:*** *Apply whole-Earth, big-picture thinking to all aspects of systems change.*

*Program includes project, grant, policy, or specific action.

We know that evaluations should search for unanticipated consequences and side effects, but too few designs make the case for and include adequate resources to conduct the open-ended fieldwork that is needed to do so. Evaluators are getting better at incorporating explicit ethical frameworks and making underlying values explicit, but these directions need improvement and further development. We have begun to incorporate systems and complexity thinking into evaluation designs. Again, this is by no means a comprehensive or exhaustive list, but my message is that we are continuing to develop, innovate, and adapt to deepen and expand our relevance, utility, and excellence as a profession.

The current challenge for evaluation is building on these accomplishments and adapting what we know how to do to take on evaluating transformation in the epoch of the Anthropocene. I like to point out that "evaluation grew up in the projects," as evidenced by what we do well. The profession's origins were in evaluation of projects and programs and, from my perspective, we remain in the grip of a self-limiting project mentality. Such tools as logic models and SMART goals work well for project evaluation. They do not work well, in my judgment, for evaluating systems changes and global transformation initiatives and interventions. Projects are closed systems, or at least treated as such in most evaluations, in which boundaries can be established and control can presumably be exercised within those boundaries by both program staff and evaluators. In contrast, complex dynamic interventions and transformative initiatives are open systems characterized by volatility, uncertainty, and unpredictability, all of which make control problematic. Treating these complicated and complex evaluations like simple projects is inappropriate, ineffective, and insufficient. Indeed, it can do harm by misconceptualizing the very nature of complex change and thereby generating results that are inaccurate and irrelevant. Evaluating global systems dynamics poses a particularly daunting challenge as we learn to view Earth and its inhabitants as a holistic interconnected global system. Given evaluation's history and dominant paradigm of practice, evaluation must be transformed to evaluate transformation.

The profession had been mostly blind to this larger pattern of Earth's systems changes until recently. The theme of the 2014 annual conference of the AEA was *Visionary Evaluation for a Sustainable, Equitable Future,* which is now a book (Parsons et al., 2020). The 2018 theme of the Australasian Evaluation Society was *Transformations,* while that of the European Evaluation Society was *Evaluation for More Resilient Societies.* The theme of the 2019 conference of the International Development Evaluation Association was *Evaluation for Transformative Change.* Evaluating transformation has arrived on the agenda of the global evaluation profession.

Global Sustainability as a Universal Concern Makes Evaluating Sustainability a Universal Concern

The notion of making global sustainability a universal criterion in evaluations flows from articles appearing in nonprofit journals arguing that addressing climate change should be part of the mission of every nonprofit (Conway, 2019). As the crises of the Anthropocene deepen, understanding that we all have skin in the game will become more universal. In the midst of the storm, everything becomes about the storm. Evaluators need to be ready for the global storm and prepared to make addressing the realities of the Anthropocene a part of everything we do.

Blue Sky Methods for Blue Marble Evaluation

Adopting and adapting new technologies to serve Blue Marble evaluations (number

18 in the vision and agenda above) moves us from just Blue Marble thinking to Blue Sky thinking (imagining the future). Big Data, artificial intelligence (AI), systems mapping, remote sensing, geographic information systems (GIS), robotics, animation, foresight scenarios, and blockchain technology are examples of new technologies that the Blue Marble bricoleur will need to understand and use as appropriate.

Summary of Blue Marble Principles

We began with the iconic image of Earth as seen from space—the Blue Marble. Absorbing that imagery and being enveloped in its wholeness inspired this journey into imagining a world in which Blue Marble evaluators contribute to global sustainability and equity. Exhibit 15.2 shows where we've ended up—the full set of Blue Marble principles.

A Vision for the Future of Blue Marble Evaluation

I invite you to imagine a transformed evaluation as the entropic force that brings together, helps work together, and focuses the many and diverse initiatives engaged on different trajectories toward transformation. Each evaluator, every evaluation, all contributing toward critical mass, adding energy, insight, learning, and knowledge toward the tipping point of transformative sustainability. We, as evaluators, are not outside the system, independent from it, but rather a part of it. The theory of transformation explains, justifies, and puts muscle on Blue Marble evaluation. Evaluating transformation requires transforming evaluation, especially and centrally, changing the criteria for evaluating sustainability from a mechanical, static engineering conceptualization to an organic, complexity-based, highly adaptive conceptualization where paradigms and mindsets are being changed and not just knowledge, behavior, and attitudes.

Big Data machine by Chris Lysy.

EXHIBIT 15.2. Blue Marble Principles

OVERARCHING BLUE MARBLE PRINCIPLES 1–4

1. Global Thinking principle: *Apply whole-Earth, big-picture thinking to all aspects of systems change.*	**2. Anthropocene as Context principle:** *Know and face the realities of the Anthropocene and act accordingly.*	**3. Transformative Engagement principle:** *Engage and evaluate consistent with the magnitude, direction, and speed of transformations needed and envisioned.*

4. Integration principle: *Integrate the Blue Marble principles in the design, engagement with, and evaluation of systems change and transformation initiatives.*

BLUE MARBLE OPERATING PRINCIPLES 5–16

5. Transboundary Engagement principle: *Act at a global scale.*	**6. GLOCAL principle:** *Integrate complex interconnections across levels.*	**7. Cross-Silos principle:** *Engage across sectors and issues for systems change.*
8. Time Being of the Essence principle: *Act with a sense of urgency in the present, support adaptive sustainability long term, grounding both in understanding the past.*	**9. Yin–Yang principle:** *Harmonize conceptual opposites.*	**10. Bricolage Methods principle:** *Conduct utilization-focused evaluations incorporating Blue Marble principles to match methods to the evaluation situation.*
11. World Savvy principle: *Engage in ongoing learning relevant to Blue Marble principles and practices.*	**12. Skin in the Game principle:** *Acknowledge and act on your stake in how the Anthropocene unfolds.*	**13. Theory of Transformation principle:** *Design and evaluate transformation based on an evidence-supported theory of transformation.*
14. Transformation Fidelity principle: *Ensure that what is called transformation constitutes transformation.* **Corollary:** *Evaluate whether and how what is called transformational engagement constitutes a trajectory toward transformation.*	**15. Transformational Alignment principle:** *Transform evaluation to evaluate transformation.*	**16. Evaluation as Intervention principle:** *Integrate and network evaluations to inform and energize transformation.*

A Vision for Evaluation and Evaluators Contributing to Global Transformation

Imagine a network of Blue Marble evaluators and others involved in evaluating transformations of all kinds at all levels, evaluators working on initiatives and interventions around the world in all sectors, on all SDGs, across issues, from all disciplines, working alone and in teams, engaged independently and as part of organizations. Imagine that they are sharing information, evaluation processes and findings, innovative methods, insights about challenges and solutions, and synthesizing trajectories and trends of transformation, and then feeding that knowledge back into the networks of people working on transformation, to further catalyze and propel the intersection of transformational efforts toward critical mass and tipping points.

Imagine a global network of bricoleurs, data analysts, methods mavens, Big Data specialists, blockchain technology experts, AI developers, science innovators, Blue Marble diplomats, and others engaged in generating, analyzing, and communicating information about how the world is unfolding. Imagine these diverse global and GLOCAL actors, connected together, learning from one another, debating important issues, distinguishing signal from noise, sense making, pattern detecting, and visually depicting findings. Imagine the results and insights used to inform those engaged in transformation about how transformational engagements are unfolding worldwide, where the gaps are, where the opportunities are, and where the resistance threatens to undermine and turn back systems change.

For the most part, evaluators, data managers, organizational consultants, and others generating, analyzing, and managing information report only to those who commission their work. They share findings or publications and conferences, but the time lags are significant, the presentations are at a high level, and the applications are limited to narrow audiences that read those publications and attend those conferences. Imagine instead a network actively facilitated and engaged, brought together by shared values, a common sense of urgency, a commitment to inclusion rather than marginalizing those with different perspectives, and the capacity and savvy to generate useful and relevant knowledge in real time to propel the transformation processes. This is indeed underway. As of the writing of this book, we are preparing the

Global networks with BME evaluators by Simon Kneebone.

Past to future by Simon Kneebone. Used with permission of the copyright holder, the Australian Evaluation Society (*aes.asn.au*).

scaffolding of such an enterprise and will need many to co-create what it actually becomes and how it is transformative for the field of evaluation.

Networks of Blue Marble Evaluators

The Hage hypothesis states that "successful transformation requires diversity integrated into a strongly connected and coordinated systemic network." Imagine Blue Marble evaluators and other data people of all kinds representing diversity of expertise, methods, and transformational engagements, integrated into a strongly connected and coordinated systemic network aimed at contributing to global transformation. Image engaging together based on the evaluation as an intervention principle.

Evaluation as Intervention Principle

Integrate and network evaluations to inform and energize transformation.

Imagine that such a global network had the resources, technology, and staffing to be significant players on the global stage as stories of transformations realized, or transformations failed, unfold. Imagine that what holds such a network together, energizes it and its participants, and provides direction is a realization that we all have skin in the game that the network holds up, adheres to, and makes operational the principle that we are all in this together as one humanity, all affected by what we do together, for better or worse.

Imagine that the *principle of Ubuntu* made such a network possible and held it together.

My humanity is caught up and is inextricably bound up in yours. I'm human because I belong. The spirit of *Ubuntu* speaks about wholeness. It is knowledge that we belong to a greater whole and are diminished when others are humiliated or diminished, when others are tortured or oppressed, or treated as if they were less than who they are. Our purpose is social and communal harmony and well-being.

—ARCHBISHOP DESMOND TUTU, explaining *Ubuntu* in Nguni languages, or *botho* in Sotho

References

Adger N., & Barnett, J. (2009). Four reasons for concern about adaptation to climate change. *Environment and Planning A, 41,* 2800–2805.

A'Hearn, T. (2017, August 30). *One planet transformation.* Keynote address, Transformation 2017 Conference, University of Dundee, Scotland, UK.

Alter, C., & Hage, J. (1993). *Organizations working together: Coordination in interorganizational networks.* Newbury Park, CA: SAGE.

American Evaluation Association. (2011). Public statement on cultural competence in evaluation. Fairhaven, MA: Author. Retrieved from *www.eval.org.*

American Evaluation Association. (2018). Evaluator competencies. Retrieved from *www.eval.org/p/do/sd/topic=12&sid=14371.*

Arena, M. (2018). *Adaptive space: How GM and other companies are positively disrupting themselves and transforming into agile organizations.* New York: McGraw-Hill Education.

Attfield, R. (2018). *Environmental ethics.* Oxford, UK: Oxford University Press.

Augustin, S. (2010, January 22). People, places, and things: Independence and interdependence [Blog post]. *Psychology Today.* Retrieved from *www.psychologytoday.com/us/blog/people-places-and-things/201001/first-places-and-place-rules-independence-and-interdependence.*

Azzam, T., & Evergreen, S. (Eds.). (2013a). *Data visualization: Part 1* (New Directions for Evaluation No. 139). Hoboken, NJ: Wiley Periodicals.

Azzam, T., & Evergreen, S. (Eds.). (2013b). *Data visualization: Part 2* (New Directions for Evaluation No. 140). Hoboken, NJ: Wiley Periodicals.

Badr, A. (2019, February 21). Why brand is essential to business transformation. *Business Matters.* Retrieved from *www.bmmagazine.co.uk/marketing/why-brand-is-essential-to-business-transformation.*

Baker, A. (2018, February 19). Where the taps run dry. *Time,* pp. 30–37.

Bamberger, M. (2016). *Integrating big data into the monitoring and evaluation of development programmes.* New York: UN Global Pulse and Rockefeller Foundation.

Bamberger, M., & Segonem, M. (2011). How to design and manage equity-focused evaluations. New York: UNICEF Evaluation Office. Retrieved from *http://mymande.org/sites/default/files/EWP5_Equity_focused_evaluations.pdf.*

Bamberger, M., Vaessen, J., & Raimondo, E. (2016). *Dealing with complexity in development evaluation: A practical approach.* London: SAGE.

Barry, J. (2017, November). How the horrific 1918 flu spread across America. *Smithsonian Magazine.* Retrieved from *www.smithsonianmag.com/history/journal-plague-year-180965222/.*

Baser, H., & Morgan, P. (2008). Capacity, change

and performance: Study report (ECPDM Discussion Paper No. 59B). Retrieved from *http://ecdpm.org/publications/capacity-change-performance-study-report*.

Belay, M. (2017, October 11). Is transformation on the horizon? [Blog post]. Kampala, Uganda: Alliance for Food Sovereignty in Africa. Retrieved from *http://transgressivelearning.org/2017/10/28/is-transformation-on-the-horizon*.

Berg, R. D. van den (2017). Mainstreaming impact evidence in climate change and sustainable development. In J. I. Uitto, J. Puri, & R. D. van den Berg (Eds.), *Evaluating climate change action for sustainable development* (pp. 37–52). Cham, Switzerland: Springer.

Berry, W. (2017a). Wendell Berry quotations. Retrieved from *www.globalstewards.org/world-quotes.htm*.

Berry, W. (2017b). Wendell Berry quotations. Retrieved from *www.goodreads.com/author/quotes/8567.Wendell_Berry*.

Blumer, H. (1954). What is wrong with social theory? *American Sociological Review, 19*(1), 3–10.

Bragg, D. D., Kirby, C., Witt, M. A., Richie, D., Mix, S., Feldbaum, M., et al. (2014, February). *Transformative change initiative*. Champaign: Office of Community College Research and Leadership, University of Illinois at Urbana–Champaign.

Brannen, P. (2018). *The ends of the world: Volcanic apocalypses, lethal oceans and our quest to understand Earth's past mass extinctions*. London: Oneworld.

Bronson, R. (2018). Doomsday clock statement. *Bulletin of the Atomic Scientists*. Retrieved from *https://thebulletin.org/2018-doomsday-clock-statement*.

Brooks, D. (2011). *The social animal: The hidden sources of love, character, and achievement*. New York: Random House.

Buffett, W. (2018, January 15). The genius of America. *Time*, pp. 20–22.

Buffett, W., & Dimon, J. (2018, June 7). Stop giving quarterly earnings guidance. *Fortune*. Retrieved from *http://fortune.com/2018/06/07/buffett-dimon-quarterly-earnings-guidance-short-term-thinking*.

Caballero, P. (2015, May 27). *Connecting the dots in 2015 for sustainable development (Voices for development)*. Washington, DC: World Bank.

Cahill, G., & Spitz, K. (2017). *Social innovation generation: Fostering a Canadian ecosystem for systems change*. Montreal, ON, Canada: McConnell Family Foundation.

Campos, A. (2017, March 16). Slave labor in the Amazon has been linked to suppliers of Lowe's and Walmart. *Pacific Standard*. Retrieved from *https://psmag.com/slave-labor-in-the-amazon-has-been-linked-to-suppliers-of-lowes-and-walmart-7519eb7a1e2b#.1syai0e5v*.

Capra, F., & Luisi, L. (2014). *A systems view of life: A unifying vision*. Cambridge, UK: Cambridge University Press.

Carey, D., Dumaine, B., Useem, M., & Zemmel, R. (2018). *Go long: Why long-term thinking is your best short-term strategy*. Philadelphia: Wharton Digital Press.

Carrington, D. (2016, August 29). The Anthropocene epoch: Scientists declare dawn of human-influenced age. *The Guardian*. Retrieved from *www.theguardian.com/environment/2016/aug/29/declare-anthropocene-epoch-experts-urge-geological-congress-human-impact-earth*.

Casey, N., & Haner, J. (2018, December 18). As seas warm, Galápagos Islands face a giant evolutionary test. *New York Times*. Retrieved from *www.nytimes.com/interactive/2018/12/18/climate/galapagos-islands-ocean-warming.html?emc=edit_nn_p_20181219&nl=morning-briefing&nlid=44499219section%3DlongRead&section=longRead&te=1*.

CERN. (2019). Dark matter. Retrieved from *https://home.cern/science/physics/dark-matter*.

Charli-Joseph, L., Siqueiros-Garcia, J. M., Eakin, H., Manuel-Navarrete, D., & Shelton, R. (2018). Promoting agency for social-ecological transformation: A transformation-lab in the Xochimilco social-ecological system. *Ecology and Society, 23*(2), 46.

China purchases U.S. soybeans and sorghum, as trade talks face hurdles. (2019, March 10). *Farm Policy News*. Retrieved from *https://farmpolicynews.illinois.edu/2019/03/china-purchases-u-s-soybeans-and-sorghum-as-trade-talks-face-hurdles*.

Chouinard, J., & Hopson, R. (2016). Decolonizing international development evaluation. *Canadian Journal of Program Evaluation, 30*(3), 237–247.

Conway, M. (2019, February 11). Put climate in every nonprofit mission [Blog post]. *Nonprofit Quarterly*.

COP24: The UN's latest climate meeting ends positively. (2018, December 16). *The Econo-*

mist. Retrieved from *www.economist.com/ science-and-technology/2018/12/16/the-uns- latest-climate-meeting-ends-positively?cid1=cust/ ddnew/email/n/n/20181217n/owned/n/n/ ddnew/n/n/n/nNA/Daily_Dispatch/ email&etear=dailydispatch&utm_ source=newsletter&utm_medium=email&utm_ campaign=Daily_Dispatch&utm_ term=20181217*.

Corntassel, J. (2012). Re-envisioning resurgence: Indigenous pathways to decolonization and sustainable self-determination. *Decolonization: Indigeneity, Education and Society, 1*(1), 86–101.

Cristiano, S., & Proietti, P. (2018, July 1). *Evaluating interactive innovation processes: Towards a developmental-oriented analytical framework*. 13th European IFSA Symposium, Chania, Greece.

Cronbach, L. J. (1980). *Toward reform of program evaluation*. San Francisco: Jossey-Bass.

Davidson, E. J. (2004). *Evaluation methodology basics: The nuts and bolts of sound evaluation*. Thousand Oaks, CA: SAGE.

Davidson, E. J. (2012). *Actionable evaluation basics: Getting succinct answers to the most important questions*. Auckland, New Zealand: Real Evaluation.

Davidson, E. J. (2014). How "beauty" can bring truth and justice to life. *New Directions for Evaluation, 142*, 31–43.

Davis, J. H. (2015). The past and future of light dark matter direct detection. *International Journal of Modern Physics, 30*(15).

Davis, N. (2018, August 27). Climate change will make hundreds of millions more people nutrient deficient. *The Guardian*. Retrieved from *www.theguardian.com/science/2018/aug/27/ climate-change-will-make-hundreds-of-millions- more-people-nutrient-deficient?CMP=share_btn_ tw*.

Deaton, A. (2016, February 8). *Angus Deaton on foreign aid and inequality*. New York: Council on Foreign Relations. Retrieved from *www. cfr.org/event/angus-deaton-foreign-aid-and-in- equality*.

Denzin, N. K., & Lincoln, Y. S. (Eds.). (2000). *Handbook of qualitative research* (2nd ed.). Thousand Oaks, CA: SAGE.

Development Assistance Committee. (1991). *Quality standards for development evaluation* (DAC Guidelines and Reference Series). Paris: Organisation for Economic Co-opera-

tion and Development. Retrieved from *www. oecd.org/dac/evaluation/qualitystandardsforde- velopmentevaluation.htm*.

Dewey, J. (1944). *Democracy and education*. New York: Free Press/Simon & Schuster.

Dickens, C. (1843). *A Christmas carol*. London: Chapman & Hall.

Duvernay, A. (Ed.). (2019, February 18/25). The art of optimism. *Time*, pp. 60–94.

Earth Day Network. (2018). Where does your plastic waste go? Retrieved from *www.earth- day.org/2018/04/06/where-does-your-waste-go*.

Easterly, W. (2013). *The tyranny of experts: Economists, dictators, and the forgotten rights of the poor*. New York: Basic Books.

El-Gendi, L. S. (2016). Illusory borders: The myth of the modern nation-state and its impact on the repatriation of cultural artifacts. *John Marshall Review of Intellectual Property Law, 15*, 486–521.

Ellis, E. C. (2018). *Anthropocene: A very short introduction*. Oxford, UK: Oxford University Press.

Ellsberg, D. (2018). *The doomsday machine: Confessions of a nuclear war planner*. New York: Bloomsbury.

England, K. V. L. (1994). Getting personal: Reflexivity, positionality, and feminist research. *The Professional Geographer, 46*(1), 80–89.

Eoyang, G. H., & Holladay, R. J. (2013). *Adaptive action: Leveraging uncertainty in your organization*. Stanford, CA: Stanford Business Books.

Evergreen, S. (2017). *Presenting data effectively: Communicating your findings for maximum impact* (2nd ed.). Los Angeles: SAGE.

Evergreen, S. (2019). *Effective data visualization: The right chart for the right data* (2nd ed.). Los Angeles: SAGE.

Farrell, S. (2019, February 21). Poundland creates transformation team to reinvent proposition. *The Grocer*. Retrieved from *www.thegrocer. co.uk/people/movers/poundland-creates-transfor- mation-team-to-reinvent-proposition/576875.ar- ticle*.

Fazey, I., Schäpke, N., Caniglia, G., Patterson, J., Hultman, J., van Mierlo, B., et al. (2018). Ten essentials for action-oriented and second order energy transitions, transformations and climate change research. *Energy Research and Social Science, 40*, 54–70.

The Fed acts: Workers in Mexico and merchants in Malaysia suffer. (2017, March 16).

New York Times. Retrieved from *www.nytimes. com/2017/03/16/business/federal-reserve-inter- est-rates-china-mexico.html.*

Fletcher, S. (2019). *Einstein's shadow: A black hole, a band of astronomers, and the quest to see the unseeable.* New York: HarperCollins.

Freire, P. (1970). *Pedagogy of the oppressed.* New York: Herder & Herder.

Freire, P. (1997). *Pedagogia da autonomia: Saberes necessários à prática educativa* [Pedagogy of freedom: Ethics, democracy and civic cour- age]. Lantham, MD: Rowman & Littlefield.

Freire, P. (2004). *Pedagogy of indignation.* Boul- der, CO: Paradigm.

Funnell, S. C., & Rogers, P. J. (2011). *Purposeful program theory: Effective use of logic models and theories of change.* San Francisco: Jossey-Bass.

Gates, B. (Ed.). (2018, January 15). The opti- mists. *Time,* pp. 16–32.

Gates, B. (2019, February 18–25). Why I'm hope- ful: Because innovation is an art form. *Time,* pp. 63–64.

Gellender, M. (2017). *Science that changed our lives: Five scientific revolutions that changed the way we live and understand the world.* Brisbane, Australia: University of the Third Age.

Gemmill-Herren, B., Leippert, F., Pondini, S., Isler, C., Töndury, N., & Bamert, M. (2018). *Beacons of hope: A sustainability transitions framework for sustainable food systems.* Toronto, ON, Canada: Global Alliance for the Future of Food.

Ghosh, A. (2016). *The great derangement: Climate change and the unthinkable.* Chicago: Univer- sity of Chicago Press.

Gilligan, C. (1982). *In a different voice: Psycho- logical theory and women's development.* Cam- bridge, MA: Harvard University Press.

Global Alliance for the Future of Food. (2019). Monitoring and evaluation. Retrieved from *https://futureoffood.org/about-us/monitoring- evaluation.*

Goldin, I., & Kutarna, C. (2016). *Age of discovery: Navigating the risks and rewards of our new re- naissance.* New York: St. Martin's Press.

Google Online. (2019). Transformation, defini- tion. Retrieved from *www.google.com/search?q =transformation+definitoon&oq=transformation +definitoon&aqs=chrome..69i57j0l5.11231j1j8& sourceid=chrome&ie=UTF-8.*

Gould, D. (2019, January 7). Introducing biodi- versity: The intersection of taste and sustain- ability [Blog post]. Retrieved from *https:// foodtechconnect.com/2019/01/07/biodiverse- food-intersection-taste-sustainability.*

Greenland's fast-melting ice sheet. (2019, Febru- ary 8). *The Week,* p. 20.

Griffs, D. J., Nilsson, M., Stevance, A., & McCol- lum, D. (Eds.). (2017). *A guide to SDG inter- actions: From science to implementation.* Paris: International Council for Science. Retrieved from *https://council.science/cms/2017/05/ SDGs-Guide-to-Interactions.pdf.*

Groopman, J. (2018). The bugs are winning. *New York Review of Books, 65*(11), 54–56.

Gunderson, L. H., & Holling, C. S. (2002). *Pan- archy: Understanding transformations in human and natural systems.* Washington, DC: Island Press.

Guth, R. A. (2010, April 23). Gates rethinks his war on polio. *Wall Street Journal.* Retrieved from *www.wsj.com/articles/SB10001424052702 3033485045751840932396150 22.*

Hage, J. (1972). *Techniques and problems of theory construction in sociology.* New York: Wiley.

Hage, J. (1980). *Theories of organizations: Form, process, and transformation.* New York: Wiley.

Hage, J. (Ed.). (1988). *Futures of organizations: In- novating to adapt strategy and human resources to rapid technological change.* Lexington, MA: Lexington Books.

Hage, J. (2011). *Restoring the innovative edge: Driving the evolution of science and technology.* Stanford, CA: Stanford Business Books.

Hage, J., & Aiken, M. (1970). *Social change in com- plex organizations.* New York: Random House.

Hage, J., & Finsterbusch, K. (1987). *Organiza- tional change as a development strategy: Models and tactics for improving third world organiza- tions.* London: Rienner.

Hage, J., & Meeus, M. (Eds.). (2006). *Innova- tion, science, and institutional change: A research handbook.* New York: Oxford University Press.

Hall, J. (2017). *Demonstrating outcomes and im- pact across different scales.* Brisbane: Australian Council for International Development.

Hanson, T. (2018). *Buzz: The nature and necessity of bees.* New York: Basic Books.

Harnish, V. (2014). *Scaling up: How a few compa- nies make it . . . and why the rest don't.* Ashburn, VA: Gazelles.

Heider, C. (2016). Transformational develop- ment projects—what makes them different? Retrieved from *https://ieg.worldbankgroup. org/blog/transformational-development-projects- what-makes-them-different.*

Heider, J. (1985). *The tao of leadership.* Atlanta, GA: Humanics New Age.

Heras, M., & Tàbara, J. D. (2014). Let's play transformations!: Performative methods for sustainability. *Sustainability Science, 9*(3), 379–398.

Heron, S. F., van Hooidonk, R., Maynard, J., Anderson, K., & Day, J. C. (2008) *Impacts of climate change on World Heritage coral reefs: Update to the first global scientific assessment.* Paris: UNESCO World Heritage Centre.

Hertz, R. (Ed.). (1997). *Reflexivity and voice.* Thousand Oaks, CA: SAGE.

Hervey, A. (2017, December 6). 99 reasons 2017 was a great year. Retrieved from *https://medium.com/future-crunch/99-reasons-2017-was-a-good-year-d119d0c32d19.*

Hickman, S. C. (2016, April 1). The Anthropocene: A return to grand narratives? [Blog post]. Retrieved from *https://socialecologies.wordpress.com/2016/04/01/the-anthropocene-a-return-to-grand-narratives.*

Hoffman, A. (2015). *How culture shapes the climate debate.* Stanford, CA: Stanford University Press.

Holley, J. (2012). *Network weaver handbook: A guide to transformational networks.* Network Weaver Publishing.

Houle, D. (2012). *Entering the shift age: The end of the information age and the new age of transformation.* Naperville, IL: Sourcebooks.

House, E. R. (1977). *The logic of evaluative argument* (CSE Monograph in Evaluation, Vol. 7). Los Angeles: UCLA Center for the Study of Education.

House, E. R. (1980). *Evaluating with validity.* Beverly Hills, CA: SAGE.

House, E. R. (2014). Origin of the ideas in *Evaluating with validity. New Directions for Evaluation, 142,* 9–15.

Howard, C. (2018, January 4). Healthy planet, healthy people [TEDx talk]. Retrieved from *www.youtube.com/watch?v=FgIYaklWOK4.*

Hrvolova, M., & Jedwab, E. L. (2019, March 5). Developing a collaboration tool to assess collective action coalitions [Blog post]. Retrieved from *https://aea365.org/blog/developing-a-collaboration-tool-to-assess-collective-action-coalitions-by-martina-hrvolova-and-elizabeth-lenz-jedwab.*

Huang, L. (2016, June 8). Interpersonal harmony and conflict for Chinese people: A yin–yang perspective. *Frontiers in Psychology.* Retrieved from *www.frontiersin.org/articles/10.3389/fpsyg.2016.00847/full.*

Independent Evaluation Group. (2016). Supporting transformational change for poverty reduction and shared prosperity. Retrieved from *http://ieg.worldbankgroup.org/evaluations/supporting-transformational-change-poverty-reduction-and-shared-prosperity.*

Independent Evaluation Group. (2017). *Transformational engagements: Accelerating progress to achieve development goals.* Washington, DC: World Bank.

Independent Evaluation Group. (2018). *Toward a clean world for all: An evaluation of the World Bank Group's support to pollution management.* Washington, DC: World Bank. Retrieved from *https://ieg.worldbankgroup.org/evaluations/pollution.*

Institute for Economics and Peace. (2018). Global Terrorism Index. Retrieved from *www.economicsandpeace.org.*

Intergovernmental Panel on Climate Change. (2018, October). *Global warming of 1.5°C.* New York: Author. Retrieved from *www.ipcc.ch/sr15.*

Intergovernmental Science-Policy Platform on Biodiversity and Ecosystem Services. (2018). Biodiversity loss. Retrieved from *www.iucn.org/theme/global-policy/our-work/ipbes.*

International Institute for Applied Systems Analysis. (2018). *Transformations to achieve the Sustainable Development Goals Report prepared by The World in 2050 initiative.* Laxenburg, Austria: Author.

Itad. (2018). Evaluation of transformational change in the Climate Investment Funds. Hove, UK: Author. Retrieved from *www.climateinvestmentfunds.org/sites/cif_enc/files/knowledge-documents/evaluation_of_transformational_change_in_the_cif_final_w_mresp_jan_2019.pdf.*

Jarvis, B. (2018, December 2). The insect apocalypse is here. *New York Times Sunday Magazine,* pp. 38–45.

Kahneman, D. (2011). *Thinking, fast and slow.* New York: Farrar, Straus & Giroux.

Kaiser, O., & Budinich, V. (2015). *Scaling up business solutions to social problems.* New York: Palgrave Macmillan.

Kates, R. W., Travis, W. R., & Wilbanks, T. J. (2012). Transformational adaptation when incremental adaptations to climate change are insufficient. *Proceedings of the National Academy of Sciences of the USA, 109*(19), 7156–7161.

Kerouac, J. (1958). *The Dharma Bums*. New York: Random House

Knight, A. T., Cook, C. N., Redford, K. H., Biggs, D., Romero, C., Ortega-Argueta, A., et al. (2019). Improving conservation practice with principles and tools from systems thinking and evaluation. *Sustainability Science, 14,* 1–12.

Knutson, B. (2014). Scientific idea ready for retirement: Emotion is peripheral. Retrieved from *www.edge.org/responses/whatscientific-idea-is-ready-for-retirement*.

Kofler, N., Collins, J. P., Kuzma, J., Marris, E., Esvelt, K., Nelson, M. P., et al. (2018). Editing nature: Local roots of global governance. *Science, 362,* 527–529.

Kolbert, E. (2014). *The sixth extinction*. New York: Macmillan.

Kormann, C. (2019, February 4). The widening gyre. *The New Yorker,* pp. 42–49.

Kristof, N. (2018, January 7). Why 2017 was the best year in human history. *New York Times,* p. SR9.

Kushner, T. (1994). *Angels in America, Part Two: Perestroika*. New York: Theatre Communications Group.

Kutarna, C. (2016, December 21). How to manage anxiety post-2016 [Canadian Broadcast Corporation (CBC) interview]. Retrieved from *www.cbc.ca/embed/?embed_type=customhtml&content_id=1.3907614&position=0&api=prod*.

Ladendorf, B., & Ladendorf, B. (2018). Wildlife apocalypse. *Skeptical Inquirer, 42*(4), 30–39.

Lamielle, G. (2010, August 20). A One Health approach to public health [GlobalVet blog]. Retrieved from *https://globalhealthvet.com/2010/08/20/hello-world/*.

Larkin, M. (2013, May 15). What is the 7th generation principle? [Blog]. Retrieved from *www.mollylarkin.com/what-is-the-7th-generation-principle-and-why-do-you-need-to-know-about-it-3*.

Laycock, S. (2014). *All the countries that we've ever invaded: And the few we never got around to*. London: History Press.

Leach, M. (2015). What is green?: Transformation imperatives and knowledge politics. In I. Scoones, M. Leach, & P. Newell (Eds.), *The politics of green transformations*. New York: Routledge.

Lechner, F. J., & Boli, J. (Eds.). (2015). *The globalization reader*. New York: Wiley.

Leeuw, F. L., & Donaldson, S. I. (2015). Theory in evaluation: Reducing confusion and encouraging debate. *Evaluation, 21*(4), 467–480.

Lemire, S., Christie, C. A., Donaldson, S. I., & Kwako, A. (2019). *The role and promise of theory knitting to improve evaluation practice: A systematic review of theory-based evaluations*. Manuscript submitted for publication.

Lévi-Strauss, C. (1966). *The savage mind* (2nd ed.). Chicago: University of Chicago Press.

Liberman, E. (2005). Nested analysis as a mixed-method strategy for comparative research. *American Political Science Review, 99*(2), 435–452.

Liu, J. J., Dietz, T., Carpenter, S., Alberti, M., Folke, C., Moran, E., et al. (2017a). Complexity of coupled human and natural systems. *Science, 317,* 1513–1516.

Liu, J., Dietz, T., Carpenter, S. R., Folke, C., & Alberti, M. (2007b). Coupled human and natural systems. *AMBIO: A Journal of the Human Environment, 36*(8), 639–649.

Mani, M., Bandyopadhyay, S., Chonabayashi, S., Markandya, A., & Mosier, T. (2018). *South Asia's hotspots: Impacts of temperature and precipitation changes on living standards*. Washington, DC: World Bank.

Mann, M., & Toles, T. (2018). *The madhouse effect: How climate change denial is threatening our planet, destroying our politics, and driving us crazy*. New York: Columbia University Press.

Marra, M. (2011). Micro, meso and macro dimensions of change: A new agenda for the evaluation of structural policies. In K. Forss, M. Marra, & R. Schwartz (Eds.), *Evaluating the complex: Attribution, contribution and beyond*. New Brunswick, NJ: Transaction.

Marshall, A. (2017). *Two-eyed seeing*. Sydney, NS, Canada: Cape Breton University, Institute for Integrative Science and Health. Retrieved from *www.youtube.com/watch?v=_CY-iGduw5c*.

McKenna, M. (2017). *Big chicken: The incredible story of how antibiotics created modern agriculture and changed the way the world eats*. Washington, DC: National Geographic Partners.

McKibben, B. (2019). *Falter: Has the human game begun to play itself out?* New York: Henry Holt.

McLeod, K., & Leslie, H. (Eds.). (2009). *Ecosystem-based management for the oceans*. Seattle, WA: Island Press.

Mead, G. H. (1936). *Movements of thought in the nineteenth century*. Chicago: University of Chicago Press.

Meadows, D. H. (2008). *Thinking in systems: A primer.* White River Junction, VT: Sustainability Institute.

Mertens, D. (2007). Transformative paradigm: Mixed methods and social justice. *Journal of Mixed Methods Research, 1*(3), 212–225.

Merton, R. K. (1976). Social knowledge and public policy. In *Sociological ambivalence and other essays.* New York: Free Press.

Merton, R. K. (1995). The Thomas theorem and the Matthew effect. *Social Forces, 74*(2), 379–424.

Midgley, G. (Ed.). (2003). *Systems thinking.* Thousand Oaks, CA: SAGE.

Midgley, G., & Pinzon, L. A. (2011). Boundary critique and its implications for conflict prevention. *Journal of Operational Research Society, 62,* 1543–1554.

Miller, K. (2019, March 4). Customer experience transformation [Blog]. Retrieved from *www.intergen.co.nz/blog/Kevin-Miller/dates/2019/3/Key-considerations-for-people-central-to-Customer-Experience-CX-transformation.*

Minnich, E. K. (2005). *Transforming knowledge* (2nd ed.). Philadelphia: Temple University Press.

MOAP. (2013). History of Europe: 6013 years in 3 minutes [YouTube video]. Retrieved from *www.youtube.com/watch?v=uxDyJ_6N-6A.*

Monbiot, G. (2018, March 7). You can deny environmental calamity: Until you check the facts. *The Guardian.* Retrieved from *www.theguardian.com/commentisfree/2018/mar/07/environmental-calamity-facts-steven-pinker.*

Moore, M.-L., Westley, F. R., & Olsson, P. (2019). Resilience roots for radical change: Transformations in social–ecological systems. In E. Boyd (Ed.), *Routledge handbook of social and ecological resilience.* Abingdon, UK: Taylor & Francis.

Mora, C., Spirandelli, D., Franklin, E. C., Lynham, J., Kantar, M. B., Miles, W., et al. (2018). Broad threat to humanity from cumulative climate hazards intensified by greenhouse gas emissions. *Nature Climate Change, 8,* 1062–1071.

Moser, S. (2017, August 30). *If it is like we want.* Keynote address, Transformations 2017 Conference, University of Dundee, Scotland, UK.

Moser, S. C., & Ekstrom, J. A. (2010). A framework to diagnose barriers to climate change adaptation. *Proceedings of the National Academy of Sciences of the USA, 107,* 22026–22031.

Nagel, T. (2018, April 5). As if! *New York Review of Books, 65*(6), 36–38.

Naidoo, K. (2017, August 31). *Transformation and affluenza in an unjust, unequal and unsustainable world.* Keynote address, Transformations 2017 Conference, University of Dundee, Scotland, UK.

Nakicenovic, N., Rockström, J., Gaffney, O., & Zimm, C. (2016). *Global commons in the Anthropocene: World development on a stable and resilient planet.* Laxenburg, Austria: International Institute for Applied Systems Analysis. Retrieved from *http://pure.iiasa.ac.at/id/eprint/14003.*

National Oceanic and Atmospheric Administration. (2018). Global climate change indicators. Retrieved from *www.ncdc.noaa.gov/monitoring-references/faq/indicators.php.*

Natsios, A. (2010). *The clash of the counter-bureaucracy and development.* Washington, DC: Center for Global Development. Retrieved from *www.hudson.org/content/researchattachments/attachment/812/clash_of_counterbureaucracy_and_developmen_final_text_pdf.pdf.*

Nelson, R. J., Coe, R., & Haussmann, B. I. G. (2016). Farmer research networks as a strategy for matching diverse options and contexts in smallholder agriculture. *Experimental Agriculture, 1,* 1–20.

Nesbit, J. (2018, October 18). Searching for water across borders: Saudi Arabia and China are among the countries that have turned to the United States and elsewhere. *New York Times.* Retrieved from *www.nytimes.com/2018/10/18/opinion/climate-change-saudi-arabia-water.html.*

Nicolls, A., Simon, J., & Gabriel, M. (Eds.). (2015). *New frontiers in social innovation research.* New York: Palgrave Macmillan.

Niles, M., Esquivel, J., Ahuja, R., & Mango, N. (2017). *Climate change and food systems: Assessing impacts and opportunities.* Washington, DC: Meridian Institute. Retrieved from *www.merid.org/~/media/CCFS/CC-FS%20Final%20Report%20November%202017.*

Nilsson, M., Griggs, D., Visbeck, M., Ringler, M. C., & McCollum, D. (2018). *A guide to SDG interactions: From science to implementation.* Paris: International Science Council. Retrieved from *https://council.science/cms/2017/05/SDGs-Guide-to-Interactions.pdf.*

O'Banion, T. (Ed.). (2019). *13 ideas that are transforming the community college world.* Lanham, MD: Rowman & Littlefield.

Ofir, Z. (2018, December 18). What do you count

as "success"? [Blog]. Retrieved from *http://ze-ndaofir.com/evaluationg-for-transformation*.

Olsen, S. B., Page, G. G., & Ochoa, E. (2009). *The analysis of governance responses to ecosystem change: A handbook for assembling a baseline* (LOICZ Reports and Studies No. 34). Gees-thacht, Germany: GKSS Research Center.

Orzel, C. (2019). *Breakfast with Einstein: The exotic physics of everyday objects*. Dallas, TX: Ben-Bella Books.

Oxfam. (2019). Public good or private wealth. Retrieved from *https://oxfamilibrary.openre-pository.com/bitstream/handle/10546/620599/ bp-public-good-or-private-wealth-210119-summ-en.pd*f.

Paris Agreement on Climate Change. (2015). New York: United Nations Climate Change. Retrieved from *https://unfccc.int/process-and-meetings/the-paris-agreement/what-is-the-paris-agreement*.

Parsons, B., Dhillon, L., & Keene, M. (2020). *Visionary evaluation for a sustainable, equitable future*. Charlotte, NC: Information Age.

Patton, M. Q. (2008). Advocacy impact evaluation. *Journal of Multidisciplinary Evaluation, 5*(9), 1–10.

Patton, M. Q. (2011). *Developmental evaluation: Applying complexity concepts to enhance innovation and use*. New York: Guilford Press.

Patton, M. Q. (2012). *Essentials of utilization-focused evaluation*. Thousand Oaks, CA: SAGE.

Patton, M. Q. (2014). What brain sciences reveal about integrating theory and practice. *American Journal of Evaluation, 35*(2), 237–244.

Patton, M. Q. (2015). *Qualitative research and evaluation methods*. Los Angeles: SAGE.

Patton, M. Q. (Ed.). (2017). *Pedagogy of evaluation* (New Directions for Evaluation No. 155). Hoboken, NJ: Wiley Periodicals.

Patton, M. Q. (2018a). Evaluation science. *American Journal of Evaluation, 39*(2), 183–200.

Patton, M. Q. (2018b). *Facilitating evaluation: Principles in practice*. Los Angeles: SAGE.

Patton, M. Q. (2018c). A historical perspective on the evolution of evaluative thinking. In A. T. Vo & T. Archibald (Eds.), *Evaluative thinking* (New Directions for Evaluation No. 158). Hoboken, NJ: Wiley Periodicals.

Patton, M. Q. (2018d). *Principles-focused evaluation: The GUIDE*. New York: Guilford Press.

Patton, M. Q. (2018e). Principles-focused pedagogy of evaluation: Inspired by Freirean pedagogy. In *Principles-focused evaluation: The GUIDE* (pp. 141–149). New York: Guilford Press.

Patton, M. Q. (2019). Expanding futuring foresight through evaluative thinking. *World Futures Review*. [EPub ahead of print]

Patton, M. Q., & Guimarães, V. (Eds.). (2018). *Pedagogia da avaliação e Paulo Freire*. Rio de Janeiro, Brazil: Fundação Roberto Marinho.

Payne, L. (2019, February 21). Total transformation: Designer turns garage into a dining room. *New Jersey Monthly*. Retrieved from *https://njmonthly.com/articles/jersey-living/ home-garden/total-transformation-designer-turns-garage-into-a-dining-room*.

Pelling, M. (2011). *Adaptation to climate change: From resilience to transformation*. New York: Routledge.

Picciotto, R. (2005). The evaluation of policy coherence for development. *Evaluation, 11*(3), 311–330.

Picciotto, R. (2019). Is evaluation obsolete in a post-truth world? *Evaluation and Program Planning, 73*, 88–96.

Pinker, S. (2018). *Enlightenment now: The case for reason, science, humanism, and progress*. New York: Viking.

Plastrik, P., Taylor, M., & Cleveland, J. (2014). *Connecting to change the world: Harnessing the power of networks for social impact*. Washington, DC: Island Press.

Poppick, L. (2018, November 12). Why is the Gulf of Maine warming faster than 99% of the ocean? *Earth and Space Science News*. Retrieved from *https://eos.org/features/why-is-the-gulf-of-maine-warming-faster-than-99-of-the-ocean*.

Purdey, S. J. (2018, October 25). The metanarrative project: Constructing a new global narrative about planetary sustainability [Web blog]. Retrieved from *https://metanarrative.ca*.

Quackenbush, C. (2019, January 20). Global wealth inequality widened in 2018. *Time*. Retrieved from *https://time.com/5508393/global-wealth-inequality-widens-oxfam*.

Raufman, J., & Machalaba, C. (2018, December 7). One Health: Global lessons to support healthier people [*The Doctor's Tablet* blog]. Retrieved from *http://blogs.einstein.yu.edu/one-health-global-lessons-to-support-healthier-people*.

Reiss, F. (2017, February 10). Why can 12-year-olds still get married in the United States? *Washington Post*. Retrieved from *www.wash-*

ingtonpost.com/posteverything/wp/2017/02/10/ why-does-the-united-states-still-let-12-year-old-girls-get married/?noredirect=on&utm_term=. fcd380befa91.*

Resilience Alliance. (2019). Who are we? Retrieved from *www.resalliance.org.*

Rheingold, H. (1988). *They have a word for it: Untranslatable words and phrases.* New York: St. Martin's Press.

Rich, N. (2019). *Losing Earth.* New York: Macmillan.

Richardson, R. (2019). *About us: Our vision.* Toronto, ON, Canada: Global Alliance for the Future of Food. Retrieved from *https://future-offood.org/about-us.*

Riddell, D., & Moore, M.-L. (2015). *Scaling out, scaling up, scaling deep: Advancing systemic social innovation and the learning processes to support it.* Montreal, ON, Canada: McConnell Family Foundation and Tamarack Institute.

Rigaud, K. K., de Sherbinin, A., Jones, B., Bergmann, J., Clement, V., Ober, K., et al. (2018). *Groundswell: Preparing for internal climate migration.* Washington, DC: World Bank.

Ringhofer, L., & Kohlweg, K. (2019, February 15). Has the theory of change established itself as the better alternative to the logical framework approach in development cooperation programmes? *Progress in Development Studies, 19*(2), 112–122.

Rogers, E. (1962). *Diffusion of innovations.* New York: Free Press of Glencoe.

Rogers, E. (2003). *Diffusion of innovations* (5th ed.). New York: Simon & Schuster.

Rogers, E., & Shoemaker, F. (1971). *Communication of innovations: A cross-cultural approach.* New York: Free Press.

Rogers, K. (2014). *WWF's new strategy.* Retrieved from *www.devex.com/news/wwf-s-new-strategy-to-affect-focus-staffing-82791.*

Rogers, P. J. (2000a). Developing and using a program theory matrix for program evaluation and performance monitoring. In P. J. Rogers, T. A. Hacsi, A. Pettosino, & T. A. Huebner (Eds.), *Program theory in evaluation: Challenges and opportunities* (New Directions for Evaluation No. 87). Hoboken, NJ: Wiley Periodicals.

Rogers, P. J. (2000b). Program theory evaluation: Not whether programs work but how they work. In G. Madaus, D. Stufflebeam, & T. Kelieghan (Eds.), *Evaluation models* (pp. 209–231). New York: Kluwer Press.

Rogers-Wright, A. (2018, August 17). White supremacy and climate: A sinister symbiosis [Blog]. Retrieved from *https://medium.com/@ARdubbs108/white-supremacy-and-climate-change-a-sinister-symbiosis-d4358da1241c.*

Rogge, P. (2018). My climate change crisis. *Science, 359,* 706.

Rosling, H. (2018). *Factfulness: Ten reasons we're wrong about the world–and why things are better than you think.* New York: Flatiron Books.

Safire, W. (2006, September 17). Skin in the game. *New York Times Sunday Magazine.* Retrieved from *www.nytimes.com/2006/09/17/magazine/17wwln_safire.html.*

Sandlin, D. T. (2019). *Ethical science and indigenous sustainability* [Internship Report for EPA Region 10]. Washington, DC: Office of Environmental Assessment, Environmental Protection Agency. Retrieved from *www.academia.edu/38034199/ETHICAL_SCIENCE_AND_INDIGENO US_SUSTAINABILITY?email_work_card=title.*

Schäpke, N., Stelzer, F., Caniglia, G., Bergmann, M., Wanner, M., Singer-Brodowski, M., et al (2018). Jointly experimenting for transformation?: Shaping real-world laboratories by comparing them. *GAIA, 27*(Suppl. 1), 85–96.

Schendler, A., & Jones, A. (2018, October 6). Stopping climate change is hopeless: Let's do it. *New York Times,* p. SR10.

Schmidt, L., Hartberger, K., Kobbe, S., Falk, T., Wesselow, M., & Schumann, C. (2018). Stakeholder involvement in transdisciplinary research: Lessons from three projects on sustainable land management in a north-south setting. *GAIA, 27*(3), 312–320.

Schorr, L. B. (1989). *Within our reach: Breaking the cycle of disadvantage.* New York: Doubleday.

Schorr, L. B. (1997). *Common purpose: Strengthening families and neighborhoods to rebuild America.* New York: Anchor.

Schorr, L. B. (2009). *Realizing President Obama's promise to scale up what works to fight urban poverty.* Washington DC: Center for the Study of Social Policy. Retrieved from *www.vacap.org/assets/content/Documents/ObamaPromise-March09.pdf.*

Schorr, L. B. (2012, Fall). Broader evidence for bigger impact. Retrieved from *https://ssir.org/articles/entry/broader_evidence_for_bigger_impact.*

Schröter, D. C. (2009). Sustainability evaluation website. Retrieved from *www.sustainabilityeval.net*.

Schwandt, T. (1997). *Qualitative inquiry: A dictionary of terms*. Thousand Oaks, CA: SAGE.

Schwandt, T. (2001). *Qualitative inquiry: A dictionary of terms* (2nd ed.). Thousand Oaks, CA: SAGE.

Schwandt, T., D'Errico, S., Ofir, Z., Lucks, D., & El-Saddick, K. (2018, May). Embedding evaluation in national plans and policies to foster transformative development [Briefing]. London: International Institute for Environment and Development with EVALSDGs, EvalPartners. Retrieved from *http://pubs.iied.org/17464IIED*.

Schwartz, J., & Popovich, N. (2019, February 6). It's official: 2018 was the fourth warmest year on record. *New York Times*. Retrieved from *www.nytimes.com/interactive/2019/02/06/climate/fourth-hottest-year.html?emc=edit_nn_p_20190207&nl=morning-briefing&nlid=44499219tion%3DtopNews&section=topNews&te=1*.

Scoones, I., Stirling, A., Abrol, D., Atela, J., Charli-Joseph, L., Eakin, H., et al. (2018). *Transformations to sustainability* (STEPS Working Paper No. 104). Brighton, UK: STEPS Centre.

Scriven, M. (1993). *Hard-won lessons in program evaluation* (New Directions for Program Evaluation No. 58). San Francisco: Jossey-Bass.

Scriven, M. (2008). The concept of a transdiscipline: And of evaluation as a transdiscipline. *Journal of Multidisciplinary Evaluation, 5*(10), 65–66.

Scriven, M. (2013). Conceptual resolutions and evaluation: Past, present, and future. In M. Alkin (Ed.), *Evaluation roots* (2nd ed., pp. 167–179). Los Angeles: SAGE.

SDG Transformations Forum. (2017, September 1). *Draft manifesto on transforming evaluation* [SDG Transformations Forum]. University of Dundee, UK.

Seager, G. (2018, June 9). What are vertical and horizontal approaches to health? [Christian Health Service Corp blog]. Retrieved from *www.healthservicecorps.org/what-are-vertical-and-horizontal-approaches-to-health*.

Segone, M., & Tateossian, F. (2017). No one left behind: A focus on gender and social equity. In R. D. van den Berg, I. Naidoo, & S. D. Tamondong (Eds.), *Evaluation for Agenda 2030: Providing evidence on progress and sustainability*. Exeter, UK: International Development Evaluation Association.

Sengupta, S., & Popovich, N. (2018, June 28). Global warming in South Asia: 800 million at risk. *New York Times*. Retrieved from *www.nytimes.com/interactive/2018/06/28/climate/india-pakistan-warming-hotspots.html?emc=edit_clim_20180704&nl=&nlid=4449921920180704&te=1*.

Sharpe, B. (2013). *Three horizons: The patterning of hope*. Axminster, UK: Triarchy Press.

Sinclair, R., & Coe, R. (2019). The options by context: A paradigm shift in agronomy. *Experimental Agriculture, 4*, 11–30.

Slatin, C., Galizzi, M., Melillo, K. D., & Mawn, B. (2004). Conducting interdisciplinary research to promote healthy and safe employment in health care: Promises and pitfalls. *Public Health Reports, 119*(1), 60–72.

Smyth, J. (2018, December 29). China ban on importing contaminated waste leaves Australia awash in rubbish. *Financial Times*. Retrieved from *www.ft.com/content/54749bae-fe9f-11e8-aebf-99e208d3e521*.

Stake, R. (2004). How far dare an evaluator go toward saving the world? *American Journal of Evaluation, 25*(1), 103–107.

Steger, M. B. (2013). *Globalization: A very short introduction*. Oxford, UK: Oxford University Press.

Sutton, R. I., & Rao, H. (2014). *Scaling up excellence: Getting to more without settling for less*. New York: Crown.

Sweeney, C., & Gosfield, J. (2013). *The art of doing: How superachievers do what they do and how they do it so well*. New York: Plume.

Systems in Evaluation. (2018). Principles for effective use of systems thinking in evaluation, Systems in Evaluation Topical Interest Group, American Evaluation Association. Retrieved from *www.systemsinevaluation.com/wp-content/uploads/2018/10/SETIG-Principles-FINAL-DRAFT-2018-9-9.pdf*.

Taleb, N. N. (2018). *Skin in the game: Hidden asymmetries in daily life*. New York: Random House.

Tepperman, J. (2016). *The fix: How nations survive and thrive in a world in decline*. New York: Duggan.

Thomas, C. D. (2018). *Inheritors of the earth: How nature is thriving in an age of extinction*. New York: Public Affairs.

Thomas, W. I., & Thomas, D. S. (1928). *The child in America: Behavior problems and programs.* New York: Knopf.

Transformational Change Leadership. (2019). Vision and methodology. Retrieved from *https://tcleadership.org/introduction.*

Tversky, A., & Kahneman, D. (1974). Judgment under uncertainty: Heuristics and biases. *Science, 185,* 1124–1131.

Uitto, J. I. (2019). Sustainable development evaluation: Understanding the nexus of natural and human systems. In G. Julnes (Ed.), *Evaluating sustainability: Evaluative support for managing processes in the public interest* (New Directions for Evaluation No. 162) (pp. 49–67). Hoboken, NJ: Wiley Periodicals.

United Nations. (2014). The millennium development goals report. Retrieved from *www.un.org/millenniumgoals/2014%20MDG%20report/MDG%202014%20English%20web.pdf.*

United Nations Children's Fund. (2015). *Unless we act now: The impact of climate change on children.* New York: Author.

United Nations Development Programme. (2015). Evaluation of the role of the UNDP in support of the MDGs (2002–2012). Retrieved from *http://web.undp.org/evaluation/evaluations/thematic/mdg.shtml.*

Waddell, S. (2011). *Global action networks: Creating our future together.* New York: Palgrave Macmillan.

Walker, B., Holling, C. S., Carpenter, S. R., & Kinzig, A. (2004). Resilience, adaptability and transformability in social–ecological systems. *Ecology and Society, 9*(2), 5.

Walker, J., Risen, J. L., Gilovich, T., & Thaler, R. (2018, February 4). Force overtime?: Or go for it? *New York Times,* p. SR6.

Wallace-Wells, D. (2019). *The uninhabitable Earth: Life after warming.* New York: Tim Duggan Books.

Waller, J. (2004). *Fabulous science: Fact and fiction in the history of scientific discovery.* New York: Oxford University Press.

Walt, V., & Meyer, S. (2018, August 23). Blood, sweat, and batteries. *Fortune.* Retrieved from *http://fortune.com/longform/blood-sweat-and-batteries.*

Wang, R. R. (2012). *Yinyang: The way of heaven and earth in Chinese thought and culture.* New York: Cambridge University Press.

Watson, S. K. (2018, June 28). China has refused to recycle the West's plastics: What now? [Radio broadcast]. National Public Radio. Retrieved from *www.npr.org/sections/goatsandsoda/2018/06/28/623972937/china-has-refused-to-recycle-the-wests-plastics-what-now.*

Weiss, C. H. (1995). Nothing as practical as good theory: Exploring theory-based evaluation for comprehensive community initiatives for children and families. Washington, DC: Aspen Institute. Retrieved from *https://pdfs.semanticscholar.org/ff5a/3eea8d1d4e07a768ded6b426b425efde8f7c.pdf.*

Weizsäcker, E. U., & Wijkman, A. (2018). *Come on!: Capitalism, short-termism, population and the destruction of the planet.* New York: Springer.

Werz, M., & Hoffman, M. (2016). Europe's twenty-first century challenge: Climate change, migration and security. *European View, 15*(1), 145–154.

Westhorp, G. (2012). Using complexity-consistent theory for evaluating complex systems. *Evaluation, 18*(4), 405–420.

Westley, F., & Antadze, N. (2010). Making a difference: Strategies for scaling social innovation for greater impact. *Innovation Journal: The Public Sector Innovation Journal, 15*(2), article 2.

Westley, F., McGowan, K., & Tjornbo, O. (Eds.). (2017). *The evolution of social innovation: Building resilience through transitions.* Northampton, MA: Elgar.

Westley, F., Olsson, P., Folke, C., Homer-Dixon, T., Vredenburg, H., Loorbach, D., et al. (2011, November). Tipping toward sustainability: Emerging pathways of transformation. *AMBIO: A Journal of the Human Environment, 40*(7), 762–780.

Westley, F., Tjornbo, O., Olsson, P., Folke, C., Crona, B., Schultz, L., et al. (2013). A theory of transformative agency in linked social–ecological systems. *Ecology and Society, 18*(3), 27.

Westley, F., Zimmerman, B., & Patton, M. Q. (2007). *Getting to maybe: How the world is changed.* Toronto, ON, Canada: Random House Canada.

Williams, B. (2005). Systems and systems thinking. In S. Mathison (Ed.), *Encyclopedia of evaluation.* Thousand Oaks, CA: SAGE.

Williams, B. (2008). Systemic inquiry. In L. M. Given (Ed.), *The SAGE encyclopedia of qualitative research methods* (Vol. 2). Thousand Oaks, CA: SAGE.

Williams, B. (2019). *Systemic evaluation design: A*

workbook (2nd ed.). Wellington, New Zealand: Author.

Williams, B., & Hummelbrunner, R. (2011). *Systems concepts in action: A practitioner's toolkit.* Stanford, CA: Stanford University Press.

Williams, B., & Iman, I. (2007). *Systems concepts in evaluation: An expert anthology* (American Evaluation Association Monograph No. 6). Point Reynes, CA: EdgePress.

Wilson, J. (2018). Principles-focused evaluation at the grassroots in Africa: Inspirational examples and reflections. In M. Q. Patton, *Principles-focused evaluation: The GUIDE* (pp. 127–136). New York: Guilford Press.

Woodland, R. H., & Hutton, M. S. (2012). Evaluating organizational collaborations: Suggested entry points and strategies. *American Journal of Evaluation, 33*(3), 366–383.

World Bank. (2015). The millennium development goals. Retrieved from *www.worldbank.org/mdgs.*

World Savvy. (2019). What is global competence? Retrieved from *www.worldsavvy.org/global-competence.*

Wurtz, B. (2017). History of the entire world, I guess [Video file]. Retrieved from *www.youtube.com/watch?v=xuCn8ux2gbs.*

Zavala, K. (2019, June 2). Buen vivir as a pathway to durable peace and a healthy planet [Alliance blog]. Retrieved from *www.alliancemagazine.org/blog/buen-vivir-as-a-pathway-to-durable-peace-and-a-healthy-planet.*

Author Index

Subject Index

Note. f or *t* following a page number indicates a figure or a table.

About the Author

 **Michael Quinn Patton, PhD,** is an independent consultant who has been conducting program evaluations since the 1970s. Based in Minnesota, he was on the faculty of the University of Minnesota for 18 years and is a former president of the American Evaluation Association (AEA). Dr. Patton's books include *Developmental Evaluation, Developmental Evaluation Exemplars, Principles-Focused Evaluation, Qualitative Research and Evaluation Methods* (now in its fourth edition), and *Utilization-Focused Evaluation* (now in its fourth edition), among others. He is a recipient of the Alva and Gunnar Myrdal Evaluation Practice Award and the Paul F. Lazarsfeld Evaluation Theory Award, both from AEA, as well as the Lester F. Ward Distinguished Contribution to Applied and Clinical Sociology Award from the Association for Applied and Clinical Sociology. Dr. Patton is an active trainer and workshop presenter who has conducted applied research and evaluation on a broad range of issues and has worked with organizations and programs at the international, national, state, provincial, and local levels.